First World War
and Army of Occupation
War Diary
France, Belgium and Germany

41 DIVISION
Headquarters, Branches and Services
Adjutant and Quarter-Master General
17 August 1916 - 31 October 1917

WO95/2620/1

The Naval & Military Press Ltd
www.nmarchive.com
Published in association with The National Archives

Published by

The Naval & Military Press Ltd

Unit 10 Ridgewood Industrial Park,

Uckfield, East Sussex,

TN22 5QE England

Tel: +44 (0) 1825 749494

www.naval-military-press.com

www.nmarchive.com

This diary has been reprinted in facsimile from the original. Any imperfections are inevitably reproduced and the quality may fall short of modern type and cartographic standards.

© Crown Copyright
Images reproduced by permission of The National Archives, London, England, 2015.

Contents

Document type	Place/Title	Date From	Date To
Heading	WO95/2620 41 Div A & Q. May 16-Oct 17		
Heading	41 Div A & Q Branch May 1916-Oct 1917 To Italy		
Miscellaneous	D.A.G. 3rd Echelon Base	02/07/1916	02/07/1916
Miscellaneous	41st. Division Administrative Instructions Amendment.	01/06/1917	01/06/1917
Miscellaneous	41st. Divn. No. Q/335/S.	03/06/1917	03/06/1917
Miscellaneous	41st Division.		
Miscellaneous	Confidential	01/07/1916	01/07/1916
Miscellaneous	Numbers Of Men Washed At Divisional Baths During The Month Of June 1916		
Heading	Original War Diary Of 41st Division "A" From July 1st 1916 To July 31st 1916		
War Diary	Steenwerck		
Miscellaneous	41st. Division.		
Miscellaneous	41st. Division. Courts-Martial During July 1916		
Miscellaneous	41st. Division. List Of Officer Casualties For Month Of July 1916		
Miscellaneous	41st. Division. Artillery Ammunition Expended During July. 1916		
Miscellaneous	41st. Divisional Baths. Numbers Bathed-July 1916		
Miscellaneous	41st. Divisional Baths. Articles Repaired-July 1916		
Miscellaneous	41st Divisional Baths. Articles Destroyed-July 1916		
Heading	Original War Diary Of 41st Division "A & Q" From August 1st 1916 To Aug 31st 1916		
War Diary	Fletre	17/08/1916	23/08/1916
War Diary	Ailly-Le-Haut-Clocher	25/08/1916	28/08/1916
Miscellaneous	Programme Of Move Of 41st Division Via Calais	16/08/1916	16/08/1916
Miscellaneous	Table "D" 41st Division.		
Miscellaneous	Distribution Of Units. 41st. Division.	16/08/1916	16/08/1916
Miscellaneous	41st Division. Officer Casualties-August 1916		
Miscellaneous	The Following Table Shows Numbers Of Killed Wounded Missing And Evacuated Sick During The Month Of August 1916 (to 12 Noon 31st)	03/09/1916	03/09/1916
Miscellaneous	41st Division. Courts-Martial During August 1916		
Miscellaneous	41st Division. Ammunition Expended During August 1916		
Heading	Original War Diary Of 41st Division Headquarters "A" & "Q" Branch From Sept 1-1916 To Sept 30 1916		
War Diary		01/09/1916	28/09/1916
Miscellaneous	Administrative Arrangements Of The Division Moving Into The Line.	10/09/1916	10/09/1916
Miscellaneous	41st Divn. No. A/524/3	13/09/1916	13/09/1916
Miscellaneous	Positions Of Wagon And Transport Lines.		
Miscellaneous	Administrative Arrangements On And Subsequent To September 15th 1916	13/09/1916	13/09/1916
Miscellaneous	Location Of Units Of 41st. Division.	12/09/1916	12/09/1916
Miscellaneous		13/09/1916	13/09/1916
Miscellaneous	Clearing The Battlefield.	15/09/1916	15/09/1916
Map			
Miscellaneous	208/S.7.	05/09/1916	05/09/1916
Miscellaneous	Estimated Casualties.		

Miscellaneous	41st. Division. Courts Martial During September 1916		
Miscellaneous	The Following Table Shows Numbers Of Killed Wounded Missing And Evacuated Sick During The Month Of September 1916 (to 12 Noon 30th.)		
Heading	Original War Diary Of 41st Division "A & Q" October 1st 1916 To October 31st 1916		
War Diary	Ribemont.	01/10/1916	26/10/1916
Miscellaneous	41st Divn. No. 288/S.7.	17/10/1916	17/10/1916
Miscellaneous	Move Of 41st Division (Less Artillery).	16/10/1916	16/10/1916
Miscellaneous	Table "D" Move Of 41st Division Less Artillery.	16/10/1916	16/10/1916
Miscellaneous	41st. Division. Courts Martial During October 1916.		
Miscellaneous	The Following Table Shows Number Of Killed, Wounded, Missing And Evacuated Sick During The Month Of October 1916		
Miscellaneous	Administrative Arrangements In Connection With Coming Operations	02/10/1916	02/10/1916
War Diary	Reninghelst	01/11/1916	30/11/1916
Miscellaneous	41st. Division. Courts-Martial During November 1916		
Miscellaneous	The Following Table Shows Numbers Of Killed, Wounded, Missing And Evacuated Sick During The Month Of November 1916 (to 12 Noon 30th.)		
War Diary	Reninghelst.		
Miscellaneous	41st. Division. Return Of Courts Martial During December 1916		
Miscellaneous	The Following Table Shows Numbers Of Killed Wounded Missing And Evacuated Sick During The Month Of December 1916 (to Noon 31st.)		
War Diary	Reninghelst.		
Miscellaneous	Statement Showing Courts Martial For The Month Of January 1917		
Miscellaneous	Statement Showing Reinforcements And Weekly Strength January 1917		
Miscellaneous	The Following Table Shows Numbers Of Killed, Wounded, Missing, And Evacuated Sick, During The Month Of January 1917-(to Noon 31st)		
War Diary	Reninghelst.		
Miscellaneous	Statement Showing Courts Martial For The Month Of February 1917		
Miscellaneous	Statement Showing Reinforcements And Weekly Strength. February 1917		
Miscellaneous	The Following Table Shows Numbers Killed Wounded Missing And Evacuated Sick During The Month Of February 1917-(to Noon 28th.)		
Miscellaneous	Statement Showing Courts Martial For The Month Of February 1917		
Heading	War Diary Of H.Q. 41st Div (A+Q) For Month Of March 1917 Vol XI		
Miscellaneous	Reninghelst.		
Miscellaneous	Statement Showing Courts Martial For The Month Of March 1917		
Miscellaneous	Statement Showing Reinforcements And Weekly Strength. March 1917		
Miscellaneous	The Following Table Shows Numbers Killed, Wounded, Missing, And Evacuated Sick duting the Month Of March 1917 (to 12 Noon 31st).		
War Diary	Reninghelst.		

Miscellaneous	Statement Showing Courts Martial For The Month Of March 1917		
Miscellaneous	The Following Table Shows Numbers Killed Wounded Missing And Evacuated Sick duting The Month Of March 1917 (to 12 Noon 31st)		
Miscellaneous	Statement Showing Reinforcements And Weekly Strength. March 1917		
War Diary	Reninghelst.		
Miscellaneous	Statement Showing Courts Martial For The Month Of April 1917		
Miscellaneous	The Following Table Shows Numbers Killed Wounded Missing And Evacuated Sick During The Month Of April 1917 (to 12 Noon 31st.)		
Miscellaneous	Statement Showing Reinforcements And Weekly Strength. April 1917		
Map			
Heading	Cover for Documents. Nature of Enclosures. HQ A&Q 41d Vol 13		
Heading	Copies for War Diary		
War Diary	Reninghelst.	25/05/1917	31/05/1917
Miscellaneous	Statement Showing Courts Martial For The Month Of May 1917		
Miscellaneous	The Following Table Shows Numbers Killed Wounded Missing And Evacuated Sick During The Month Of May 1917 (to 12 Noon 31st.)		
Miscellaneous	Statement Showing Reinforcements And Weekly Strength. May 1917		
Miscellaneous	41st. Division. Administrative Instructions In Connection With Forthcoming Operations.	19/05/1917	19/05/1917
Miscellaneous	Index To 41st. Divisional Administrative Arrangements.		
Miscellaneous	I. Personnel.		
Miscellaneous	Return Of Personnel At Reinforcement Camp.		
Miscellaneous	V. Rations.		
Miscellaneous	VI. Water.		
Miscellaneous	(VIII). Ordinance.	21/05/1917	21/05/1917
Miscellaneous	(X). Burials.		
Miscellaneous	(XII). Communications		
Miscellaneous	(XIII). Traffic Control.		
Miscellaneous	(XIV). Trench Tramway Traffic.		
Miscellaneous	(XV). First Line Transport.		
Miscellaneous	(XVII). Salvage.		
Miscellaneous	(XVIII) Baths And Laundry.		
Miscellaneous	(XX) R. E. Stores.		
Miscellaneous	(XXI). Reports And Returns.		
Miscellaneous	41st. Divn. No. Q/335/S.	25/05/1917	25/05/1917
Miscellaneous	(XXII). Packs And Surplus Baggage.		
Miscellaneous	Xth. Corps. No. 570.A. 41st. Division No. A.29/115 Appendix A	28/12/1916	28/12/1916
Miscellaneous	Appendix. "B"		
Miscellaneous	Appendix. "D" 14th Corps Burial Instructions.		
Miscellaneous	Appendix ('E').		
Map			
Miscellaneous	122nd Infantry Brigade.	28/05/1917	28/05/1917
Miscellaneous	Advance Of Wagon And Transport Lines. (Addenda To XV First Line Transport)		
Miscellaneous	122nd Infantry Brigade.	29/05/1917	29/05/1917

Miscellaneous	41st. Division No. Q/335/S.	29/05/1917	29/05/1917
Miscellaneous	Amendment To 41st. Divisional Administrative Instructions In Connection With Forthcoming Operations.		
Map			
Miscellaneous	122nd Infantry Brigade.	28/05/1917	28/05/1917
Miscellaneous	Advance Of Wagon And Transport Lines. (Addenda To XV First Line Transport)		
Miscellaneous	122nd Infantry Brigade.	29/05/1917	29/05/1917
Miscellaneous	41st. Division No. Q/335/S.	29/05/1917	29/05/1917
Miscellaneous	41st. Division Administrative Instructions Amendment	01/06/1917	01/06/1917
Miscellaneous	Amendment To 41st Division Administrative Instructions In Connection With Forthcoming Operations.	03/06/1917	03/06/1917
Map			
Miscellaneous	Amendment To 41st. Divisional Administrative Instructions In Connection With Forthcoming Operations.		
Miscellaneous	Index To 41st. Divisional Administrative Arrangements.		
Miscellaneous	41st. Division. Administrative Instructions In Connection With Forthcoming Operations.	19/05/1917	19/05/1917
Miscellaneous	I. Personnel.		
Miscellaneous	Return Of Personnel At Reinforcement Camp.		
Miscellaneous	V. Rations.		
War Diary	VI. Water.		
Miscellaneous	(4). Washing Water.		
Miscellaneous	VII. Medical.		
Miscellaneous	(VIII). Ordnance.	21/05/1917	21/05/1917
Miscellaneous	(X). Burials.		
Miscellaneous	(XII). Communications.		
Miscellaneous	(XIII). Traffic Control.		
Miscellaneous	(XIV). Trench Tramway Traffic.		
Miscellaneous	(XV). First Line Transport.		
Miscellaneous	(XVII). Salvage.		
Miscellaneous	(XVIII) Baths And Laundry,		
Miscellaneous	(XX) R.E. Stores.		
Miscellaneous	(XXI). Reports And Returns.		
Miscellaneous	(XXII). Packs And Surplus Baggage.		
Miscellaneous	Xth. Corps. No. 570.A. 41st. Division No. A.29/115. Appendix A	28/12/1916	28/12/1916
Miscellaneous	Appendix. "B".		
Miscellaneous	Appendix. 'D' Xth Corps Burial Instructions.		
Miscellaneous	Appendix ('E').		
War Diary	Reninghelst	07/06/1917	07/06/1917
War Diary	Westoutre	22/06/1917	30/06/1917
War Diary	Reninghelst	07/06/1917	07/06/1917
War Diary	Westoutre	22/06/1917	30/06/1917
Miscellaneous			
Miscellaneous	Statement Showing Reinforcements And Weekly Strength During The Month-June 1917.		
Miscellaneous	The Following Table Shows Numbers Killed Wounded Missing And Evacuated Sick During The Month Of June 1917 (to 12 Noon 30th).		
Miscellaneous	Statement Showing Courts Martial For The Month Of June 1917		
Miscellaneous	A Form. Messages And Signals.	31/07/1917	31/07/1917

War Diary	Berthen	01/07/1917	23/07/1917
War Diary	Westoutre	25/07/1917	31/07/1917
Heading	Administrative Instructions In Connection 41st Div O.O. 140		
Miscellaneous	122nd Infantry Brigade.	14/07/1917	14/07/1917
Miscellaneous	Administrative Arrangements For Forthcoming Operations Reference 41st Division Operation Order No. 140 Of 9th Instant		
Miscellaneous	Appendix "A".		
Miscellaneous	Appendix "B".		
Miscellaneous	Appendix "C". Return Of Personnel Infantry Brigade.		
Miscellaneous	122nd Infantry Brigade.	17/07/1917	17/07/1917
Miscellaneous	41st. Division No. Q/411/14.	21/07/1917	21/07/1917
Miscellaneous	122nd Infantry Brigade.	21/07/1917	21/07/1917
Miscellaneous	Clearing The Battlefield.		
Miscellaneous	Appendix "D" Burial Instructions.		
Miscellaneous	Further Administrative Arrangements For Forthcoming Operations In Continuation And Amendment To Those Dated 14/7/17	23/07/1917	23/07/1917
Miscellaneous	41st Division. Statement Showing Reinforcements And Weekly Strength During July 1917		
Miscellaneous	The Following Table Shows Numbers Killed Wounded. Missing. And Evacuated Sick During The Month Of July 1917 (to Noon 31st).		
Miscellaneous	41st Division. Statement Showing Courts Martial Held During July 1917		
War Diary	Westoutre.	11/08/1917	11/08/1917
War Diary	Berthen	19/08/1917	19/08/1917
War Diary	Wizernes.	21/08/1917	21/08/1917
Miscellaneous	122nd Infantry Brigade. Appendix A	11/08/1917	11/08/1917
Miscellaneous	Embussing Table.		
Miscellaneous	Administrative Instructions Reference 41st Division Order No. 152 Of 11th August 1917	11/08/1917	11/08/1917
Miscellaneous	Billeting Schedule.		
Miscellaneous	41st Division No. Q. 64/186/3	19/08/1917	19/08/1917
Miscellaneous	41st Division No. Q/64/186/1 Appendix B	19/08/1917	19/08/1917
Miscellaneous	41st Division No. Q.64/186/2	19/08/1917	19/08/1917
Miscellaneous	The Following Table Shows Numbers Killed Wounded Missing And Evacuated Sick During The Month Of August 1917 (to Noon 31st).		
Miscellaneous	41st. Division. Statement Showing Courts Martial Held During August 1917 Appendix D		
War Diary	Wizernes.	12/09/1917	12/09/1917
War Diary	Zevecoten.	17/09/1917	22/09/1917
War Diary	Caestre.	24/09/1917	24/09/1917
War Diary	La Panne.	04/10/1917	04/10/1917
War Diary	Wizernes.	12/09/1917	12/09/1917
War Diary	Zevecoten.	17/09/1917	22/09/1917
War Diary	Caestre.	24/09/1917	24/09/1917
War Diary	La Panne.	04/10/1917	04/10/1917
Miscellaneous	Administrative Instructions In Connection With 41st Division Instruction No. 4 Of 11/9/17	12/09/1917	12/09/1917
Miscellaneous	Addendum To 41st Divisional Administrative Instructions In Connection With 41st Division Instruction No. 4 Dated September 11th 1917	14/09/1917	14/09/1917

Miscellaneous	Addendum And Corregenda To Administrative Instructions In Connection With 41st. Division Instruction No. 4 of 11/9/17	12/09/1917	12/09/1917
Miscellaneous	Administrative Instructions In Connection With 41st Division Instruction No. 4 Of 11/9/17	12/09/1917	12/09/1917
Miscellaneous	Addendum To 41st Divisional Administrative Instructions In Connection With 41st Division Instruction No. 4 Dated September 11th 1917	14/09/1917	14/09/1917
Miscellaneous	Addendum And Corregenda To Administrative Instructions In Connection With 41st. Division Instruction No. 4 Of 11/9/17	12/09/1917	12/09/1917
Miscellaneous	Index To Administrative Instructions Issued In Connection With 41st Division Order No. 166 Dated 10th Sept. 1917	17/09/1917	17/09/1917
Miscellaneous	(1). S.A.A., Grenades And L.T.M. Ammunition.		
Miscellaneous	(2). Supplies. Rations.		
Miscellaneous	(3). R. E. Stores.		
Miscellaneous	(4). Medical.		
Miscellaneous	(5). Veterinary.		
Miscellaneous	(6). Water.		
Miscellaneous	(7). Roads & Tracks.		
Miscellaneous	Addendum To Administrative Instructions Issued In Connection With 41st Division Order No. 166 Dated 10th September 1917	18/09/1917	18/09/1917
Miscellaneous	(8). Tramways		
Miscellaneous	Addendum To Administrative Instructions Issued In Connection With 41st Division Order No. 166 Dated 10th September 1917	18/09/1917	18/09/1917
Miscellaneous	(9). Provost Instructions.		
Miscellaneous	(10). Clearing The Battlefield.		
Miscellaneous	(11). Surplus Kits.		
Miscellaneous	122nd. Infantry Brigade.	13/09/1917	13/09/1917
Miscellaneous	(12). Details.		
Map			
Miscellaneous	Approximate Contents Of Ammunition Dumps Shown On Reverse.		
Map			
Miscellaneous	Appendix "D" Burial Instructions.		
Miscellaneous	(14). Ordnance.	17/09/1917	17/09/1917
Miscellaneous	Appendix "E". Return Of Personnel Infantry Brigade.		
Miscellaneous	Index To Administrative Instructions Issued In Connection With 41st Division Order No. 166 Dated 10th Sept 1917	17/09/1917	17/09/1917
Miscellaneous	(1). S.A.A., Grenades And L.T.M. Ammunition.		
Miscellaneous	(2). Supplies. Rations.		
Miscellaneous	(3). R. E. Stores.		
Miscellaneous	(4). Medical.		
Miscellaneous	(5). Veterinary.		
Miscellaneous	(6). Water.		
Miscellaneous	(7). Roads & Tracks.		
Miscellaneous	Addendum To Administrative Instructions Issued In Connection With 41st Division Order No. 166 Dated 10th September 1917	18/09/1917	18/09/1917
Miscellaneous	(8). Tramways.		

Miscellaneous	Addendum To Administrative Instructions Issued In Connection With 41st Division Order No. 166 Dated 10th September 1917.	18/09/1917	18/09/1917
Miscellaneous	(9). Provost Instructions.		
Miscellaneous	(10). Clearing The Battlefield.		
Miscellaneous	(11). Surplus Kits.		
Miscellaneous	122nd. Infantry Brigade.	13/09/1917	13/09/1917
Miscellaneous	(12). Details.		
Miscellaneous	(14). Ordnance.	17/09/1917	17/09/1917
Miscellaneous	Approximate Contents Of Ammunition Dumps Shown On Reverse.		
Map			
Miscellaneous	41st Division. Statement Showing Courts Martial Held During September 1917		
Miscellaneous	The Following Table Shows Numbered Killed Wounded Missing And Evacuated Sick During The Month Of September 1917 (to Noon 30th)		
Miscellaneous	Appendix "D" Burial Instructions.		
Miscellaneous	Appendix "E" Return Of Personnel Infantry Brigade.		
Miscellaneous	Administrative Instructions In Connection With 41st Division Order No. 175	22/09/1917	22/09/1917
Miscellaneous	March Table. Divisional Transports	22/09/1917	22/09/1917
Miscellaneous	41st Divn. No. Q. 64/187/1.		
Miscellaneous	Administrative Instructions In Connection With 41st Division Order No. 175	22/09/1917	22/09/1917
Miscellaneous	March Table. Divisional Transports		
Miscellaneous	41st Divn. No. Q. 64/187/1.		
Miscellaneous	Administrative Instructions Reference 41st Division Warning Order No. 16 Dated 24th September 1917	24/09/1917	24/09/1917
Miscellaneous	Instructions For Embussing In Continuation Of 41st Division Administrative Instructions Reference 41st Division Warning Order No 16	25/09/1917	25/09/1917
Miscellaneous			
Miscellaneous	Administrative Instructions Reference 41st Division Warning Order No. 16 Dated 24th September 1917	24/09/1917	24/09/1917
Miscellaneous	41st Division No. Q/420/2.	26/09/1917	26/09/1917
Miscellaneous			
War Diary	St Idasbalde	28/10/1917	31/10/1917
Miscellaneous	41st Division No. G. 103/1/1	28/10/1917	28/10/1917
Miscellaneous	41st Division Administrative Instructions In Connection With Warning Order No. 18	28/10/1917	28/10/1917
Miscellaneous	41st. Division. Statement Showing Casualties And Sick Evacuations During The Month Of October		
Miscellaneous	Administrative Instructions Reference 41st Division Order No. 177 Of 4th Oct 1917	04/10/1917	04/10/1917
Miscellaneous	Location Of Units 41st Division.		
Miscellaneous	Administrative Instructions Reference 41st Division Order No. 177	04/10/1917	04/10/1917
Miscellaneous	Location Of Units 41st Division.		

WO95/2620 ①
41 DIV. A & Q.
May '16 – Oct '17

41 DIV

A & Q BRANCH

MAY 1916 - OCT 1917

TO ITALY

D/A.
3rd Echelon
    Base

      Herewith War Diary
for the months of May & June –

                    W Bingel Trumbull
                         Captn.
2/7/16   o.c. 41/ Signal Coy.

SECRET

41st. Division Administrative Instructions

AMENDMENT

Administrative Instructions, section XXI "Reports and Returns" para vi first paragraph delete " The Officer in charge Ammunition refilling point will wire Divisional Headquarters "Q" the amount of Artillery ammunition (including T.M.Ammunition) issued", and substitute "C. R. A. and Brigades will wire to D.H.Q. "Q" the quantities of Artillery and T.M.Ammunition expended".

[signature]

1st. June 1917.

Captain,
D. A. Q. M. G.
41st. Division.

Copies to :-
122nd Infantry Brigade.
123rd Infantry Brigade.
124th Infantry Brigade.
R.A.
R.E.
Signals.
Pioneers
Xth. Corps Q.
47th Division.
Divisional Train
War Diary

A. D. M. S.
A. D. V. S.
A. P. M.
D. A. D. O. S.
Salvage Officer
Area Comm'dt.
"G"
Reserve Division.
19th Division.
S.S.O.
Spare.

41st.Divn.No.Q/335/S.

AMENDMENT TO 41st.DIVISION ADMINISTRATIVE INSTRUCTIONS IN CONNECTION WITH FORTHCOMING OPERATIONS.

Add to Section (VIII) a new subsection (4) as under :-

(4). Attention is drawn to the necessity of preventing revolvers, field glasses, wire cutters, compasses, watches, etc., from disappearing with wounded.

These must accompany wounded to the Divisional Collecting Station at VOORMEZEELE or Advanced Dressing Station at DICKEBUSCH and on no account be evacuated further.

D.A.D.O.S. will arrange to collect them periodically from the above places.

Captain,
D. A. Q. M. G.
41st. Division.

June 3rd. 1917.

Copies to :-
122nd.Inf.Brigade.	A.D.M.S.
123rd.Inf.Brigade.	A.D.V.S.
124th.Inf.Brigade.	A.P.M.
R.A.	D.A.D.O.S.
R.E.	Salvage Officer
Signals.	Area Commandant.
Pioneers.	"G".
Xth Corps Q.	24th.Division.
47th.Division.	19th.Division.
Divisional Train.	S.S.O.
War Diary.	Spare.

41st DIVISION.

List of Officer Casualties for Month of June 1916.

Date.	Rank.	Name.	Unit.	Nature of Casualty.
3rd.	Lieut.	J.S.Barker.	20th Durham L.Infy.	Wounded.
6th.	Captain.	W.E.Day.	233rd Field Coy., R.E.	Killed.
9th.	Captain.	C.J.Hogan.	11th Queens.	Wounded (slight at duty).
10th	Brig.Gen.	W.F.Clemson D.S.O.	H.Q., 124th Infy.Bde.	Wounded.
11th	Captain.	F.C.Vignoles.	11th Queens.	Wounded.
12th	2nd Lt.	H.L.Tate.	187th Brigade R.F.A.	Killed.
14th	Lieut.	F.W.Parrish.	18th K.R.R.Corps.	Missing.
18th	2nd Lieut.	D.Adams.	26th Royal Fusiliers.	Wounded.
19th	Capt.	J.F.Bretherton.	Warwicks att.10th Queens.	Wounded.
19th	2nd Lt.	F.R.Hoggett.	10th Queens.	Wounded.
19th	2nd Lt.	J.K.G.Ground.	10th R.W.Kents.	Killed.
20th	2nd Lt.	G.G.Samuel.	10th R.W.Kents.	Wounded.
21st	2nd Lt.	H.D.Hart.	26th Royal Fusiliers.	Wounded.
23rd	Lieut.	M.C.L.Porter.	11th Queens.	Wounded.
24th	Major.	L.Tenbosch.	12th E.Surreys.	Wounded, Shell Shock.
24th	Lieut.	E.C.Lambert.	R.A.M.C. att.12th E.Surreys.	Wounded.
25th	Capt.	J.S.Ryan.	18th K.R.R.Corps.	Killed.
"	2nd Lt.	W.G.Langford.	18th K.R.R.Corps.	Wounded.
"	Capt.	C.H.Wickham.	10th R.W.Kents.	Wounded Shell Shock.
"	2nd Lieut.	F.T.Licence.	10th R.W.Kents.	-do-
28th	2nd Lieut.	J.A.Tennyson-Smith	10th R.W.Kents.	Wounded.
30th	2nd Lieut.	C.F.Snow.	187th Brigade R.F.A.	Killed.
"	2nd Lieut.	B.Morris.	R.F.A. T.M.B. X/41.	Wounded.
"	Lieut.	A.C.Bender.	15th Hampshires.	Wounded slight at duty.
"	2nd Lieut.	S.H.Wigmore.	15th Hampshires.	Wounded.
"	Capt	M Wayman	20th Durham L.I.	Wounded

CONFIDENTIAL.

War Diary

The following Table shows numbers of killed, wounded, missing, and evacuated sick, during the month of June. (to 12 noon 30th).

UNIT.	OFFICERS.				OTHER RANKS.			
	Killed.	Wounded.	Missing.	Evacuated Sick.	Killed.	Wounded.	Missing.	Evacuated Sick.
Divisional Headquarters.	-	-	-	-	-	-	-	-
H.Q., 122nd Infy. Bde.	-	-	-	-	-	1	-	1
12th E. Surrey Regt.	-	4	-	-	13	49	-	27
15th Hampshire Regt.	-	2*	-	-	7	41	-	21
11th R.W.Kent Regt.	-	2	-	-	7	20	-	15
18th K.R.R.Corps.	1	1	-	-	10	30	-	11
123rd Bde. M.G.Coy.	-	-	-	-	-	4	-	4
H.Q., 123rd Infy. Bde.	-	3	-	-	-	-	-	-
11th Queens R.W.Surrey Regt.	1	4	-	-	14	31	-	13
10th R.W.Kent Regt.	-	1	-	-	7	59	-	10
23rd Middlesex Regt.	-	2	-	-	4	22	-	6
20th Durham L.Infantry.	-	1	-	-	4	17	-	9
123rd Bde. M.G.Coy.	-	-	-	-	-	-	-	-
H.Q., 124th Infantry Bde.	-	1	-	-	8	42	-	24
10th Queen's R.W.Surrey Regt.	-	3	-	-	7	24	-	14
26th Royal Fusiliers.	-	2	-	-	6	17	-	7
32nd Royal Fisiliers.	-	-	-	-	9	30	-	14
21st K.R.R.Corps.	-	-	-	-	1	-	-	1
19th Middlesex Regt.	-	1	-	-	1	16	-	14
H.Q., Divl. R.A.	-	-	-	-	-	-	-	-
183rd Brigade R.F.A.	2	-	-	-	1	3	-	6
187th " "	-	-	-	-	1	3	-	9
189th " "	-	-	-	-	-	3	-	8
190th " "	-	-	-	-	-	4	-	5
Divl. Ammn. Column.	-	-	-	-	-	4	-	5
T.M.B. X/41.	-	1	-	-	-	-	-	1
" Y/41.	-	-	-	-	-	-	-	1
" Z/41.	-	-	-	-	-	-	-	-
Heavy T.M.B. V/41.	-	-	-	-	-	5	-	3
Carried forward:-	4	21	-	-	98	422	-	228

P.T.O.

UNIT.	OFFICERS.			OTHER RANKS.			Evacuated Sick
	Killed.	Wounded.	Missing.	Killed	Wounded.	Missing.	
Brought forward:-	4	21	1	98	422	1	228
H.Q., Divl. R.E.							
228th Field Coy., R.E.							6
233rd " " "	1				1		3
237th " " "				1	4		1
41st Divl. Signal Coy., R.E.					4		1
41st Divisional Train.					1		2
138th Field Ambulance.							11
139th " "							1
140th " "					1		4
84th Sanitary Section.5							1
52nd Mobile Voty. Section.							1
Total.	5	21	1	99	432	1	257

* Includes Medical Officer.

H.Q., 41st Division.
1st July 1916.

NUMBERS OF MEN WASHED AT DIVISIONAL BATHS, during the month of June 1916.

Date.	Nieppe.	Papot.	Piggeries.	Steenwerck.	Total.
June 1.	377	45	103	30	555.
" 2.	1005	190	174	115	1484
" 3	1909	120	115	155	2299
" 4	335	210	193	175	913
" 5	845	200	139	210	1394
" 6	938	115	135	201	1389
" 7	1045	90	112	213	1460
" 8	1334	104	90	114	1642
" 9	753	84	72	130	1039
" 10	561	106	121	70	858
" 11	300	195	145	227	865
" 12	1287	115	97	112	1611
" 13	1164	110	128	25	1427
" 14	906	44	94	192	1236
" 15	541	90	89	169	889
" 16	753	125	107	436	1421
" 17	808	104	151	215	1258
" 18	389	103	75	209	776
" 19	1021	109	140	180	1450
" 20	1250	98	150	144	1642
" 21	1167	84	101	143	1495
" 22	751	176	135	311	1373
" 23	983	38	79	329	1429
" 24	351	200	180	224	955
" 25	537	190	40	159	926
" 26	1357	220	113	288	1978
" 27	1290	200	110	253	1853
" 28	1050	40	90	267	1447
" 29	659	50	170	322	1201
" 30	980	100	190	235	1505
				Grand total.	39770.

SECRET

Original.
War Diary
of
41st Division "A"
from
July 1st 1916 to July 31st 1916.

Army Form C. 2118

WAR DIARY
or
INTELLIGENCE SUMMARY
(Erase heading not required.)

Instructions regarding War Diaries and Intelligence Summaries are contained in F.S. Regs., Part II. and the Staff Manual respectively. Title Pages will be prepared in manuscript.

Place	Date	Hour	Summary of Events and Information	Remarks and references to Appendices
Stenwerck			Attached is (1) Roll of officers killed and wounded during month (2) Numbers of other ranks killed, wounded and evacuated sick missing during month (3) Numbers of men bathed at the divisional Baths during month (4) Numbers of articles of clothing mended at baths during month (5) Numbers of articles of clothing destroyed at the divisional baths during the month. (6) List of Cmt martials (No names) There is nothing else to record during the month.	22

Thos. __ Lt Col
A.D. & S.M.S.

CONFIDENTIAL.

41st Division.

The following Table shows numbers of killed, wounded, missing, and evacuated sick, during the month of July 1916. (to 12 noon 31st).

UNIT.	OFFICERS.				OTHER RANKS.			
	Killed.	Wounded.	Missing.		Killed.	Wounded.	Missing.	Evacuated Sick.
Divisional Headquarters.	-	-	-		-	-	-	-
H.Q., 122nd Infy. Brigade.	-	-	-		-	-	-	9
122nd M.G. Company.	-	-	-		4	4	-	15
12th E.Surrey Regt.	2	2	-		9	24	-	14
15th Hampshire Regt.	-	2	-		9	58	-	11
11th R.W.Kent Regt.	1	1	-		9	25	1	17
18th K.R.Rif.Corps.	-	-	-		-	32	-	-
H.Q., 123rd Infy. Brigade.	-	1	-		1	4	-	22
123rd M.G. Company.	-	6	-		12	45	-	19
11th R.W.Surrey Regt.	1	1	-		13	65	4	12
10th R.W.Kent Regt.	-	4	-		10	68	-	18
23rd Middlesex Regt.	1	5	-		11	103	10	-
20th Durham L. Infy.	-	-	-		-	5	-	4
H.Q., 124th Infy. Brigade.	-	6	-		10	55	4	20
124th M.G. Company.	-	1	-		8	25	-	11
10th R.W.Surrey Regt.	1	3	-		6	35	-	13
26th Royal Fusiliers.	-	2	-		12	44	-	12
32nd Royal Fusiliers.	-	2	-		-	7	-	9
21st K.R.Rif.Corps.	-	-	-		1	-	-	-
19th Middlesex Regt.(Pioneers).	-	2	-		2	5	-	4
H.Q., Divl. R.A.	-	-	-		-	16	-	6
187th Brigade R.F.A.	-	2	-		1	2	-	6
189th " " "	-	-	-		1	8	-	9
190th " " "	-	2	-		1	1	-	8
183rd " " "	-	-	-		-	6	-	-
41st Divl. Ammn. Column.	-	-	-		-	-	-	6
228th Field Coy., R.E.	-	2	-		1	5	-	6
233rd " " "	-	-	-		-	7	-	-
237th " " "	-	-	-		-	-	-	-
41st Divl. Signal Coy.	-	-	-		-	-	-	-
Carried forward.—	6	43	-		118	649	19	245

UNIT.	OFFICERS.			OTHER RANKS.			Evacuated Sick.
	Killed.	Wounded.	Missing.	Killed.	Wounded.	Missing.	
Brought forward.	6	43	-	118	649	19	245
41st Divisional Train.	-	-	-	-	7	-	7
138th Field Ambulance.	-	-	-	-	-	-	-
139th " "	-	-	-	-	1	-	5
140th " "	-	-	-	-	-	-	3
52nd Mobile Vety. Section.	-	-	-	-	1	-	1
T.M.B. V/41.	-	-	-	1	4	-	1
" X/41.	-	-	-	1	4	-	-
" Y/41.	-	-	-	-	-	-	-
41st Divl. Supply Column.	-	-	-	-	-	-	-
T.M.B. Z/41.	-	-	-	-	6	-	1
TOTAL.	6	43	-	120	665	19	262

41st DIVISION.

Courts-Martial during July 1916.

Unit.	No.	Particulars of Charge.	Sentence.
12th E. Surreys.	3	1. Carelessly firing a rifle. 2. " " " 3. Disobeying a lawful command.	1. 7 days F.P. No.2 2. 3 mos. F.P. No.1 3. 3 years P.S.
15th Hants. Rgt.	4	1. Asleep when on duty as a Signaller. 2. Carelessly handling a rifle. 3. Sleeping on his post when acting as sentinel. 4. Drunkenness.	1. 2 years Impt. with hard labour. 2. 3 mos. F.P. No.1. 3. 3 years P.S. 4. Reduced to the ranks (Sgt) and 3 mos. F.P. No.1.
18th K.R.R.Corps.	1	Failing to deliver a registered letter, and opening a letter not addressed to him.	Reduced to the ranks (Cpl), and 10 days F.P. No. 1.
11th R.W.Kent Rgt.	4	1. Desertion. 2. Leaving his guard without orders from his superior Off. 3. Sleeping on his post when acting as sentinel. 4. (a) Drunkenness. (b) Resisting an escort.	1. 10 years P.S. 2. 3 mos. F.P. No.1 3. 10 years P.S. (Sentence remitted) 4. 3 mos. F.P. No.1
20th Durham L.Inf.	3	1. Sleeping on his post when acting as sentinel. 2. Conduct to the prejudice of good order and Military discipline. 3. Desertion.	1. 3 years P.S., commuted to 1 year Impt. with H.L. 2. 90 days F.P. No.1 3. 5 years P.S., commuted to one year Impt. H.L.
23rd Middlesex Rt.	4	1. Drunkenness. 2. Sleeping on his post when acting as sentinel. 3. -do- 4. -do-	1. Reduced to ranks (Sgt) and fined £1. 2. 3 years P.S. 3. 3 mos. Impt. H.L. 4. 1 year Impt. H.L. Commuted to 90 days F.P. No. 1.
11th R.W.Surreys.	7	1. Neglect to the prejudice of good order and Mil. discipline 2. Disobeying a lawful command. 3. Using threatening language to his superior officer. 4. Disobeying a lawful command. 5. " " " 6. Discharging his rifle, thereby wounding a comrade. 7. Neglect to the prejudice of good order and Mil.discipline.	1. 56 days F.P. No.1 2. 3 mos. F.P. No.1 3. 14 days F.P. No.1 4. 28 days F.P. No.1 5. 3 mos. F.P. No.1 6. 14 days F.P. No.2 7. 56 days F.P. No.2

P.T.O.

Unit.	No.	Particulars of Charge.	Sentence.
10th R.W.Kent Rgt.	3	1. (a) Striking his superior Offr. (b) Disobeying a lawful command. 2. Disobeying, in such a manner as to show wilful defiance of authority, a lawful command. 3. --do--	1. 2 years Imp. H.L. 2. 3 years P.S. 3. 2 years Impt. H.L..
26th Roy.Fuslrs.	Nil.		
32nd " "	1.	(a) Drunkenness. (b) Resisting an escort.	Reduced to the ranks (Sgt), and 60 days F.P.No.1.
10th R.W.Surreys.	Nil.		
21st K.R.R.Corps.	1	Sleeping on his post when acting as sentinel.	6 mos. Impt. H.L. commuted to 90 days F.P. No. 1.
183rd Brigade R.F.A.	2	1. Leaving his post without being regularly relieved. 2. Drunkenness.	1. 14 days F.P.No. 1. 2. 42 days F.P.No. 1.
187th Brigade R.F.A.	2	1. (a) Theft. (b) Receiving goods knowing them to be stolen. 2. Conduct to the prejudice of good order and Mil.discipline.	1. 30 days F.P. No. 1 and to forfeit 60 days pay. 2. Reduced to the ranks (Sgt).
189th Brigade R.F.A.	Nil.		
190th Brigade R.F.A.	Nil.		
237th Field Coy.R.E.	1	(a) Using threatening language. (b) Drunkenness.	Reduced to the ranks (2nd Cpl).
41st Div.Signal Coy.	1	Drunkenness.	14 days F.P.No.1.
41st Divl. Train.	1	Disobeying a lawful command.	3 mos. F.P. No.1.
122nd T.M.B.	1	Drunkenness.	Reduced to the ranks (Sgt,)
228th Field Coy.R.E.	Nil.		
233rd " " "	"		
138th Field Ambulance	"		
139th " "	"		
140th " "	"		
52nd Mobile Vety. Section.	"		

41st DIVISION.

List of Officer Casualties for Month of July 1916.

Date.	Rank.	Name.	Unit.	Nature of Casualty.
1st.	Lieut.	J.W.James.	15th Hampshire Regt.	Wounded.(Slight at duty).
1st.	Lieut.	C.B.Smith.	11th R.W.Kent Regt.	Wounded.
1st.	Lieut.	J.Thompson-Hopper.	20th Durham L.Infy.	Killed.
1st.	Captain.	A.Pumphrey.	20th Durham L.Infy.	Wounded.
3rd.	2nd Lieut.	F.Wayman.	20th Durham L.Infy.	Wounded. (Slight at duty).
3rd.	2nd Lieut.	L.T.Garratt.	32nd Royal Fusiliers.	Wounded. (Died of wounds).
3rd.	Major.	H.H.Hulton.	187th Brigade R.F.A.	Wounded.
3rd.	2nd Lieut.	L.H.Easton.	187th Brigade R.F.A.	Wounded.
6th.	2nd Lieut.	R. Love.	11th R.W.Surrey Rgt.	Wounded. (Shell shock).
6th.	2nd Lieut.	R.W.R.Law.	21st K.R.Rif.Corps.	Wounded. (Slight at duty).
7th.	Lieut.	F.W.Roberts.	10th R.W.Kent Regt.	Wounded.
8th.	2nd Lieut.	G.H.Fawcett.	123rd M.G.Company.	Wounded.
9th.	Captain.	R.L.Pillman.	10th R.W.Kent Regt.	Died of wounds.
10th.	2nd Lieut	T.L.Wills.	32nd Royal Fusiliers.	Wounded.
10th.	Lieut.	G.J.L.Burton.	21st K.R.Rif.Corps.	Wounded.
11th.	2nd Lieut.	C.A.Lindup.	11th R.W.Surrey Regt.	Wounded.
11th.	2nd Lieut.	H.J.Snell.	23rd Middlesex Regt.	Wounded.
11th.	Lieut.	K.G.Livingstone.	23rd Middlesex Regt.	Wounded.(accidentally).
12th.	Captain.	W.E.Heydeman.	183rd Brigade R.F.A.	Wounded.
12th.	2nd Lieut.	J.Gibbs.	183rd Brigade R.F.A.	Wounded.
13th.	2nd Lieut.	W.H.Morgan.	15th Hampshire Regt.	Killed.
13th.	2nd Lieut.	G.H.Wingfield.	16th K.R.Rif.Corps.	Killed.
14th.	Lt.Colonel	H.H.Lee, D.S.O.	12th E.Surrey Regt.	Wounded.
14th.	2nd Lieut.	B.F.Dodd.	12th E.Surrey Regt.	Wounded. (Slight at duty).
14th.	Captain.	O.J.Hogan.	11th R.W.Surrey Regt.	Wounded. (Slight at duty).
14th.	Captain.	W.Hoad.	23rd Middlesex Regt.	Wounded.
14th.	Lieut.	W.G.F.Challis.	15th Hampshire Regt.	Killed.
15th.	Lieut.	O.L.Roberts.	19th Middlesex Regt.	Wounded.
15th.	2nd Lieut.	T.H.Pebworth.	19th Middlesex Regt.	Wounded.
15th.	Lieut.	E.T.G.Carter.	228th Field Coy., R.E.	Wounded. (Slight at duty).
22nd	Lt.Colonel	K.J.W.Leather.	20th Durham L.Infy.	Wounded.
23rd.	2nd Lieut.	G.L.Smetham.	32nd Royal Fusiliers.	Wounded.
24th.	Captain.	C.J.Hogan.	11th R.W.Surrey Regt.	Wounded.
25th.	Lieut.	S.C.J.Martin.	15th Hants. Rgt.(att'd 122nd T.M.B.)	Wounded.
25th.	2nd Lieut.	T.H.Fryer.	18th K.R.Rif.Corps.	Wounded.
25th.	2nd Lieut.	W.H.G.Chapman.	11th R.W.Surrey Regt.	Wounded. (Shell shock).
25th.	2nd Lieut.	A.F.Leslie.	228th Field Coy.,R.E.	Wounded.
26th.	2nd Lieut.	A.L.Keep.	11th R.W.Surrey Regt.	Wounded.
27th.	2nd Lieut.	E.W.Britton.	20th Durham L.Infy.	Wounded.
27th.	Captain.	D.E.Jessop.	20th Durham L.Infy.	Wounded. (Slight at duty).
27th.	Captain.	F.Sutherland.	10th R.W.Surrey Regt.	Wounded.
27th.	Lieut.	J.A.L.Hopkinson.	10th R.W.Surrey Regt.	Wounded.

Date.	Rank.	Name.	Unit.	Nature of Casualty.
27th.	2nd Lieut.	S.J.Ranson.	10th R.W.Surrey Regt.	Wounded.
27th.	2nd Lieut.	W.F.Serby.	10th R.W.Surrey Regt.	Wounded.
27th.	2nd Lieut.	H.G.D.Ereckson.	10th R.W.Surrey Regt.	Wounded.
30th.	Lieut.	C.C.Birch.	26th Royal Fusiliers.	Wounded.
31st.	2nd Lieut.	M.C.M.Fenton.	23rd Middlesex Regt.	Wounded.
31st.	Lieut.	G.A.Webb.	10th R.W.Surrey Regt.	Wounded.

41st. DIVISION.

ARTILLERY AMMUNITION EXPENDED DURING JULY, 1916.

Date.	18 pr. Shrapnel.	18 pr. H.E.	4.5 How. Shrapnel.	4.5 How. H.E.
1st.	5319	4486	61	1678
2nd.	567	497	19	147
3rd.	3117	1450	7	533
4th.	760	399	105	393
5th.	83	102	-	99
6th.	78	106	-	122
7th.	921	956	6	411
8th.	203	154	2	129
9th.	1488	286	23	185
10th.	688	744	48	276
11th.	443	564	40	464
12th.	652	462	2	257
13th.	2314	510	6	389
14th.	903	521	2	374
15th.	1438	147	-	243
16th.	2545	1314	10	524
17th.	2422	1376	6	868
18th.	1250	699	2	396
19th.	213	47	5	77
20th.	1458	116	-	-
21st.	3	-	-	-
22nd.	82	15	-	-
23rd.	93	30	16	15
24th.	386	40	-	-
25th.	1553	231	-	87
26th.	1906	567	-	21
27th.	2444	2903	-	1402
28th.	1140	733	-	-
29th.	125	99	-	-
30th.	114	64	9	-
31st.	120	90	-	-
Total.	34,828	19,708	369	9090

41st DIVISIONAL BATHS.

Numbers Bathed - July 1916.

Date.	Pont de Nieppe.	Papot.	Piggeries.	Steenwerck.	Total.
1st.	462	200	190	185	1037
2nd.	505	200	50	281	1036
3rd.	1262	250	210	155	1877
4th.	1126	180	104	234	1644
5th.	1223	200	12	215	1650
6th.	715	180	32	143	1070
7th.	757	70	130	277	1234
8th.	756	120	124	124	1124
9th.	646	160	51	399	1256
10th.	806	350	387	238	1781
11th.	698	180	226	288	1392
12th.	1175	250	205	204	1834
13th.	749	260	165	244	1418
14th.	577	200	182	378	1337
15th.	1163	100	175	327	1765
16th.	787	100	178	171	1236
17th.	1148	110	170	226	1654
18th.	1033	190	114	286	1623
19th.	1478	180	119	261	2038
20th.	714	90	102	576	1482
21st.	614	40	14	300	968
22nd.	419	150	50	325	944
23rd.	784	-	39	419	1242
24th.	1228	-	20	468	1716
25th.	1463	-	-	510	1973
26th.	1629	-	-	893	2522
27th.	1106	-	-	401	1507
28th.	1135	70	-	293	1498
29th.	972	150	-	388	1510
30th.	1109	150	200	381	1840
31st.	1158	120	-	490	1768
				T O T A L.	46976.

41st DIVISIONAL BATHS.

Articles Repaired - July 1916.

Date.	Socks. (Pairs).	Shirts.	Drawers.	Cardigans.
1st.	720	98	82	
3rd.	767	135	41	
4th.	633	122	36	
5th.	802	108	54	
6th.	546	138	26	
7th.	734	115	73	
8th.	619	156	62	
10th.	627	139	59	
11th.	855	140	53	
12th.	730	120	82	
13th.	768	128	78	
14th.	691	140	68	
15th.	561	147	60	31
17th.	657	200	40	3
18th.	721	132	28	
19th.	658	150	32	
20th.	640	132	62	
21st.	852	135	36	
22nd.	850	139	39	
24th.	819	174	51	
25th.	763	159	52	
26th.	985	124	46	
27th.	907	117	74	
28th.	886	123	62	
29th.	900	119	45	
31st.	692	176	45	
	19,383	3666	1386	34

41st DIVISIONAL BATHS.

Articles Destroyed - July 1916.

Date.	Socks. (Pairs).	Shirts.	Drawers.
1st.	42	12	9
3rd.	59	8	16
4th.	46	11	-
5th.	39	10	13
6th.	60	14	14
7th.	54	7	22
8th.	65	8	19
10th.	73	-	7
11th.	70	-	12
12th.	56	-	-
13th.	52	10	16
14th.	58	9	8
15th.	39	14	15
17th.	46	36	5
18th.	45	20	-
19th.	33	22	-
20th.	40	12	10
21st.	45	18	12
22nd.	48	8	14
24th.	49	30	8
25th.	70	25	10
26th.	60	45	14
27th.	45	47	15
28th.	53	42	8
29th.	60	52	8
31st.	32	52	11
	1,339.	512.	266.

~~Secret~~ A&Q Vol A

Original

War Diary

of

41st. Division "A & Q"

from

August 1st 1916 to Aug 31st 1916

WAR DIARY or INTELLIGENCE SUMMARY

Army Form C. 2118

Place	Date	Hour	Summary of Events and Information	Remarks and references to Appendices
FLÊTRE	17.	6 p.m.	Moved from STEENWERCK. The division moved into huts in area METEREN — MONT-DES-CATS — FLETRE — EECKE, divisional headquarters being established at FLETRE	Nil
FLÊTRE	23rd		The division commenced entraining to join the Fourth army in accordance with attached table	Nil A
AILLY-LE-HAUT-CLOCHER	25th		The detrainment was complete by 8 a.m. The distribution of the division in in huts is shown in the attached	Nil B
AILLY-LE-HAUT-CLOCHER	28th		Major (T/Lt Col) C.F. POTTER R.A assumed duties of A.A. and Q.M.G Southern Command vice Lt Col J.S. KNOX appt. D.Q. Southern Command	C

WAR DIARY
or
INTELLIGENCE SUMMARY

Army Form C. 2118

Place	Date	Hour	Summary of Events and Information	Remarks and references to Appendices
			Attached table C shows officer casualties during the month	C
			Attached table D shows casualties to other ranks during the month	D
			Attached table E shows contraventions during the month	E
			Attached table F shows ammunition expended during the month	F

R Matthews o'Carroll
Major
DA+QMG
1st Division
Lt of Division

PROGRAMME OF MOVE OF 41ST DIVISION VIA CALAIS

23.8.16 – 24.8.16

From Second Army
Entraining Stations
A = BAILLEUL MAIN 123/122
B = BAILLEUL WEST 124/122
C = GODEWAERSVELDE RA

To Fourth Army
Detraining Stations
A LONGPRE
B PONT REMY
C ABBEVILLE.

Train No. from stations			Serial No. (p=part)	Time of dep. from Ent.St'n	Date	Marche	Time of arr. at Det'ing Station	Date
A	B	C						
1	2	3	4	5	6	7	8	9
1			4121	2.28	23.8	HT 6	10.22	23rd 11 Queens
	2		4190,93	3.28	"	7	11.05	145 F.A. 4 ASC
		3	4141,79p	4.13	"	8	11.40	A/183 23 MSec
4			4122	5.28	"	9 L	13.22	23 Sex
	5		4131	6.18	"	10 RR	13.55	10 Queens
		6	4142,79p	7.05	"	11 A	14.40	B/183
7			4120,25,26,27	7.58	"	12 L	16.02	123 Bde MG TMB
	8		4132	9.28	"	13 RM	17.05	26 RF
		9	4143,79p	10.13	"	14 A	17.30	C/183
10			4189,92	11.28	"	15 L	19.22	139 FA 3 ASC
	11		4130,35,36,37	12.28	"	16 PR	20.05	124 Bde MG Coy TMB
		12	4144,79p	13.13	"	17 A	20.40	D/183
13			4183,85	14.28	"	CRE+ 18 L	22.22	233 Coy RE
	14		4133	15.28	"	19 PR	23.05	32 RF
		15	4151,80p	16.13	"	20 A	23.40	A/187
16			4123	17.28	"	21 L	1.22	24th 10 Kents
	17		4134	18.28	"	22 PR	2.05	21 KRRC
		18	4152,80p	19.13	"	23 A	2.40	D/187
19			4124	20.28	"	24 L	4.22	20 DLI
	20		4186	21.28	"	1 PR	5.05	237 7 Coy RE
		21	4153,80p	22.13	"	2 A	5.40	C/187
22			4111	23.28	"	3 L	7.22	12 E. Sussex
	23		4101,02,05,08	0.28	24.8	RA Sigs & Salvage 4 PR	8.05	DHQ
		24	4154,80p	1.13	"	5 A	8.40	D/187
25			4112	2.28	"	6 L	10.22	15 Hants
	26		4104	3.28	"	7 PR	11.05	19 Mx
		27	4140,50,60,70 and 78	4.13	"	8 A	11.40	HQ RA Bdes
28			4110,15,16,17	5.28	"	M.V.S Sansec & 1 Coy 1 Mxsec 9 L	13.22	122 Bde
	29		4187,94,95,04a	6.18	"	10 PR	13.55	HQ Coy Train
		30	4161,4181p	7.05	"	11 A	14.40	A/189
31			4113	7.58	"	12 L	16.02	11 Kents
	32		4171,82c	9.28	"	13 PR	17.05	A/190
		33	4162,81p	10.13	"	14 A	17.30	B/189
34			4184	11.28	"	15 L	19.22	226 7 Coy RE
	35		4172,82d	12.28	"	16 PR	20.05	B/190
		36	4163,81p	13.13	"	17 A	20.40	C/189
37			4188,91	14.28	"	18 L	22.22	138 7A 2 Coy ASC
	38		4173,82e	15.28	"	19 PR	23.05	C/190
		39	4164,81p	16.13	"	20 A	23.40	D/189
40			4114	17.28	"	21 L	1.22	25th 18 KRRC
	41		4174,82f	18.28	"	22 PR	2.05	D/190
		*42	4182a,96,97	19.13	"	23 A	2.40	1/2 B/ch/DAC
*43			4182b,98	20.28	"	24 L	4.22	1/2 B/ch/DAC

SUMMARY.

BAILLEUL MAIN (A) = 14 T.C's and 1 T.P.
BAILLEUL WEST (B) = 14 T.C's
GODEWAERSVELDE (C) = 13 T.C's and 1 T.P.
Trains 1 to 41 inc. are T.C's.
Trains 42 and 43 are T.P's

HAZEBROUCK. 16. 8. 16.

J.C. Owen Capt. R.E.
for Lieut. Colonel.
A.D.R.T. II

TABLE "D"   41ST DIVISION.

UNIT	Serial No.	DESCRIPTION
Divisional Units.	4101	Divisional Headquarters.
	02	H.Q., Divisional R.A.
	04	19th Middlesex (Pioneers) less 04a
	04a	1 Co. 4 G.S.Waggons & teams.
	05	H.Q. & H.Q.Section Div. Sig. Co.
	08	Salvage Co. and details.
122nd Infantry Bde.	4110	Brigade Headquarters.
	11	12th E.Surreys.
	12	15th Hants.
	13	11th R.W.Kents.
	14	18th K.R.R.C.
	15	Signal Section.
	13	Brigade M.G.Co.
	17	Light T.M.Battery.
123rd Infantry Bde.	4120	Brigade Headquarters.
	21	11th R.W.Surreys.
	22	23rd Middlesex.
	23	10th R.W.Kents.
	24	20th D.L.I.
	25	Signal Section.
	26	Brigade M.G.Co.
	27	Light T.M.Battery.
124th Infantry Bde.	4130	Brigade Headquarters.
	31	10th R.W.Surreys.
	32	26th Royal Fusiliers.
	33	32nd Royal Fusiliers.
	34	21st K.R.R.C.
	35	Signal Section.
	36	Brigade M.G.Co.
	37	Light T.M.Battery.
185rd Brigade R.F.A.	4140	Brigade Headquarters.
	41	A Battery.
	42	B "
	43	C "
	44	D "
187th Brigade R.F.A.	4150	Brigade Headquarters.
	51	A Battery.
	52	B "
	53	C "
	54	D "
189th Brigade R.F.A.	4160	Brigade Headquarters.
	61	A Battery.
	62	B "
	63	C "
	64	D "

DISTRIBUTION OF UNITS. 41st. DIVISION.

Divisional Headquarters.   AILLY LE HAUT CLOCHER.

122nd. Infantry Brigade Group.
Brigade Headquarters.	VAUCHELLES LES DOMART.
12th. East Surrey Regt.	MOUFLERS.
15th. Hampshire Regiment.	VILLERS SOUS AILLY.
11th. Royal West Kent Regt.	BRUCAMPS.
18th. K.R.R.Corps.	BRUCAMPS.
228th. Field Co. R.E.	BOUCHON.
122nd. Machine Gun Co.	VAUCHELLES LES DOMART.
122nd. T. Mortar Battery.	-do- -do-
138th. Field Ambulance.	BOUCHON.

123rd. Infantry Brigade Group.
Brigade Headquarters.	GORENFLOS.
11th. R.West Surrey Regt.	BUSSUS.
10th. R.West Kent Regt.	BUSSUS.
23rd. Middlesex Regt.	GORENFLOS
20th. Durham Light Infantry.	YAUCOURT.
233rd. Field Company.	ERGNIES.
123rd. Machine Gun Co.	-do-
123rd. T.Mortar Battery.	-do-
139th. Field Ambulance.	-do-

124th. Infantry Brigade Group.
Brigade Headquarters.	BOIS DE L'ABBEY.
10th. Royal West Surrey Regt.	BUIGNEY L'ABBE
26th. Royal Fusiliers.	VAUCHELLES LES QUESNOY.
32nd. Royal Fusiliers.	BELLANCOURT.
21st. K.R.R.Corps.	FRANCIERES.
257th. Field Company.	BAUCOURT.
124th. M.Gun Co.	MONFLIERS.
124th. T.Mortar Battery.	-do-
140th. Field Ambulance.	BAUCOURT.

Royal Field Artillery.
Headquarters.	PONT REMY.
183rd. Brigade.	PONT REMY.
187th. Brigade.	PONT REMY.
189 th.Brigade.	COCQUEREL.
190th. Brigade.	L'ETOIL.
"A" ECHELON D.A.C.	-do-
"B" ECHELON D.A.C.	EPAGNE.
T.M.B. V/41.	PONT REMY.
T.M.B's X/41,Y/41,Z/41.	EPAGNE.

Divisional Troops.
19th. Bn. Middlesex Regt.	AILLY LE HAUT CLOCHER.
Divisional Train.	LONG.
84th. Sanitary Section.	AILLY LE HAUT CLOCHER.
52nd.Mobile Veterinary Section.	EPAGNE.
Divisional Supply Column.	VAUCHELLES LES DOMART.

Copies to, G, Q, A, A.D.M.S.,A.D.V.S.,D.A.D.O.S.,A.P.M.,
122/123/124 Brigade H.Q.,C.R.A.,M.V.S.,Corps"Q",Salvage.,
C.R.E.,Camp Commandant, Claims Officer,Signals,2Spare.

U N I T.	Serial No.	DESCRIPTION.
190th Brigade R.F.A.	4170	Brigade Headquarters.
	71	A Battery.
	72	B "
	73	C "
	74	D "
Divisional Ammunition Column.	4178	Headquarters.
	79	No. 1 Section.
	80	No. 2 "
	81	No. 3 "
	82a	½ No.4 Section less 8 G.S.Wgns & teams
	82b	do.
	82c	4 G.S.Waggons and teams No.4 Section.
	82d	do.
	82e	do.
	82f	do.
Divisional Engineers.	4183	H.Q., Div'l R.E.
	84	228 Field Co. R.E.
	85	233 do.
	86	237 do.
Divisional Train.	4187	H.Q. & H.Q.Co. Train.
	4188	No. 2 Company.
	4189	No. 3 "
	4190	No. 4 "
Medical Units.	4191	138th Field Ambulance.
	4192	139th " "
	4193	140th " "
	4194	Sanitary Section.
	4195	Mobile Veterinary Section.
Trench Mortar Batteries.	4196	X T.M.Battery (Medium).
	4197	Y ditto
	4198	Z ditto

16. 8. 16.

41st DIVISION.
Officer Casualties – August 1916.

Date.	Rank.	Name.	Regiment.	Nature of Casualty.
4th.	Lieut.	J.W.C.Stares.	15th Hants. Rgt.	Wounded (Slight, at duty).
5th.	2nd Lt.	Menzies Calder.	15th Hants. Rgt.	-do- -do-
6th.	Lieut.	R.G.Rogers.	11th R.W.Kent Rgt.	Wounded.
6th.	2nd Lt.	M.H.Allen.	" " " "	Wounded.
6th.	2nd Lt.	R.W.Wheeler.	187th Bde. R.F.A.	Wounded.
14th.	Capt.	H.A.Robinson.	26th Royal Fuslrs.	Wounded.
17th.	2nd Lt.	N.T.Johnson.	" " "	Killed.
31st.	Lt.Col.	C.E.Stewart.	190th Bde. R.F.A.	Killed.

CONFIDENTIAL.

The following Table shews numbers of killed, wounded, missing and evacuated sick, during the month of August 1916 (to 12 noon, 31st).

UNIT.	OFFICERS.				OTHER RANKS.			
	Killed.	Wounded.	Missing.		Killed.	Wounded.	Missing.	Evacuated Sick.
Divisional Headquarters.	-	-	-		-	-	-	1
H.Q., 122nd Infantry Bde.	-	-	-		-	-	-	-
122nd Machine Gun Coy.	-	-	-		-	-	-	7
12th E.Surrey Regt.	-	-	-		-	4	-	19
15th Hampshire Regt.	-	2	-		2	7	-	21
11th R.W.Kent Regt.	-	2	-		1	7	-	30
18th K.R.R.Corps.	-	-	-		-	5	-	21
H.Q., 123rd Infantry Bde.	-	-	1		-	1	-	1
123rd Machine Gun Coy.	-	-	-		9	31	-	4
11th R." Surrey Regt.	-	-	-		2	6	-	50
10th R." Kent Regt.	-	-	-		5	3	-	31
23rd Middlesex Regt.	-	-	-		-	-	-	8
20th Durham L.Infantry.	-	-	-		3	13	-	19
123rd T.M.Battery.	-	-	-		-	-	-	2
H.Q., 124th Infantry Bde.	-	-	-		-	-	-	-
124th Machine Gun Coy.	-	-	-		4	1	-	5
10th R." Surrey Regt.	1	1	-		1	5	-	34
26th Royal Fusiliers.	-	-	-		-	3	-	25
32nd -do-	-	-	-		3	21	-	9
21st K.R.R.Corps.	-	1	-		1	8	-	15
19th Middlesex Regt. (Pioneers).	-	-	-		1	5	-	17
H.Q., 41st Divl. R.A.	-	-	-		-	-	-	12
187th Brigade R.F.A.	-	-	-		-	3	-	8
189th Brigade R.F.A.	-	-	-		-	4	-	8
190th Brigade R.F.A.	-	-	-		-	-	-	3
41st Divl. Ammn. Column.	-	-	-		-	1	-	3
T.M.B. V/41.	-	1	-		-	1	-	1
" X/41.	-	-	-		-	1	-	7
" Y/41.	-	-	-		-	-	-	-
183rd Brigade R.F.A.	1	-	-		-	1	-	7
Carried forward:-	2	8	-		32	130	-	331

UNIT.	OFFICERS.			OTHER RANKS.			
	Killed.	Wounded.	Missing.	Killed.	Wounded.	Missing.	Evacuated Sick.
Brought forward:-	2	6	-	32	130	-	331
229th Field Coy., R.E.	-	-	-	-	1	-	-
233rd Field Coy., R.E.	-	-	-	-	1	-	8
237th Field Coy., R.E.	-	-	-	-	-	-	-
41st Divl. Signal Coy., R.E	-	-	-	-	-	-	-
41st Divisional Train.	-	-	-	-	-	-	5
138th Field Ambulance.	-	-	-	-	-	-	2
139th Field Ambulance.	-	-	-	-	-	-	1
140th Field Ambulance.	-	-	-	-	-	-	4
52nd Mobile Vety. Section.	-	-	-	-	-	-	-
TOTALS.	2	6	-	32	132	-	351

H.Q., 41st Division.
3rd Sept. 1916.

41st DIVISION.

Courts-Martial during August 1916.

Unit.	No.	Particulars of Charge	Sentence.
12th E.Surreys.	Nil.		
15th Hants.	1	(a). Disobedience. (b). Attempting to escape from custody.	28 days F.P.No.1
18th K.R.R.Corps.	2	1. Carelessly firing a rifle, thereby wounding a comrade. 2. Drunkenness.	1. 5 mos. F.P.No.1. 2. Reduced to rank of Sgt. (R.Q.M.S.)
11th R.W.Kents.	1	Sleeping on his post when acting as sentinel.	10 years P.S. Sentence remitted.
20th Durham L.I.	5	1. Carelessly wounding himself in the left foot. 2. Drunkenness. 3. Drunkenness. 4. Drunkenness. 5. Drunkenness, and striking his superior Officer.	1. 28 days F.P.No.1. 2. Reduced to the ranks (Sgt). 3. 28 days F.P.No.1 and fined £1. 4. Fined 5/-. 5. 3 years P.S.
23rd Middlesex.	5	1. By neglecting to unload his rifle before cleaning, wounding a comrade. 2. Using insubordinate language to his superior Officer. 3. Drunkenness. 4. Negligently discharging his rifle, thereby wounding a comrade. 5. Drunkenness.	1. 56 days F.P.No.1. Sentence remitted 2. 18 mos. Impt.H.L. Commuted to 3 mos. F.P. No.1. 3. Reduced to the ranks (Cpl), and fined £1. 4. 90 days F.P.No.1. 5. 14 days F.P.No.1.
11th R.W.Surreys.	3	1. When acting as a sentinel, sleeping on his post. 2. -do- -do- 3. Drunkenness.	1. 5 years P.S. 2. 5 years P.S. 3. Fined 10/-.
10th R.W.Kent Regt.	4	1. Firing his rifle and wounding a comrade. 2. -do- -do- 3. Drunkenness. 4. -do-	1. 56 days F.P.No.1. 28 days F.P.Remitted. 2. 56 days F.P.No.1. 3. Reduced to the ranks (Sgt). 4. Fined £1.
32nd Royal Fusiliers.	1.	Drunkenness.	40 days F.P.No.1.
10th R.W.Surreys.	1.	Manslaughter.	1 year Impt.H.L.

P. T. O.

Unit.	No.	Particulars of Charge.	Sentence.
26th Royal Fuslrs.	Nil.		
21st K.R.R.Corps.	2.	1. Sleeping on his post when acting as sentinel. 2. -do- -do-	1. 1 year Impt. without H.L. 2. 1 year detention
183rd Brig.R.F.A.	Nil.		
187th -do-	1	(a). Using insubordinate language to a superior. (b). Offering violence to a superior Officer.	5 years P.S.
189th -do-	Nil.		
190th -do-	Nil.		
41st Div.A.Col.	1	Drunkenness.	Fined 10/-.
228th Field Coy.	1	Drunkenness.	12 mos. Impt.H.L. and to be reduced to the ranks (Cpl).
233rd Field Coy.	Nil.		
237th Field Coy.	Nil.		
138th Fd.Ambce.	Nil.		
139th Fd.Ambce.	Nil.		
140th Fd.Ambce.	1	Drunkenness.	28 days F.P.No.1.
41st Div.Train.	Nil.		
41st Div.Signal Coy.	Nil.		
52nd Mobile Voty. Section.	Nil.		
Divl.Headqiarters	1	(a). Drunkenness. (b). Absence from duty.	90 days F.P.No.1.

41st DIVISION.

Ammunition Expended during August 1916.

Date.	18 pr. Shrapnel.	18 pr. H.E.	4.5 How. Shrapnel.	4.5 How. H.E.	Stokes Mortars.
1st	114	64	9	-	-
2nd	83	102	-	99	-
3rd	120	90	-	-	-
4th	549	497	28	44	-
5th	386	40	-	-	-
6th	688	203	19	147	-
7th	959	1039	102	420	240
8th	384	642	9	65	296
9th	1492	421	10	211	90
10th	662	505	24	229	110
11th	192	279	23	20	3
12th	40	38	-	-	40
13th	14	-	-	-	13
14th	2	4	10	73	-
15th	138	170	20	232	-
16th	153	196	7	84	-
17th	423	245	69	98	-
18th	-	-	-	-	-
19th	-	-	-	-	-
20th	-	-	-	-	-
21st	-	-	-	-	-
22nd	-	-	-	-	-
23rd	-	-	-	-	-
24th	-	-	-	-	-
25th	-	-	-	-	-
26th	-	-	-	-	-
27th	-	-	-	-	-
28th	-	-	-	-	-
29th	-	-	-	-	-
30th	-	-	-	-	-
31st	-	-	-	-	-
TOTALS.	6399	4535	330	1722	792.

Vol 5

SECRET

Original
War Diary of
41st Division Headquarters
"A" & "Q" Branch
From Sept 1– 1916, to Sept 30 1916

WAR DIARY
INTELLIGENCE SUMMARY

(Erase heading not required.)

Army Form C. 2118

41 Divn H.Q.
"P" Branch

Place	Date	Hour	Summary of Events and Information	Remarks and references to Appendices
	1st Sept.		Transport of 228th and 233rd Field Companies R.E. and 19th Middlesex (Pioneers) proceeded by road to XV. Corps area.	Neil
	2nd Sept.		Dismounted personnel of above proceeded by bus to XV. Corps area bivouacing in Square F 9 c., Sheet 62.D. for work under C.E., XV. Corps. The 41st Divisional Artillery moved to XV. Corps area.	Neil
	5th Sept.		First Line Transport of Divisional Headquarters, 122nd and 123rd Infantry Brigades, 138th and 139th Field Ambulances, and 237th Field Coy., R.E., H.Q. and Nos. 2 and 3 Companies Divisional Train proceeded to XV. Corps area by road, billeting at ARGOEUVRES and LONGPRE the night of 5th/6th September, and reaching XV. Corps area the following day.	Neil
	6th Sept.		122nd and 123rd Infantry Brigades with dismounted personnel of Divisional Headquarters and 138th and 139th Field Ambulances proceeded by tactical trains from Xth Corps area, entraining at LONGPRE LES CORPS SAINTS, and detraining in XV. Corps area at MERICOURT, camping in XV. Corps reserve area A, with 123rd Brigade at BECORDEL; Divisional Headquarters at BUIRE. Transport 124th Infantry Brigade, 140th Field Ambulance and 52nd Mobile Veterinary Section, and No. 4 Company 41st Divisional Train, proceeded by road to XV. Corps area, billeting night 6th/7th Sept. at ARGOEUVRES and LONGPRE.	Neil
	7th Sept.		Dismounted personnel of 124th Infantry Brigade and 140th Field Ambulance proceeded by tactical train from X. Corps area, entraining at LONGPRE LES CORPS Saints, and detraining in XV. Corps area at MERICOURT bivouacing NORTH of BERNACOURT.	Neil
	9th Sept.		123rd Infantry Brigade moved to FRICOURT Camp. 124th Infantry Brigade moved to BECORDEL Camp.	
	10th Sept.		Administrative arrangements issued - copies attached. 123rd Infantry Brigade took over Sector of Front Line.	
	11th Sept.		124th Infantry Brigade moved to BECORDEL.	

Army Form C. 2118

WAR DIARY
INTELLIGENCE SUMMARY
(Erase heading not required.)

Instructions regarding War Diaries and Intelligence Summaries are contained in F.S. Regs., Part II. and the Staff Manual respectively. Title Pages will be prepared in manuscript.

Place	Date	Hour	Summary of Events and Information	Remarks and references to Appendices
	12th.		Arrangements for dealing with battle stragglers made and notified to all concerned. - Copy attached.	new
	13th.		Administrative Orders in case of an advance issued. Artillery wagon and Infantry etc. Transport Lines selected in forward area between MAMETZ and MONTAUBAN. One Troop Wiltshire Yeomanry, attached to the Division for tactical purposes, joined Divisional Headquarters and was camped with them. Administrative arrangements on and subsequent to Sept. 15th issued. Copy attached. Locations to be occupied by Battery wagon lines, Infantry Transport and Train in event of an advance selected and issued. Copy attached.	new
	14th.		A table shewing the location of units is attached.	Rem
	15th.		The Division attacked with rest of XV. Corps. Advanced Orders for clearing the battlefield and salvaging issued. Copies attached.	Rem
	16th.		Reinforcements from Brigade Transport Lines sent up to Battalions. A party of 3 Officers and 240 Infantry supplied to the A.D.M.S. to reinforce R.A.M.C. bearers who were becoming exhausted.	Rem
	17th.		Parties sent up from Transport Lines to clear battlefield. Owing to heavy shelling very little could be effected.	
	18th.		The Division was relieved during night 17th/18th, and moved back to XV. Corps Reserve Camps. Two Brigades to camp north of DERNANCOURT, one Brigade to BECORDEL Camp. Divisional Headquarters to RIBEMONT. The Divisional Artillery remained in the Line.	
	19th.		A Table shewing estimated casualty wires sent is attached.	
	21st.		The Division received Orders to hold itself in readiness to move one Brigade at 1 hour's notice, two Brigades at 2 hours notice.	
	22nd.		The Division remained in reserve.	

1875 Wt. W593/826 1,000,000 4/15 J.B.C. & A. A.D.S.S./Forms/C. 2118.

Army Form C. 2118

WAR DIARY
INTELLIGENCE SUMMARY
(Erase heading not required.)

Instructions regarding War Diaries and Intelligence Summaries are contained in F. S. Regs., Part II. and the Staff Manual respectively. Title Pages will be prepared in manuscript.

Place	Date	Hour	Summary of Events and Information	Remarks and references to Appendices
	28th		123rd Infantry Brigade moved up to Camp near MONTAUBAN and reinforced 21st Division. Table shewing casualties during month is attached. Table shewing Sick wastage during month is attached.	

1st Div.
524/A.

ADMINISTRATIVE ARRANGEMENTS OF THE DIVISION MOVING INTO THE LINE.

(1). GRENADES, STOKES AMMUNITION, S.A.A., etc.

Main Dump.   F 7 a 0 3.

Brigade Dumps:-
  Right Brigade in line.   S 23 a a a 22 d 9 2
  Left   "   "   "   S 16 d 0 6. (known as GREEN DUMP).

The Main Dump is supplied by the Corps Ammunition Park.

First Line Transport of units will be used to take up requirements from the Main Dump to Brigade Dumps. The Main Dump will be in charge of Captain MAYELL, Divisional Bombing Officer, who will be provided with a small staff including a certain number of men trained as Bombers. Each Brigade Dump will be in charge of an Officer — the Brigade Bombing Officer is suggested, who will have a small staff for unloading wagons, and detonating bombs and Stokes Ammunition.

Bombs and Stokes Ammunition can always be sent up from the Main Dump ready detonated in the event of this being necessary.

In the event of a third Brigade moving up into the line, it will draw on either Brigade Dump for bombs, etc. In any case of emergency any Brigade can draw from any Dump.

The following amounts of ammunition will be maintained at the Divisional Main Dump, and at each Brigade Dump. Officers in charge of dumps must see that these amounts are kept up

Nature of Ammunition.	Main Divl. Dump.	Each Bde. Dump.
No. 5 Mills Grenades.	10,000.	5,000.
Stokes 3" Bombs.	5,000.	2,000.
Red Cartridges.	5,000.	2,000.
Green Cartridges.	5,000.	2,000.
1" Very Lights.	4,000.	1,000.
1½" "	2,000.	500.
2" Trench Mortar.	1,000.	250.
S.A.A.	400 boxes.	100 boxes.
"P" Grenades.	1,000.	500.
Rifle Grenades.	4,000.	1,000.
Rockets "S.O.S." and sticks	50.	25.
Flares (yellow).	100.	50.
" (green).	100.	50.
Petrol tins, 2 galls	1,000.	400.
No 5 mills Rifle Grenades	5000	

* This includes those issued under Brigade orders to units in the Line.

The Divisional Dump Officer will issue to units on the indent of the Officers i/c. Brigade Dumps.

Normally bombs and Stokes ammunition will be detonated at Brigade Dumps.

It is hoped that the Main Dump will be in direct telephonic communication with Divisional and Brigade Headquarters.

A reserve of Gas Helmets will be kept at the Divl. Dump.

(2). R. E. STORES.

The main Divisional R.E. Dump will be close to FRICOURT Siding at F 5 c.2 5. [MAMETZ] Units will draw their requirements in trench material here and send it up in the transport wagons in the normal way.

In addition the Officers i/c. Brigade Dumps will arrange to maintain at Brigade Dumps a small reserve of sandbags, barbed-wire, and entrenching tools.

(3). WATER.

Two sources:-

(i). FRICOURT - 4 standpipes for filling water carts, tank for filling petrol tins (6 taps), and troughs for horses.

(ii). BECORDEL - Standpipes for water carts and troughs for horses.

Horses watering at these places must conform to local orders as regards tracks to be used going to and from watering.

All watering parties are to be in charge of an Officer whenever possible, or when an Officer is not available of a senior N.C.O.

For the trenches, supply will have to be by petrol tins, units sending up full petrol tins on their wagons and returning with empty tins. Petrol tins are filled up from water carts in the Transport Lines of units.

In addition, each Brigade will keep a reserve of 400 tins at the Brigade Dump. To ensure a daily turnover, the daily requirements will be sent up to the front trenches from the reserve supply at the Brigade dump and replenished by the tins that come up on the Transport Wagons.

It is hoped to be able to arrange for 2 or 3 tanks at each Brigade dump for use as a further reserve in case of necessity

(4). SUPPLIES.

Units attached to the Divisional Headquarter group will continue to be fed from ALBERT, the normal procedure being followed.

In the case of Infantry Brigade groups, supplies are brought by the metre gauge railway direct to FRICOURT Siding where the Supply Column Supply Officer will hand over to the S.S.O. Here they are dumped under Divisional arrangements and loaded direct into 1st Line Transport of units.

With the exception of those in Strong Points no reserve dumps of rations will be maintained either in the trenches or in Divisional Dumps, and units must rely on the current day's rations and the iron ration. The importance, therefore, of taking care of the iron ration cannot be too strongly impressed on all ranks.

(5). SALVAGE.

A Divisional Salvage Dump, at which the Divl. Salvage Officer and his staff will be located, will be established at the Main Divisional Grenade Dump at F 7 a 0 3.

Brigade Salvage Dumps will be established at Brigade Grenade Dumps, and will be supervised by the Officers i/c. the latter.

Brigades are responsible for salvaging in their own Brigade areas (including Transport Lines and their immediate vicinity).

Each Brigade will appoint a Brigade Salvage Officer, who will be placed in charge of all temporary unfit men or any men too old or otherwise unavailable for work in the forward trenches. This party will be located in the Brigade Transport Lines, and will be used for salvage or any other work as required. In the event of any special salvage work being required to be done, Divisional Headquarters, will call on Brigade Salvage Companies to furnish the necessary men.

In addition to the above, each Brigade will maintain one N.C.O. and 2 men at the Brigade Salvage Dump (i.e. Brigade Grenade Dump). They will be under the supervision of the Officer i/c. Brigade Dump, and will be used to take care of, sort and load all salvaged material.

All salvaged articles will be sent back in the empty ration and ammunition wagons, and will be handed over to the Divisional Salvage Officer at the Divisional Dump.

The Divisional Salvage Officer will render every morning to the D.A.D.O.S., 41st Division, a rough return showing what he has at the Dump. After the D.A.D.O.S. has notified what he requires for fitting out the Division, the remainder will be sent to the Corps Salvage Dump at HERICOURT (Square J 3 d.).

One G.S. wagon from Divl. Train will be allotted to the Divl. Salvage Officer and will remain at the Divisional Dump.

Commanding Officers must impress on all ranks the importance of doing all they can to assist in salving. The waste of equipment and material in the present operations has been enormous, and there is still a very large amount lying about, such as rifles, Lewis Gun magazines, steel helmets, etc., etc.

No man should return from the front line without bringing some article of salvage with him.

(6). RUM.

The S.S.O. of the Division always maintains a one day's stock on hand, which will be issued on the authority of the Divisional Commander.

(7). REINFORCEMENTS.

Railhead for reinforcements is EDGEHILL (Square E 12 d.).

All reinforcements will be sent direct to Brigade Transport lines. Each Brigade will arrange for an orderly to be sent to EDGEHILL at once to report to the R.T.O. He will be used as a permanent guide to conduct reinforcements to their respective transport lines. These guides will be accommodated and rationed by the R.T.O.

4.

The Gas Officer will visit all reinforcements immediately after their arrival at the transport lines to inspect gas helmets and see that each man is thoroughly conversant with gas drill.

No reinforcements are to be sent to the trenches without the Divisional Commander's sanction. To enable him to keep in touch with the numbers available, Brigade Transport Officers will forward daily to Divl. Headquarters direct a statement showing the total number of reinforcements, by units, available in the transport lines, under 2 headings :-

 (i) Those who have previous experience of the war, and

 (ii) Those who have never been in the trenches before.

This statement will be made up to noon daily and will be forwarded as soon as possible after that hour.

(C) CEMETERIES.

A list of the authorised cemeteries will shortly be published. As far as possible burials should take place in those cemeteries only.

Units are responsible for the collection and burial of dead in their own areas. In the event of any special assistance being required application will be made to Divisional Headquarters.

Lieut-Colonel,
A.A. & Q.M.G.
41st Division.

10.9.16.

Copies to :-

Infantry Brigades
17th Middlesex Regt.
C. R. A.
C. R. E.
41st Divl. Train.
17th Supply Column
A. D. M. S.
41st Signal Coy.
A. D. V. S.
D. A. D. O. S.
52nd Mobile Veterinary Section.
A. P. M.
Camp Commandant.
"G".
Divl. Salvage Officer.

SECRET.   41st Divn. No. A/524/3.

1.   In the event of an advance, battery wagon lines, the D.A.C., Train, M.V.S. and Infantry group transport lines will move to positions as shown on attached list.

2.   These positions should be reconnoitred at once, and working parties, found from reinforcements and unfits at the transport lines, sent forward on the morning of the 14th, to carry out any necessary work.

3.   Among other works necessary are the following :-

(a) Making road ways from main road to sites of lines.
(b) Making roads over old trenches and through wire entanglements.
(c) Burying cables; the ground is covered with telegraph and telephone cables. Where any of these cross routes which have to be followed to obtain entrances to the transport lines, the greatest care must be taken to bury them one foot deep in order to avoid breaking them, which would in many cases have the most serious consequences.

4.   All wagon and transport lines etc. must close up and not occupy more ground than necessary.

5.   It must be clearly understood that on no account are any tents or shelters to be taken from present lines.

13. 9. 16.

Lieut-Colonel,
A.A. & Q.M.G.
41st Division.

Copies to :-

Inf. Bdes.
17th Middlesex Regt.
C.R.A.
C.R.E.
Divl. Train.
S.S.O.
Supply Cln.
A.D.V.S.
A.D.M.S.
A.P.M.
D.A.D.O.S.

"G"
Camp Commandant
41st Signal Coy.
52nd Mobile Vety. Section.

POSITIONS OF WAGON AND TRANSPORT LINES.

Royal Artillery 21st and 41st Divisions.

Squares F.5.b. excluding portion allotted to Divnl. Train, part of Square F.5.d. North of main road, all F.6.a. north of main road, X.30.c. excluding N.W. corner, S.25.d., South east part of S.25.b.

Divisional Train and Mobile Veterinary Section.

Area bounded by points X.29.d.0.0., X.30.c.0.5., F.6.c.0.5, F.5.b.2.5.

122 Infantry Brigade Group (less Field Coy. R.E. and Coy. A.S.C.)

Squares S.27.a, b and c. excluding village of MONTAUBAN.

123 Infantry Brigade group (less Field Coy. R.E. and Coy. A.S.C)

Squares S.26.b and d.

124 Infantry Brigade group (less Field Coy.R.E. and Coy. A.S.C)

Squares S.26.a.and c.

D.H.Q., Signal Coy. and 3 Field Coys. R.E.

Square A.1.b. north of main road.

10th Middlesex Regt.

Part of Square A.2.a. north of main road.

SECRET.   41st Division No. A/524/2.

ADMINISTRATIVE ARRANGEMENTS ON AND SUBSEQUENT
TO SEPTEMBER 15th, 1916.
----

1. SUPPLIES.

    All troops will commence the attack on the morning of 15th with the following in their possession :-

    (a) Rations for the 15th.
    (b) One Iron Ration.
    (c) Extra soup ration.

    Rations for the 16th will be drawn on the morning of the 15th as usual, i.e. 3 Inf. Bde. Groups at FRICOURT OLD STATION and R.A. at refilling point in Square E.10.a.& b.
    As 1st Line transport of units will be filled ready for any forward move, it will not be available to carry rations from the refilling point at FRICOURT STATION to transport camp. This, therefore, will be done by the supply wagons of the train.
    The subsequent move of supply wagons depends on how the advance progresses. If a considerable advance is made entailing the movement of transport lines, then supply wagons will carry forward the food for the 16th and hand over to units in the new transport lines. If no considerable advance is made and the transport lines cannot be moved, supply wagons will hand over rations in the present transport lines, whence they will be sent forward to the trenches under regimental arrangements.
    Units should make arrangements to collect all rations of casualties in the front line trenches and so ensure a small reserve being always immediately available.
    There is already a considerable reserve of water at Brigade Dumps which can be drawn on as an immediate reserve.
    Subsequent arrangements for supplies will depend on the tactical situation.

2. BAGGAGE WAGONS.

    All baggage wagons will be returned to units by noon on 14th inst.

3. TRANSPORT & WAGON LINES.

    In the event of a considerable advance, transport lines and all Battery wagon lines will be moved forward to the ridge N of the road between MAMETZ and MONTAUBAN. Some lines may even be moved as far forward as Square S.21 but this depends on circumstances.
    Separate instructions showing allotment of transport lines in detail will follow.

4. WATER.

    Storage tanks holding 50.000 gallons have been erected on the S side of the MAMETZ-MONTAUBAN road at S.27.c.2.1. Here a certain number of water carts can be filled.

2.

WATER (continued).

Horse troughs will be available on the evening of the 15th. at a point in S.27.b.
Until further orders water carts and animals of R.A. and Divl. Train will water at the MAMETZ-FRICOURT supply; all other units will use the new supply at MONTAUBAN.
The water supply at S.27.c.2.1. will be controlled by the Division on our right, that in Square S.27.b. by the 41st Division.
A programme of hours for watering will be issued later.
On no account is the water from wells in LONGUEVAL to be used by troops for drinking purposes until it has been subjected to a strict medical test.

5. ROADS.

Particular attention is drawn to XV Corps No. AC/1005/63 dated 12/10/16 on the subject of traffic regulations which must be strictly complied with.

6. AMMUNITION.

All units must ensure that their first (regimental) echelons of S.A.A., bombs etc. are filled up and ready to move forward at a moment's notice.
No attempt will be made to move forward the Brigade and Divisional Grenade Dumps at present, though this will be done as soon as possible.

7. MEDICAL.

The Divisional Advanced Dressing Station is at the QUARRY (Square S.22.c.). Advanced reserve bearer posts are at GREEN DUMP (S.16.d.0.6) and the SHRINE (S.23.a.6.7). Walking wounded proceed to the Collecting Station at F.6.a.2.0. (just E. of MAMETZ).

8. SANITATION.

As large numbers of troops will probably use the camping area between MAMETZ and MONTAUBAN in the future the importance of strict attention to sanitation cannot be over estimated. Latrines must be carefully sited and all foul ground marked. The practice of using shell holes as latrines and receptacles for every form of rubbish must be stopped. Public latrines will shortly be erected. When ready, those latrines only and no others will be used.
Incinerators will be erected at the first possible opportunity.

Lieut-Colonel,
A.A. & Q.M.G.
41st Division.

13.9.16.

Copies to :— Inf. Bdes.
     18th Middlesex Regt.
     C.R.A.
     C.R.E.
     Divl. Train.
     D.A.D.O.S.
     "G".
     17th Supply Clm.
     A.D.M.S.
     A.D.V.S.
     A.P.M.
     41st Signal Coy.
     52nd. Mobile Vety. Sctn.
     S.S.O.
     Camp Commandant.

SECRET.

LOCATION OF UNITS OF 41st. DIVISION.

D.H.Q.	BELLEVUE FARM.
C.R.A.	-do- -do-
C.R.E.	-do- -do-
A.D.M.S.	-do- -do-
A.D.V.S.	-do- -do-
WAGON LINES R.A.	E.11.
D.A.C.	E.4.c.7.4.
FIELD COS' R.E.	F.1.c.6.7.
122nd.BRIGADE TRANSPORT LINES.	F.2.CENTRAL.
123rd.BRIGADE TRANSPORT LINES.	F.2.c.CENTRAL.
124th.BRIGADE TRANSPORT LINES.	E.12.a.
13th. MIDDLESEX	F.0.c.6.8.
H.Q.138th.FIELD AMBULANCE.	F.8.a.2.0.
H.Q.139th.FIELD AMBULANCE.	F.7.a.8.2.
140th.FIELD AMBULANCE.	BELLEVUE FARM.
84th.SANITARY SECTION.	BELLEVUE FARM.
DIVISIONAL TRAIN.	E.4.d.
MOBILE VETERINARY SECTION.	E.10.c
DIVL.SALVAGE CO. & DUMPS.	E.12.b.c.5.

```
Copies to:-   "G".  2.        R.T.O.Mericourt.   1.
      A.D.M.S.    5.          R.T.O.Edgehill     1
      A.D.V.S.    1.          Claims Offcr.      1.
      A.P.M.      1.          "Q"                3.
      San.Secn.   1.          Divl.Dump Offcr.   1.
      C.R.A.      5.          Divl Sal.Offcr.    1.
      Brigades    1.each.     M.Vet.Secn.        1.
      O.Commdt.   1.          S.H.Bryant.A.P.O.  1. R.41.
      Train.      2.          Spare              3.
      D.S.C.      1.          13th.Msex.         1.
      7th.D.Atlly. 1
      21st.-do-   1.
```

September 12th.1916.

Major,
D.A.A.&.Q.M.G.
41st.Division.

S E C R E T.

1.   Alterations to "Location of units 41st. Division". Transport 124th. Infantry Brigade to F.2.c.3.3. from tomorrow morning.

2.   Add 41st. Divisional Cavalry 1 Troop Wiltshire Yeomanry camped with Divisional Headquarters.

[Signature]

Major,
D.A.A. & Q.M.G.,
41st. Division.

September 13th. 1916.

Copies to all units.

41st Divn. No. A/82/2.

CLEARING THE BATTLEFIELD.
------------------*------------

1. 1 Officer and 50 men from each Infantry Brigade Transport Lines, with the necessary picks and shovels, will be held in readiness to proceed from their transport lines at 7 a.m. tomorrow to the battlefield to bury the dead on receipt of further orders which will be issued.

2. Areas which each Brigade party is responsible for are shewn in the attached sketch. Parties will commence at the South-west end of their areas and work North-west, as far forward as the enemy's fire allows.

3. Bodies will be buried in selected spots, provisionally indicated thus + on sketch, until the exact sites can be reconnoitred.

4. Our own dead and those of the enemy must be buried separately.

5. The following extracts from G.R.Os. must be carefully complied with:-

   (a) Officers will, as a rule, be buried with their men, but in the case of General or senior officers reference will be made to Divisional Headquarters.

   (b) The officer i/c of the burial party will personally see that each body is searched; that all effects found are tied together with the cord of the identity disc, and that the whole of packets thus made up belonging to individuals buried in the same place are secured together (in a sandbag is suggested) and forwarded to Divisional Headquarters, labelled with the position of the burial ground.

   (c) The officer in charge of the burying party will enter in his notebook the name, number, unit etc. of each body from the identity disc before it is placed in the grave. When the grave is filled in he will forward this list, together with a note giving the map reference, and describing the position of the grave as accurately as possible, to Divisional Headquarters.

6. Every effort must be made to mark all graves. A wooden peg with the name on it, or failing that a slip of paper in a cleft stick, should be used.

7. Senior Chaplains of each denomination will arrange for Chaplains to be present.

R H à Court
Major,
D.A.A. & Q.M.G.,
41st Division.

15. 9. 16.

Copies to :- A.D.M.S., C.R.A., C.R.E., 13th Middlesex Regt.
122, 123 and 124 Bde. Transport Officers,
C.R.A. 21st Division.
C. of E. Senior Chaplain.
R.C. Senior Chaplain.
Wesleyan Senior Chaplain
122, 123 and 124 Inf. Bdes. (for information)

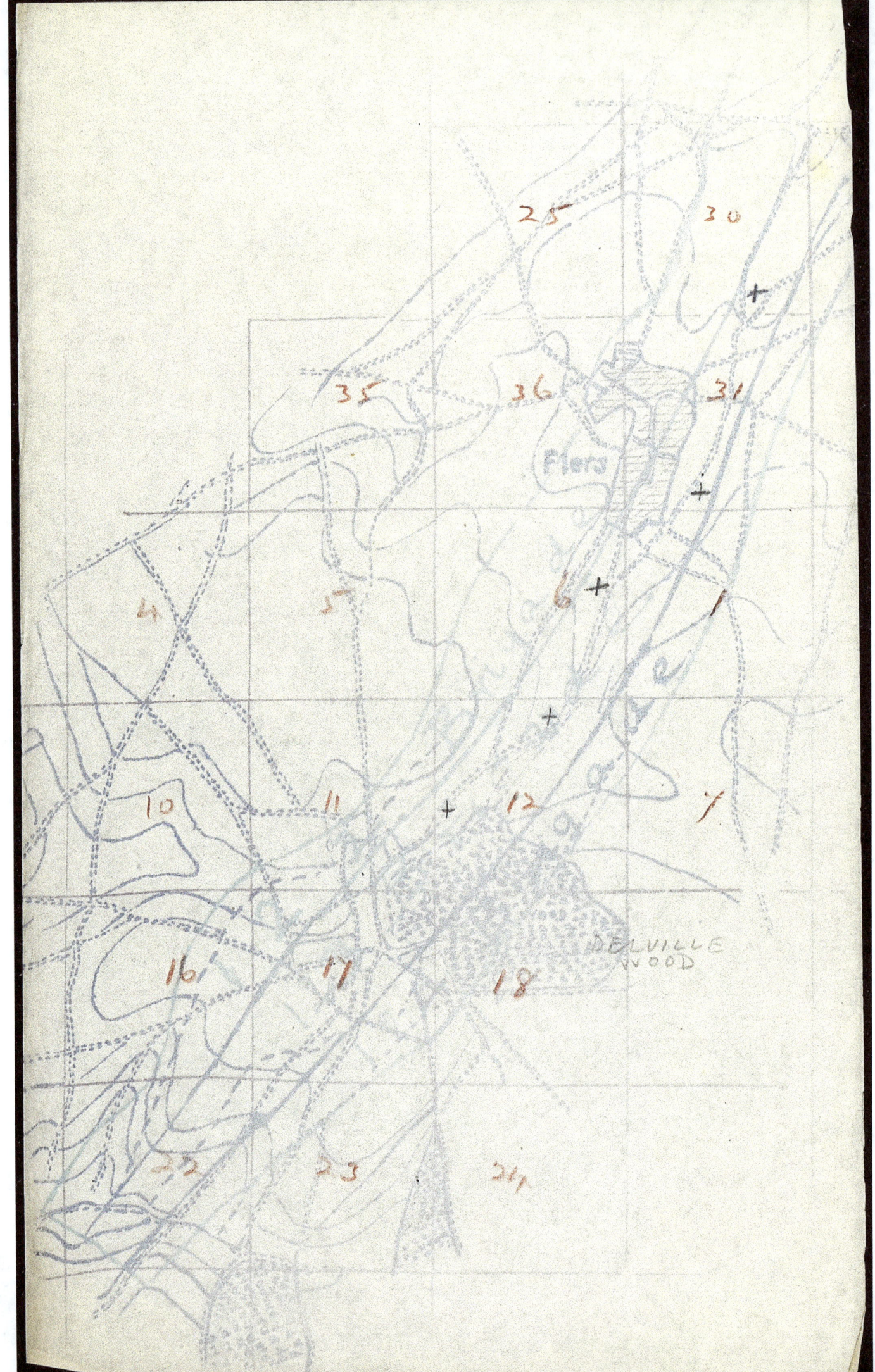

SECRET

Copy No. 1.
208/S.7.

The 122nd and 123rd Infantry Brigade Groups will entrain at LONGPRE LES CORPS SAINTS on Sept. 6th as follows:-

Train leaving at 5 a.m.
12th E.Surrey Regiment.
15th Hampshire Regiment.
122nd Brigade Headquarters.
122nd Stokes Mortar Batteries.
138th Field Ambulance.

7 a.m.
11th R.W.Kent Regiment.
18th K.R.R.Corps.
122nd Machine Gun Company.
Details, Divisional Train.

1 p.m.
Divisional Headquarters.
139th Field Ambulance.
11th Bn. "Queens."
10th Bn. R.W.Kents.
Details, 19th Middlesex Regt.

3 p.m.
123rd Brigade Headquarters.
123rd   Stokes Mortar Batteries.
23rd Middlesex Regt.
20th Durham Light Infantry Bde.
123rd M.G.Company.

In all cases Troops should be at the Station 30 minutes before the advertised hour of departure of the train.

It must be clearly understood that no baggage or transport of any kind can be carried on the trains with the exception of Lewis and Stokes Gun Handcarts and their contents.

The journey is expected to occupy about 4 hours.

Detrainment will be at MERICOURT where trains will be met by guides.

Lt.Colonel,
A.A. & Q.M.G.,
41st Division.

5th Sept. 1916.

Copy No. 1.	File.		Copy. No. 24.	G.
" Nos. 2 to 8.	122nd Infy. Bde.		" " 25	A.
" " 9 to 15.	123rd " "		" " 26	A.D.V.S.
" " 16	O.C., Details, 19th Middx.		" " 27	Camp Commdt.
" " 17	" R.E. Details.		" " 28	D.A.D.O.S.
" " 18 to 22.	A.D.M.S.		" " 29	A.P.M.
" " 23	O.C. Div.Train details.		" " 30	Spare.

ESTIMATED CASUALTIES.

Source	Original Strength O.	O.R.	Time: 1.30am Date: 15th Num/or: ES1 O.	O.R.	1.30am 16th ES2 O.	O.R.	12 noon 16th ES3 O.	O.R.	7.30pm 16th ES4 O.	O.R.	10.5am 19th EC5 O.	O.R.	TOTAL ESTIMATE CASUALTIES O.	O.R.
12/E.Surry.	400		7	400				300	14	475			14	4
15/Hants.									13	310				
18/K.R.R.		250			(Co)	250			14	449				
11/R.Knts.	8	250							12	440				
11/K.Srry.							1(Co)	150	3	150				
10/R.Knts.									4	230				
23/Msex.					12(Co)	350		350	12	350				
20/D.L.I.								100	4	250				
10/K.Srry.					1(Co)	350			18	350				
26/R.Fslrs.						300			9	300				
32/R.Fslrs.						300			13	300				
21/K.R.R.C.						300			14	300				
19/Msex.														
228/F.Coy.														
233/F.Coy.														
237/F.Coy.														
122/M.G.Co.									3	35	3	18		
123/M.G.Co.									2			40		
124/M.G.Co.														
									124	3904				

41st. DIVISION.

COURTS MARTIAL DURING SEPTEMBER 1916.

Unit.	No.	Particulars of Charge.	Sentence.
15th. Hants.	1.	Conduct prejudice to good order and military discipline.	Reduced to ranks (Cpl) 56 days F.P.No.1.
20th. D.L.I.	3.	2 Absence without leave 1.Self inflicted wound.	28 days F.P.2 2 years. imp.H.L. S.I.W. Not guilty
26th. R.Fslrs.	1.	Discharging rifle & wounding a comrade.	Fined 28 days pay
32nd. R.Fslrs.	1.	Breach of Censorship.	90 days F.P.2.
21st. K.R.R.C.	2.	Drunkenness.	Not Guilty.
187th. R.F.A.	1.	Drunkenness.	(Cpl) Reduced to ranks.
189th. Brig.R.F.A.	1	Threatening superior offr.	21 days pay fft.
122.M.G.Co.	1.	Firing revolver.	14 days F.P.1.
124.M.G.Co.	1.	-do-	28 days F.P.1.
41st. Sig.Co.	2.	Drunkenness.	1 Not Guilty. 1 56 days F.P.1.
140th. F.Ambulce.	2	1.Drunkenness 1.Stealing Drunk.Threatening.	90 days F.P.1. 1 yrs.Imp.H.L.
17th. D.S.C.	1.	Drunkenness.	2 months F.P.1 & fined 10.

CONFIDENTIAL.

The following table shows numbers of Killed, Wounded, Missing, and evacuated Sick during the month of September 1916, (to 12 noon 30th.)

UNIT.	OFFICERS.			Other Ranks.			Evacuated Sick.
	Killed.	Wounded.	Missing.	Killed.	Wounded.	Missing.	
12th. East Surrey.	8	8	—	42	224	57	7
15th. Hampshire Regt	8	5	1	32	192	59	10
11th. R.West Kents.	4	10	1	30	140	100	11
18th. K.R.R.C.	6	7	—	57	230	59	9
122nd.M.Gun Company.	1	2	—	4	19	1	3
11th. Royal West Surrey.	1	8	—	19	110	—	15.
10th. R.West Kents.	3	5	—	29	116	5	21
23rd.Middlesex.	2	11	—	12	43	215	9
20th. D.L.Infantry.	1	10	—	17	156	28	21
123rd.M.Gun Co.	2	1	—	3	19	1	15
10th. A.West Surrey.	5	13	—	28	221	65	7
24th. Royal Fusiliers	3	6	—	37	140	58	13
32nd.Royal Fusiliers.	1	12	—	29	175	38	20.
21st. K.R.R.Corps.	4	10	—	55	222	70	4
124th. M.Gun Company.	—	2	—	6	23	—	5
19th. Middlesex Regt.	—	1	7	5	39	2	3
H.Q.Royal Artillery.	1	—	—	1	1	—	—
183rd.Brigade.R.F.A.	1	2	—	4	41	—	9
187th. Brigade R.F.A.	—	10	—	2	34	—	11
189th. Brigade R.F.A.	3	3	—	3	30	—	11
190th. Brigade R.F.A.	3	3	—	10	68	—	6.
Div.A.Column.	1	—	—	3	17	—	9
T.M.B. X.41.	—	—	—	—	2	—	—
T.M.B. Y.41.	—	—	—	—	1	—	—
T.M.B. Z.41.	—	—	—	—	2	—	2.
Carr. Forward.	56	133	2	428	2308	809	211.

UNIT.	OFFICERS.			OTHER RANKS.			Evacuated Sick.
	Killed.	Wounded.	Missing.	Killed.	Wounded.	Missing.	
Brought Forward.	56	133	2	428	2308	809	211
228th. Field Co. R.E.	1	1	—	—	26	1	2
235rd. Field Co. R.E.	—	3	—	—	15	—	2
237th. Field Co. R.E.	—	—	—	—	2	—	2
41st. Signal Co. R.E.	1	—	—	—	—	—	5
41st. Div. Trains.	—	—	—	—	2	—	2
138th. Field Ambulance.	—	—	—	—	9	—	6
139th. Field Ambulance.	—	1	—	—	—	—	5
140th. Field Ambulance.	—	—	—	—	—	—	1
Mobile Vet Section.	—	—	—	—	—	—	—
TOTAL.	58	138	2	428	2362	810	235

SECRET

vol 6

27/8B

ORIGINAL WAR DIARY

of

41ˢᵗ DIVISION "A & Q"

October 1ˢᵗ 1916 to October 31ˢᵗ 1916.

Army Form C. 2118

WAR DIARY of "A & Q" Branch
INTELLIGENCE-SUMMARY 41st Division.

(Erase heading not required.)

Instructions regarding War Diaries and Intelligence Summaries are contained in F.S. Regs., Part II. and the Staff Manual respectively. Title Pages will be prepared in manuscript.

Place	Date	Hour	Summary of Events and Information	Remarks and references to Appendices
RIBEMONT.	Oct. 1st.		123rd Inf. Bde. came out of line night 1st/2nd and camped between POMMIERS REDOUBT and MONTAUBAN.	
	2nd.		Administrative arrangements published with a view to taking over line from New Zealand Division.	
	4th.		Divisional Headquarters moved, "A" Echelon to FRICOURT CHATEAU, "B" Echelon to QUARRY E.11 Central (South of ALBERT). Division relieved New Zealand Division in the line - relief being completed by 7 a.m. 4th.	
	7th.		The Division attacked. For casualties see attached.	
			Considerable difficulty experienced in evacuating wounded from front line owing to exhaustion of stretcher bearers by carrying from front line to Main Dressing Station at THISTLE DUMP, where ambulances first used. R.A.M.C. stretcher bearers reinforced by 100 infantry.	
	8th.		123rd Inf. Bde. relieved 122nd Inf. Bde. in front line. 122nd Inf. Bde. brought back to CARLTON TRENCH. All reinforcements available in transport lines sent up to 122nd and 124th Inf. Bdes. Wounded still being brought it.	
	9th.		Last of wounded brought in during night 9/10th.	
	10th.		41st Division relieved by 30th Division.	
	11th.		Divisional Headquarters moved to BUIRE.	
	16th.		The 124th Inf. Bde. entrained for X Corps Area.	
	17th.		The 124th Inf. Bde. arrived X Corps Area and billeted about AIRAINES. Trains about 20 hours late. 122nd and 123rd Inf. Bdes. entrained.	

Army Form C. 2118

WAR DIARY
of
INTELLIGENCE SUMMARY

(Erase heading not required.)

"A & Q" Branch
41st Division

Instructions regarding War Diaries and Intelligence Summaries are contained in F.S. Regs, Part II, and the Staff Manual respectively. Title Pages will be prepared in manuscript.

Place	Date	Hour	Summary of Events and Information	Remarks and references to Appendices
	18th		The 122nd and 123rd Inf. Bdes. detrained at OISEMONT in X Corps Area and went into billets, 122nd Inf. Bde. about LIMIEUX, 123rd Inf. Bde. in villages North of OISEMONT. Divisional Headquarters HALLENCOURT.	
	19th		Entrainment of the Division for 2nd Army Area commenced. Tables attached.	
	20th		Entrainment continued.	
			The Division on detrainment billeted in IX Corps Area. Divisional Headquarters at FLETRE. 122nd Inf. Bde. Group about CAESTRE. 123rd Inf. Bde. Group about GODEWAERSVELDE. 124th Inf. Bde. Group about METEREN. The Division came under orders of 1st A.N.Z.A.C.	
	21st		Detrainment of Division completed. 124th Inf. Bde.group Moved up to 1st A.N.Z.A.C. Area about BOESCHEPE.	
	22nd		123rd Inf. Bde. Group moved to 4th Australian Divisional Area into the ONTARIO group of camps 124th Inf. Bde. relieved the 12th Australian Brigade in the right sub-sector.	
	23rd		123rd Inf. Bde. relieved 13th Australian Brigade in the left sub-sector.	
	24th		Divisional Headquarters established at RENINGHELST.	
	24th		122nd Inf. Bde. group moved up to billets at MONT DES CATS.	
	25th		122nd Inf. Bde./moved up into Divisional Area and became Divisional Reserve.	
	26th		The Division came under orders of X Corps who relieved 1st A.N.Z.A.C.	
			Tables showing casualties for month attached. " sick wastage " " " " Court Martials " "	

Major,
D.A.A. & Q.M.G.
41st Division.

S E C R E T. Copy No. 24

41st Divn. No. 280/S.7.

1. The 41st Division, less Divisional Artillery and all Motor vehicles, will move by rail from the 4th Army Area to the 2nd Army Area in accordance with the attached copies of Entrainment Table and Table "D". Entrainment will commence on Oct. 19th, 1916.

2. Entraining stations will be PONT REMY and LONGPRE.
Detraining stations will be GODEWAERSVELDE and CAESTRE.

3. Troops will arrive at the station one hour and transport three hours before the advertised time of departure of the train.

4. No. 17 Supply Column, less lorries feeding 41st Divl. Artillery, will proceed to Second Army by road in detachments to be arranged by the D.D.S. & T. Fourth Army.

5. Motor vehicles (other than motor cars with Staff Officers) and Motor Ambulances will be despatched in convoys on the 19th: journey to be completed in one day.
Route :- VIGNACOURT - DOULLENS - ST POL - ANVIN - ST. HILAIRE - AIRE - HAZEBROUCK - FLETRE.

6. Supply Railhead will close in 4th Army Area on Oct. 19th and will open at CAESTRE on 20th October.

7. Units will be rationed for the day following the day of detraining. This day's rations will be carried on the Supply vehicles.

8. All Baggage and Supply wagons will entrain with the units to which they are allotted.

9. Loading parties will be detailed as follows. - They will report to the R.T.O. at the respective entraining stations three hours before the advertised time of departure of the first train.

    122nd Inf. Bde.   1 Off, 35 O.R.   at PONT REMY
    123nd "   "   1 "   35 "   LONGPRE
    123rd "   "   2 "   65 "   PONT REMY
    124th "   "   2 "   65 "   LONGPRE

    The R.T.Os. will make arrangements for accommodation; arrangements for rationing will be made by Brigades. The above parties will entrain on the last train from each station.

10. The S.S.O. will report to the D.A.A. & Q.M.G. at the TROIS CHEVAUX, HAZEBROUCK between 6 p.m. and 7 p.m. 18th inst.
The O.C. Supply Column will report similarly on the 19th inst. at mid-day.

11. Breast ropes for entrainment of horses must be provided by units. Lashings for vehicles will be provided by the railway.

12. Arrangements for policing the entraining stations will be made by the A.P.M.

17th Oct. 1916.

E.S.White

Captain,
D.A.Q.M.G.
41st Division.

P.T.O.

2.

Copies numbered.	1, 2, 3, 4.	to 122nd. Infantry Brig.
" "	5, 6, 7, 8.	to 123rd. Infantry Brig.
" "	9,10,11,12.	to 124th. Infantry Brig.
Copy number.	13	to C.R.E.
" "	14, 15	to Divisional Train.
" "	16.	to Camp Commandant.
" "	17.	to A.D.V.S. for Mob Vet Sec.
" "	18.	to A.D.M.S.
" "	19	to A.P.M.
" "	20	to D.A.D.O.S.
" "	21.	to G.
" "	22.	to 19th. Middlesex.
" "	23.	to O.C.Signals.
" "	24 and 25.	to War Diary.
" "	26.	to File.
" "	27 and 28	Spare.

---

4. Copies of Covering letter, less train times to A.D.M.T.
ARMIES.

MOVE OF 41st DIVISION (LESS ARTILLERY).

via CALAIS

From FOURTH ARMY.   To SECOND ARMY.
                19th/20th October 1916.
Entraining Stations:-   Regulating Station:-

A PONT REMY.   HAZEBROUCK.

B LONGPRE.

Train No. From Stations		SERIAL NO.	Date.	Marche.	Time due to depart.	Time due to arrive.	Remar
A	B						
1	2	3	4	5	6	7	8
1	-	4101, 05, 83	19/10	T 6	11.18		
-	2	4130, 35, 36, 37	"	7	12.31		
3	-	4120, 25, 26, 27	"	9	14.38		
-	4	4131	"	10	15.31		
5	-	4121	"	12	17.38		
-	6	4190, 93	"	13	18.21		
7	-	4123	"	15	20.28		
-	8	4193a, 32	"	16	22.11		
9	-	4192, 89	"	18	23.38		
-	10	4133	20/10	19	0.41		
11	-	4122, 92a	"	21	2.38		
-	12	4134	"	22	3.31		
13	-	4124	"	24	5.38		
-	14	4186	"	1	6.21		
15	-	4185	"	3	8.38		
-	16	4110, 15, 16, 17	"	4	9.21		
17	-	4111	"	6	11.18		
-	18	4113	"	7	12.31		
19	-	4188, 91	"	9	14.38		
-	20	4114	"	10	15.31		
21	-	4112, 91a	"	12	17.38		
-	22	4104	"	13	18.21		
23	-	4184	"	15	20.28		
-	24	4104a, 87, 94, 95	"	16	22.11		

SUMMARY.

A PONT REMY   12 T.Cs.
B LONGPRE   12 T.Cs.

F. Leslie Ditmas.
Captain
for A.D.R.T. (IV).

AMIENS.
16/10/1916.

TABLE "D".

MOVE OF 41st DIVISION LESS ARTILLERY.

UNIT.	SERIAL NO:	DESCRIPTION.
Divisional Units	4101	Divisional H.Q.
	4104	Pioneer Bn. 19th Middlesex (Pt).
	4104a	" " " (Remdr).
	4105	H.Q. and H.Q.Sect. Div'l Signals.
122nd Infantry Brigade.	4110	Brigade H.Q.
	4111	12th East Surrey Regt.
	4112	15th Hampshire Regt.
	4113	11th R. West Kent Regt.
	4114	18th K.R.R.C.
	4115	Signal Section.
	4116	Brigade M.Gun Co.
	4117	Light T.M. Battery.
123rd Infantry Brigade.	4120	Brigade H.Q.
	4121	11th R.W.Surrey Regt.
	4122	10th R.W.Kent Regt.
	4123	23rd Middx. Regt.
	4124	20th Durham L.I.
	4125	Signal Section.
	4126	Brigade M.Gun Co.
	4127	Light T.M. Battery.
124th Infantry Brigade.	4130	Brigade H.Q.
	4131	10th R.W.Surrey Regt.
	4132	26th Royal Fusiliers.
	4133	32nd Royal Fusiliers.
	4134	21st K.R.R.C.
	4135	Signal Section.
	4136	Brigade M.Gun Co.
	4137	Light T.M. Battery.
Divisional Engineers.	4183	H.Q. Divisional Engineers.
	4184	228th Field Co. R.E.
	4185	233rd Field Co. R.E.
	4186	237th Field Co. R.E.
Divisional Train	4187	H.Q. Divisional Train.
	4188	No 2 Co. Divisional Train.
	4189	No 3 Co. " "
	4190	No 4 Co. " "
Medical Units.	4191	138th Field Amblce. less 2 Field Amblces and teams.
	4191a	2 Field Amblces & teams of 138th F.A.
	4192	139th Field Amblce. less 2 Field Amblces and teams.
	4192a	2 Field Amblces & teams of 139th F.A.
	4193	140th Field Amblce. less 2 Field Amblces and teams.
	4193a	2 Field Amblces & teams of 140th F.A.
	4194	Sanitary Section.
	4195	Mobile Veterinary Section.

F. Lesley Ditmas
Captain
for A.D.R.T.(IV).

AMIENS.
16/10/1916.

41st. DIVISION.

COURTS MARTIAL DURING OCTOBER 1916.

Unit.	No.	Particulars of Charge.	Sentence.
20th. Durham L.I.	1.	Drunkenness.	Fined 10/-
10th. R.W.Kents.	4.	1. Drunkenness.	Twelve months imprisonment with hard labour.
do.		2. do.	do.
do.		3. do.	do.
do.		4. do.	do.
Attached Troops.			
Headquarters, 12th. Austn. Field Artillery Brigade.	1.	(1) Stealing goods, the property of regmtl. mess. (2) Drunkenness.	(1) Not Guilty. (2) Forfeit 90 days pay.
40th. Battery, 4th. Austn. Divl. Artillery.	1.	Neglecting to obey an order.	Not Guilty.
44th. Battery, 4th. Austn. Divl. Artillery.	1.	Assaulting an inhabitant in the Country in which he is serving.	NOT Guilty.

CONFIDENTIAL.

The following table shows number of Killed, Wounded, Missing and Evacuated Sick during the month of October 1916.

UNIT.	OFFICERS.			OTHER RANKS.			
	Killed.	Wounded.	Missing.	Killed.	Wounded.	Missing.	Evacuated Sick.
Divisional Headquarters.	–	1	–	1	–	–	25
12th. East Surrey Regt.	1	6	–	16	64	18	14
15th. Hampshire Regt.	1	8	2	54	129	12	9
11th. R.West Kent Regt.	7	8	–	62	212	85	101
18th. K.R.R.Corps.	1	3	2	42	147	15	4
122nd. M.Gun Co.	2	2	–	13	36	1	11
11th. R.West Surrey Regt.	–	1	–	10	45	3	13
10th. R.West Kent Regt.	–	4	–	16	57	14	18
23rd. Middlesex Regt.	–	3	–	40	73	21	11
20th. D.L.I.	–	6	–	13	107	10	11
123rd. M.Gun.Co.	–	–	–	4	5	5	8
10th. R.West Surrey Regt.	2	2	2	10	79	9	36
26th. R.Fusiliers.	3	8	1	39	191	20	19
32nd. R.Fusiliers.	3	8	–	28	169	45	19
21st. K.R.R.Corps.	2	4	–	28	100	13	10
124th. M.G.Co.	2	3	–	3	9	2	3
19th. Bn. Middlesex Regt.	1	2	–	7	26	5	3
H.Qtrs. R.A.	–	1	–	1	–	–	1
183rd.Brig.R.F.A.	–	5	–	5	28	–	4
187th.Brig.R.F.A.	–	2	–	2	15	1	3
189th.Brig.R.F.A.	–	2	–	1	16	–	2
190th.Brig.R.F.A.	1	6	–	15	46	–	1
D.A.Column.	–	1	–	2	9	–	4
Carried Forward.	25	74	7	405	1563	279	317

UNIT.	OFFICERS. Killed	Wounded	Missing	OTHER RANKS. Killed	Wounded	Missing	Evacuated Sick.
Brought forward.	25	74	7	405	1563	279	317
Y.41 T.Mortar Battery.	—	—	—	—	1	—	1
Z.41 " "	—	—	—	—	1	—	3
228th. Field Co.R.E.	—	—	—	1	10	—	3
233rd. Field Co.R.E.	1	1	—	3	11	4	3
237th. Field Co.R.E.	—	—	—	—	5	—	3
Signal Company.	—	—	—	—	1	—	5
Divisional Train.	—	—	—	—	1	—	4
Mob.Vet Section.	—	—	—	—	—	—	—
M.M.Police.	—	—	—	—	9	—	4
138th. Field Ambulance.	—	—	—	—	—	—	—
139th. Field Ambulance.	—	—	—	—	—	—	8
140th.Field Ambulance.	—	—	—	—	11	—	7
Divl.Supply Colmn.(17th).	—	—	—	—	—	—	1
TOTAL.	26	75	7	409	1613	283	351

SECRET.   271/S.3.

ADMINISTRATIVE ARRANGEMENTS IN CONNECTION WITH COMING OPERATIONS.

(In continuation of this Office No. 248/S.3 dated 24th. Sept. 1916.

=========================

1. SUPPLIES.

    Will be drawn in bulk from ALBERT railhead commencing (probably) tomorrow 3rd. October 1916, by the Supply Sections of the Train. Refilling will take place at BECORDEL and rations will then be delivered to transport lines in the supply wagons of the Train. Regimental transport takes rations forward from transport lines.
    The New Zealand Division have been taking wheels up as far as the advanced Grenade Dump at M.30.b.3.2.
    Route CATERPILLAR VALLEY - FLATIRON COPSE - THISTLE DUMP - LONGUEVAL - FLERS - ABBEY ROAD - Point M.30.c.8.6.

2. WATER.

    (a). Square S.20.c.

        For horses. No standpipes for water carts at present, but these are being put in and should be ready in a few days.

    (b). Montauban.

        S.21.d.5.0. for horses.
        S.27.c.5.2. for watercarts.

    (c). Longueval.

        S.17.c.7.0. for horses and watercarts.

    (d). Fricourt.

        F.9.b.3.9. for watercarts.
        F.4.d. for horses.
        F.3.d.6.7. for filling (petrol tins only).

    (e). Several good wells in FLERS (vide attached Appendix A)

    (f). A good well at FACTORY CORNER. Not yet fully exploited.

3. GRENADE AND S.A.A. DUMPS.

    (a). Main Dump at E.2.b.8.3. This is being moved forward to F.6.a.6.3. (between MAMETZ and MONTAUBAN) and should be established here by the evening of the 4th. inst.

    (b). Advanced Dumps.
        (1). South entrance to FLERS (T.1.a.1.6.). To be taken over by 124th. Infantry Brigade.
        (2). M.30.b.3.2. To be taken over by 122nd. Infantry Brigade.

(c). An intermediate dump at GREEN DUMP (S.16.c.7.0.)
This will be gradually depleted and done away with altogether. To be taken over meanwhile by the 123rd. Infantry Brigade.
Advanced dumps should as far as possible draw on GREEN DUMP until the latter is cleared.

4. STRAGGLERS.

Battle Stops as follows:-
SWITCH TRENCH (S.5.Central).
THISTLE DUMP (S.16.a.3.9.)
FLATIRON COPSE (S.14.c.4.1.)
At the latter two points stragglers can be fed and rearmed. Brigades will send an N.C.O. to each of these two latter points to march stragglers back to their Brigade Headquarters. Accommodation and rations will be arranged by the Officer i/c Advanced Dressing Station at each of these places.
Brigades must make full use of their regimental police to stop stragglers and return them to their units before they get away from the front area. Particular attention is drawn to this office No. 245/c.16 dated September 23rd. 1916.

5. PRISONERS CAGES.

Corps cage is at S.23.a.5.6. on the LONGUEVAL - BERNAFAY WOOD road.
Brigades will arrange to escort prisoners to the Corps cage. Receipts for numbers of prisoners handed over must always be taken from the Corps representative at the Corps cage.

6. MEDICAL.

Advanced Dressing Stations as follows:-
(a). THISTLE ALLEY (S.16.a.4.9.)
(b). FLAT IRON COPSE (S.14.c.4.1.)
(c). GREEN DUMP (S.16.c.7.0.)
Walking wounded to FLAT IRON COPSE.

7. R.E. STORES.

GREEN DUMP.
Divisional R.E. Dump at MAMETZ (F.11.a.5.8.) &
Small reserves of tools, sandbags, wire etc. should be maintained at advanced Grenade Dumps.

8. DIVISIONAL ORDNANCE (E.11.a.3.4.).

9. MOBILE VETERINARY SECTION (F.11.a.1.8.)

10. BURIAL OF DEAD AND SALVAGE. (vide Appendix "B" attached).

11. Transport Lines.

For Infantry Brigades Square X.30.a. and c.
Pioneers. Square S.21.b.
Divisional Train (complete) at BECORDEL village, F.7.c.
Headquarters at E.11.Central with "B" Echelon Divisional Headquarters.

for - Lieut. Colonel,
A.A. & Q.M.G.
41st. Division.

2nd. October 1916.

Army Form C. 2118

WAR DIARY
of "A" & "Q" Branch, 41st Division.
INTELLIGENCE SUMMARY
(Erase heading not required.)

Vol 7

Instructions regarding War Diaries and Intelligence Summaries are contained in F. S. Regs., Part II. and the Staff Manual respectively. Title Pages will be prepared in manuscript.

Place	Date	Hour	Summary of Events and Information	Remarks and references to Appendices
RENINGHELST	Nov. 1st to Nov. 30th. 1916.		List of Casualties, Sick and Courts Martial are attached.	

Chitzel
AA&QMG
41st Division

41ST. DIVISION.

Courts-Martial during November 1916.

UNIT.	NO.	PARTICULARS OF CHARGE.	SENTENCE.
12th. East Surrey.	2	(1) When on active service acting as a sentinel, sleeping on his post. (2) - ditto -	2 years imprisonment with hard labour. (suspended). - ditto -
20th. Durham L.I.	4	(1)(a) Absent without leave. (b) Refusing to obey an order. (2) Manslaughter. (3) Desertion. (4) Desertion.	18 months imprisonment with hard labour. (commuted to 3 months Imp.H.L.) 2 years imprisonment with hard labour. Death.(commuted to 2 years imp. H.L.) Death.(commuted to 2 years imp. H.L.)
23rd. Middlesex.	2	(1) Conduct to the prejudice of good order and military discipline. (2) Desertion.	21 days Field Punishment No. 1. Death.(Sentence carried out 1/12/16.)
10th. R.W.Kent.	3.	(1) Drunkenness. (2) Drunkenness. (3) Drunkenness.	Reduced to ranks. 28 days F.P.No. 1 and fined £1. 28 days F.P.No. 1 and fined £1.
26th. Royal Fusiliers.	2.	(1) Desertion. (2) Discharging rifle carelessly wounding a comrade.	Not guilty. 56 days detention. (commuted to 21 days F.P.No. 1.)
32nd. Royal Fusiliers.	3.	(1) Stealing public goods. (2) Receiving public goods. (3) Receiving public goods.	Not guilty. Not guilty. Not guilty.
10th. R.W.Surrey.	2	(1) Drunkenness. (2) Drunkenness.	12 months imp. H.L. & fined £1. Not guilty.

UNIT.	NO.	PARTICULARS OF CHARGE.	SENTENCE.
21st. K.R.R.C.	3	(1) Sleeping on post while acting as sentinel. (2) - ditto - (3)(a) Disobeying a lawful command. (b) Insubordinate language to a superior officer.	1 year imprisonment with H.L. - ditto - 2 years imprisonment with H.L. (commuted to 3 months F.P.No.1.)
189th. Brigade. R.F.A.	1	(1) Conduct to the prejudice of good order and military discipline.	Not guilty.
19th. Middlesex.	4	(1) Absent without leave. (2)(a) Disobeying a lawful command. (b) An act to the prejudice of good order and military discipline. (3) Drunkenness. (4) Drunkenness.	2 months F.P.No.1. Deprived of rank. & 2 months F.P.No.1. Reduced to corporal & lose 6 months seniority. - ditto -

CONFIDENTIAL.

The following Table shows numbers of killed, wounded, missing and evacuated sick during the month of November 1916 (to 12 noon, 30th.)

UNIT.	OFFICERS.				OTHER RANKS.			
	Killed.	Wounded.	Missing.	Killed.	Wounded.	Missing.	Evacuated sick.
Divisional Headquarters.	-	-	-	-	-	-	1
H.Q., 122nd. Infantry Brigade.	-	-	-	-	1	-	1
122nd. Machine Gun Coy.	-	-	-	-	-	-	42
12th. E.Surrey Regt.	-	-	2	3	10	2	43
15th. Hants. Regt.	-	-	-	3	10	-	28
11th. R.W.Kent Regt.	-	-	1	2	4	-	29
18th. K.R.R.Corps.	-	-	-	2	4	-	3
123rd. Infantry Bde. H.Q.	-	3	-	-	-	-	3
123rd. Machine Gun Coy.	-	-	-	5	16	-	21
11th. R.W.Surrey Regt.	-	1	-	2	7	-	25
10th. R.W.Kent Regt.	-	1	-	1	2	-	35
23rd. Middlesex Regt.	-	-	-	3	9	-	37
20th. Durham L.I.	-	-	-	-	2	-	4
124th. Infantry Brigade H.Q.	-	-	-	-	-	-	-
124th. Machine Gun Coy.	-	1	-	1	6	-	52
10th. R.W.Surrey Regt.	-	-	-	4	4	-	37
26th. Royal Fusiliers.	-	-	-	-	15	-	25
32nd. Royal Fusiliers.	-	-	-	2	10	-	26
21st. K.R.R.Corps.	-	-	-	-	1	-	14
19th. Middlesex Regt.	-	-	-	-	-	-	15
41st. Divl. Artillery H.Q.	-	-	-	-	-	-	6
185rd. Brigade R.F.A.	-	-	-	-	-	-	11
189th. Brigade R.F.A.	-	1	-	-	1	-	8
190th. Brigade R.F.A.	1	-	-	-	-	-	17
41st. D.A.C.	-	-	-	-	-	-	-
T.M.B. X/41.	-	-	-	-	1	-	2
" Y/41.	-	-	-	-	-	-	-
" Z/41.	-	-	-	-	-	-	-
Carried Forward:-	1	7	3	28	103	2	480

UNIT.	OFFICERS.			OTHER RANKS.			Evacuated Sick.
	Killed.	Wounded.	Missing.	Killed.	Wounded.	Missing.	
Brought Forward:-	1	7	3	28	103	2	480
228th. Field Coy. R.E.	-	-	-	-	-	-	6
233rd. Field Coy. R.E.	-	-	-	-	-	-	1
237th. Field Coy. R.E.	-	-	-	-	-	-	4
41st. Signal Company.	-	-	-	-	-	-	2
41st. Divisional Train.	-	-	-	-	-	-	9
138th. Field Ambulance.	-	-	-	-	-	-	8
139th. Field Ambulance.	-	-	-	-	-	-	4
140th. Field Ambulance.	-	-	-	-	-	-	1
52nd. Mobile Veterinary Sec.	-	-	-	-	-	-	1
17th. Supply Column.	-	-	-	-	-	-	1
84th. Sanitary Section.	-	-	-	-	-	-	1
TOTAL :-	1	7	3	28	103	2	515

Army Form C. 2118

WAR DIARY
or
INTELLIGENCE SUMMARY

(Erase heading not required.)

Headquarters,
41st.Division
"A" and "Q".

Vol 8

Instructions regarding War Diaries and Intelligence Summaries are contained in F. S. Regs., Part II. and the Staff Manual respectively. Title Pages will be prepared in manuscript.

Place	Date	Hour	Summary of Events and Information	Remarks and references to Appendices
RENINGHELST.	December 1916.		A statement showing the casualties and sick wastage for the month is attached.	
			A statement showing the Courts Martial for the month is attached.	

January 6th.1917.

Lieut Colonel,
A.A.&.Q.M.G.
41st. Division.

1875 Wt. W593/826 1,000,000 4/15 J.B.C. & A. A.D.S.S./Forms/C. 2118.

41st. DIVISION.

RETURN OF COURTS MARTIAL DURING DECEMBER 1916.

Unit.	No. of cases.	Offence.	Punishment.
12th. E. Surrey.	1.	Carelessly firing rifle.	3 weeks F.P. No.1.
15th. Hampshire.	1.	Drunkenness.	28 days F.P.1 & fined £1.
18th. K.R.R.C.	2.	(1). Drunkenness & Striking. (2). Drunkenness.	(1). 2 months F.P.1. (2). Reduced to ranks.
23rd. Middlesex.	1.	Leaving post without orders.	Not guilty.
26th. R.F.	3.	(1). Absent without leave. (2). " " " (3). discharging revolver.	(1). 6 months imp. H.L. (2). 14 days F.P.1. (3). 2 days F.P.1.
32nd. R.Fslrs.	1.	(1) Threatening language. (2) Conduct to prejudice of good order & military discipline	Not guilty. 60 days F.P.No.1
10th. Queens.	4.	(1). Drunkenness. (2). Improper remark to N.C.O. (3). Absent without leave. (4). Drunkenness.	(1). Not guilty. (2). 3 months imp. H.L. (3). 6 months imp. (4). Fined £1.
183rd. Brigade.	1.	Leaving post without orders.	2 yrs. imp. H.L.
187th. Brigade.	2.	(1). Disobeying lawful command. (2). Striking S. Officer.	90 days F.P.1. 1 yr. imp.
190th. Brig.	2.	Breach of censorship. Drunkenness.	6 months H.L. Reduced to ranks.
19th. Middlesex.	1.	Drunkenness.	reduced to Cpl. & lose 6 months seniority.
Divl. Train.	1.	Drunkenness.	-do-
Signal Co.	1.	Drunkenness.	28 days F.P.1.

CONFIDENTIAL

The following Table shows numbers of killed, wounded, missing and evacuated sick during the month of December 1916 (to noon 31st.)

UNIT.	OFFICERS.				OTHER RANKS.			
	Killed.	Wounded.	Missing.		Killed.	Wounded.	Missing.	Evctd.Sick.
Divisional Headquarters.	-	-	-		-	-	-	1
H.Q., 122nd. Infantry Brigade.	-	-	-		-	-	-	3
122nd. Machine Gun Coy.	-	-	-		-	2	-	45
12th. E.Surrey Regt.	-	1	-		2	20	-	68
15th. Hants. Regt.	-	2	-		3	3	-	41
11th. R.W.Kent Regt.	-	1	-		3	4	-	31
18th. K.R.R.Corps.	-	-	-		5	1	-	7
H.Q., 123rd. Infantry Brigade.	-	-	-		-	-	-	33
123rd. Machine Gun Company.	-	1	-		2	16	-	24
11th. R.W.Surrey Regt.	-	-	-		2	4	-	32
10th. R.W.Kent Regt.	-	-	-		3	3	-	36
23rd. Middlesex Regt.	-	-	-		2	7	-	1
20th. Durham L.I.	-	-	-		-	1	-	57
H.Q., 124th. Infantry Brigade.	-	1	-		2	10	-	24
124th. Machine Gun Company.	-	1	-		3	33	2	33
10th. R.W.Surrey Regt.	-	-	-		5	27	1	46
26th. Royal Fusiliers.	-	-	-		2	18	-	14
"	-	-	-		-	-	-	1
32nd.	-	-	-		-	3	-	24
21st. K.R.R.Corps.	-	-	-		1	2	-	16
19th. Middlesex Regt.	-	-	-		-	-	-	26
H.Q., 41st. Divl. Headquarters.	-	-	-		-	-	-	24
187th. Brigade R.F.A.	-	-	-		-	3	-	4
189th. Brigade R.F.A.	-	-	-		-	1	-	12
190th. Brigade R.F.A.	-	-	-		1	-	-	10
41st. D.A.C.	-	-	-		-	-	-	2
41st. T.M.Batteries.	-	-	-		-	-	-	2
228th. Field Coy. R.E.	-	-	-		-	-	-	6
233rd. Field Coy. R.E.	-	-	-		-	-	-	
237th. Field Coy. R.E.	-	-	-		-	-	-	
41st. Divl. Signal Company.	-	-	-		-	-	-	
41st. Divisional Train.	-	-	-		-	-	-	
Carried Forward.	1	6	1		33	158	3	622

UNIT.	OFFICERS.			OTHER RANKS.			
	Killed.	Wounded.	Missing.	Killed.	Wounded.	Missing.	Evactd. Sick.
Brought Forward.	1	6	1	33	158	3	622
38th. Field Ambulance.							4
39th. " "							6
40th. " "					2		5
2nd. Mobile Vety. Sec.							1
7th. Supply Column.							1
4th. Sanitary Section							
TOTAL.	1	6	1	33	160	3	638

Army Form C. 2118

WAR DIARY
or
INTELLIGENCE SUMMARY

(Erase heading not required.)

Headquarters,
41st. Division,
"A" and "Q".

Instructions regarding War Diaries and Intelligence Summaries are contained in F. S. Regs., Part II. and the Staff Manual respectively. Title Pages will be prepared in manuscript.

Place	Date	Hour	Summary of Events and Information	Remarks and references to Appendices
RENINGHELST.	January. 1917.		A Statement showing the Casualties and Sick evacuations for the month is attached.	
"	"		A Statement shewing the Courts Martial held during the month is attached.	
"	"		A Statement shewing the Reinforcements joined during the month and strength of Infantry each week of the month.	

Lieut Colonel,
A.A.& Q.M.G.
41st.Division.

1875 Wt. W593/826 1,000,000 4/15 J.B.C. & A. A.D.S.S./Forms/C. 2118.

STATEMENT SHOWING COURTS MARTIAL FOR THE MONTH OF JANUARY 1917.

Unit.	No.	Particulars of Charge.	Sentence.
12th E.Surrey.	1	Drunkenness & Restg Escort.	3 years P.S.
18th.K.R.RXC.	1	Conduct t the preducice of good order & Mil.Disc.	60 days F.P.1
11th.R.W.Kents.	3	(1) Violence to S.Offcr.	1 year I.H.L.
		(2) Drunkenness.	10 days F.P.1 and fined £1.
		(3) Desertion. (since killed)	6 months H.L.
20th.D.L.I.	2	(1) Manslaughter.	56 days F.P.1.
		(2) Disobeying Lawful Command.	40 days F.P.1
23rd.Middlesex.	2	(1) Leaving Post without orders.	Not Guilty.
		(2) Drunkenness.	Not Guilty.
10th.R.W.Kents.	1	Disobeying Lawful Command.	" years Imp H.L.
26th.R.Fusiliers.	4	(1) Absent without leave.(Sgt)	Forfeit 6 month seniority.
		(2) Sleeping on Post.	1 year I.H.L.
		(3) Drunkenness.	14 days F.P.1 and fined £1.
		(4). Drunkenness.	- do -
10th.Queens.	1	Obtaining leave by flase pretences. (sgt)	Reduced to ranks.
187th Brig.RFA.	1	Conduct prejudice good order and military discipline.	28 days F.P.1
189th Brig.RFA.	2	(1) Drunkenness.	Not Guilty.
		(2). Theft.	56 days F.P.1
190th Brig.RFA.	3	(".) Drunkenness and Striking.	1 year I.H.L.
		(2) Conduct to the prejudice of good order and M.Discipline.	6 months H.L.
		(3). Drunkenness & resist escort.	28 days F.P.1.
41st Signal Co.	1	Drunkenness.	3 months F.P.1.
122nd M.G.Co.	2	(1) Drunkenness.	10 days F.P.1 and fined £1.
		(2). Drunkenness.	- do -
124th M.G.Co.	1	Breach of Censorship.	31 days F.P.1.
233rd F.Co. RE.	1	Drunkenness, resisting escort and escape confinment.	2 years I.H.L.

STATEMENT SHOWING REINFORCEMENTS AND WEEKLY STRENGTH, JANUARY 1917.

UNIT.	Reinforcements.		Weekly Strength, Other Ranks.					
	Offrs.	O.R.	January 1st.	January 7th.	January 14th.	January 21st.	January 28th.	January 31st.
12th. E.Surrey.	11	136	1020	1011	1009	998	996	1090
15th. Hants.	5	142	850	926	921	962	963	947
11th. R.W.Kent.	3	179	840	998	1007	997	990	974
19th. K.R.R.Corps.	5	13	1020	1019	1011	1000	1000	989
122nd. M.G.Coy.	-	5	176	174	172	174	175	173
11th. R.W.Surrey.	5	151	960	938	959	952	1075	1059
10th. R.W.Kents.	3	71	984	985	979	992	999	1012
23rd. Middlesex.	5	17	993	995	992	993	989	969
20th. Durham L.I.	7	319	754	744	740	920	1061	1012
123rd. M.G.Coy.	-	3	168	168	170	165	165	160
10th. R.W.Surrey.	7	41	1054	1017	1010	996	990	989
26th. Royal Fus.	5	136	921	910	894	981	979	981
32nd. Royal Fus.	9	6	1016	1002	1000	993	982	977
21st. K.R.R.Corps.	8	2	1036	1030	1015	1001	988	985
124th. M.G.Coy.	1	1	173	173	173	170	171	169
19th. Middlesex.	3	72	883	870	867	853	931	920

CONFIDENTIAL.

The following Table shows numbers of Killed, Wounded, Missing, and evacuated Sick, during the month of January 1917 :- (to noon 31st.)

UNIT.	OFFICERS.			OTHER RANKS.			
	Killed.	Wounded.	Missing.	Killed.	Wounded.	Missing.	Evacuatd.Sick.
Divisional Hqtrs.	-	-	-	-	-	-	2
H.Q.122nd.I.Brigade.	-	-	-	-	-	-	8
122nd.M.Gun Co.	-	-	-	-	-	-	49
12th.East Surrey Rgt.	-	3	-	2	15	-	58
15th.Hants Regt.	-	-	-	2	5	-	33
11th.R.West Kent Regt.	-	-	-	4	8	-	36
18th.K.R.R.C.	-	-	-	3	15	-	-
H.Q.123rd.I.Brigade.	-	-	-	-	-	-	6
123rd.M.G.Co.	-	-	-	2	3	1	26
11th.R.W.Surrey Rg.t	-	-	-	6	9	-	25
10th.R.West Kent Regt.	-	-	-	2	16	-	27
23rd.Middlesex Regt.	1	-	-	5	9	-	35
20th.Durham L.I.	-	2	-	4	22	-	-
H.Q.124th.I.Brigade.	-	-	-	-	-	-	6
124th.M.G.Co.	-	-	-	1	3	1	62
10th.R.W.Surrey Regt.	-	2	-	9	34	-	52
26th.R.Fusiliers.	-	2	-	8	16	-	39
32nd.R.Fusiliers.	-	1	-	2	4	-	34
21st.K.R.R.C.	-	1	-	5	11	-	25
19th.Middlesex.	-	-	-	1	9	-	-
41st.Div R.A.	-	-	-	-	-	-	30
187th.Brigade R.F.A.	-	1	-	3	5	-	27
190th.Brigade R.F.A.	-	-	-	-	1	-	28
41st.D.A.C.	-	-	-	1	2	-	5
41st.T.Mortar Bttys.	-	-	-	-	1	-	7
228th.Field Co. R.E.	-	1	-	1	1	-	5
233rd.Field Co. R.E.	-	-	-	-	-	-	3
237th.Field Co. R.E.	-	-	-	-	-	-	2
41st. Divl. Signal Co.	-	-	-	-	2	-	10
41st.Div.Train A.S.C.	-	-	-	-	-	-	-
Carried Forwd.	1	13	-	59	189	2	640

	OFFICERS.				OTHER RANKS.			
UNIT.	Killed.	Wounded.	Missing.		Killed.	Wounded.	Missing.	Evctd. Sick.
Brought Forward.	1	13	-		59	189	2	640
138th. Field Amb Inco.	-	-	-		-	1	-	5
139th. Field Amb Inco.	-	-	-		-	-	-	26
140th. Field Amb Inco.	-	-	-		-	-	-	11
52nd Mobile Vet Secn.	-	-	-		-	-	-	1
84th. Sanitary Section.	-	-	-		-	-	-	-
17th. Supply Column.	-	-	-		-	-	-	-
TOTAL.	1	13	-		59	190	2	683
189th Brigade R.A. (Corps Artillery)	1	-	-		-	-	-	18

Army Form C. 2118

WAR DIARY
or
INTELLIGENCE SUMMARY

Headquarters,
41st Division.
"A" and "Q" Branch.

(Erase heading not required.)

Instructions regarding War Diaries and Intelligence Summaries are contained in F. S. Regs., Part II. and the Staff Manual respectively. Title Pages will be prepared in manuscript.

Place	Date	Hour	Summary of Events and Information	Remarks and references to Appendices
RENINGHELST.	February 1917.		A statement showing the Casualties, and sick evacuations for the month is attached.	
			A statement showing the reinforcements and weekly strength for the month is attached.	
			A statement showing the Courts Martial held during the month is attached.	

Lieut. Colonel,
A.A.&.Q.M.G.
41st Division.

STATEMENT SHOWING COURTS MARTIAL FOR THE MONTH OF FEBRUARY 1917.

Unit.	No.	Particulars of Charge.	Sentence.
12th. E.Surrey.	2	(1)Leaving his Post without permission.	2 years Imp H. (18 months remitted)
		(2)Drunkenness.	Reduced to Ranks. (6 mths H.L.remitted)
11th. R.W.Kents.	1	Desertion (since killed)	6 months H.L.
20th. D.L.I.	3	(1)Manslaughter.	56 days F.P.1.
		(2)Drunkenness.	28 days F.P.1. fined 10/-
		(3)Disobeying Lawful Command.	40 days F.P.1.
23rd Middlesex	2	(1)Drunkenness.	Not Guilty
		(2)Stealing Goods.	Reduced to Rank
11th.Queens	2	(1)Absent from Front Line.	35 days F.P.1. (30 days remit)
		(2) ditto	30 days F.P.2.
10th. R.W.Kents	1	Disobeying Lawful Command.	Not Guilty
26th. R.Fusiliers	6	(1)Sleeping on his Post.	1 year I.H.L.
		(2)Drunkenness.	14 days F.P.1. fined £1.
		(3)Drunkenness.	14 days F.P.1. fined £1.1.
		(4)Wounding Comrade.	56 days detent. remitd to 28 d F.P.1.
		(5)Disobeying Lawful Command.	6 mths H.L.
		(6)Asleep on Post.	Not Guilty
32nd R.Fusiliers	2	(1)Disobeying Lawful Command.	42 days F.P.2.
		(2)a.Failing to appear on Parade	28 days F.P.1.
		b.Malingering.	Not Guilty.
187th. Brig.R.F.A.	1	Conduct to the predudice of good order and Mil.Disc.	28 days F.P.1.
189th. Brig.R.F.A.	1	Knowingly making a false statement.	Not Guilty
190th. Brig.R.F.A.	1	Using threatening language.	56 days F.P.1.
10th. Corps Cyclists	1	Disrespectful langiage to N.C.O.	90 days F.P.1. 52 days remitd.
124th M.G.Co.	1	Striking two soldiers.	Reduced to Rank
122nd M.G.Co.	1	Leaving his Post.	1 year I.H.L.

STATEMENT SHOWING REINFORCEMENTS AND WEEKLY STRENGTH. FEBRUARY 1917.

UNIT.	Reinforcements		Weekly Strength, Other Ranks.					
	Offrs	O.R.	February 1st.	February 4th.	February 11th.	February 18th.	February 25th.	February 28th.
12th. E.Surrey.	2	69	1090	1106	1115	1105	1098	1078
15th. Hants.	7	33	947	955	945	930	923	891
11th. R.W.Kents.	3	34	974	1003	951	932	951	937
18th. K.R.R.Corps.	2	16	989	988	973	951	913	913
122nd. M.G.Coy.	-	4	173	174	173	171	168	169
11th. R.W.Surrey.	6	69	1059	1063	1080	1068	1071	1062
10th. R.W.Kents.	1	50	1012	992	989	956	1002	986
23rd. Middlesex	3	31	969	971	961	942	960	941
20th. D.L.Infantry.	3	18	1012	1017	1002	974	970	951
123rd. M.G.Co.	-	9	160	163	158	158	157	156
10th. R.W.Surrey.	3	124	989	986	934	954	946	891
26th. K.Fusiliers	2	27	981	975	935	922	929	924
32nd. R.Fusiliers	3	47"	977	965	943	910	942	932
21st. K.R.R.Corps.	2	19	985	982	965	964	912	912
124th. M.G.Co.	2	11	189	167	167	168	174	175
19th.Middlesex Regt.	4	53	920	919	908	950	959	941

CONFIDENTIAL

The following Table shows numbers killed, wounded, missing, and evacuated sick during the month of February 1917. (to noon 28th.)

UNIT.	OFFICERS. Killed	OFFICERS. Wounded	OFFICERS. Missing	OTHER RANKS. Killed	OTHER RANKS. Wounded	OTHER RANKS. Missing	Evacuated Sick.
Divisional Headquatrs.	-	-	-	-	-	-	-
A.Q.122nd.I.Brigade.	-	-	-	-	-	-	-
122nd.M.Gun Co.	-	-	-	-	-	-	6
2th.E.Surrey Regt.	-	1	-	3	2	-	67
5th.Hampshire.	-	3	-	7	11	-	79
11th.R.West Kents.	-	2	-	6	10	2	43
8th.K.R.R.C.	-	-	-	-	29	1	56
123rd.Inf.Brig.H.Q.	-	-	-	-	29	-	-
123rd.M.G.Company.	-	1	-	4	1	-	8
11th.Queens.	-	1	-	1	11	-	54
10th.R.W.Kents.	-	1	-	8	25	-	43
23rd.Middlesex.	1	-	-	3	11	-	35
20th.D.L.Infantry.	-	-	-	8	40	-	58
H.Q.124th.Inf.Brigade.	-	-	-	-	1	-	4
124th.M.G.Company.	-	7	-	20	117	-	74
10th.Queens.	2	1	-	9	30	12	45
26th.R.Fusiliers.	1	1	-	4	16	-	72
32nd.R.Fusiliers.	1	-	-	8	24	5	37
21st.K.R.R.C.	-	-	-	-	5	-	27
19th.Middlesex Pioneers.	-	1	-	-	4	-	31
H.Q.Divl.Artillery.	-	2	-	-	-	-	16
187th.Brigade R.A.	-	-	-	1	4	-	25
190th.Brigade R.F.A.	1	-	-	-	-	-	7
41st.D.A.C.							
41st.T.M.Batteries.							
Carrd. Forward.	6	20	-	82	370	20	783

	OFFICERS.			OTHER RANKS.			Evacuated
Unit.	Killed	Wounded	Missing	Killed	Wounded	Missing.	Sick.
Broug. Forward.	6	20	—	82	370	20	783
H.Q.Divl.Engineers.	—	—	—	—	—	—	8
228th.Fld.Co.R.E.	—	—	—	—	—	—	6
233rd.Fld.Co.R.E.	1	—	—	—	9	1	2
237th.Fld.Co.R.E.	—	—	—	—	—	—	3
41st.Signal Co.	—	—	—	—	1	—	8
41st.Divl.Train.	—	—	—	—	—	—	8
138th.Field Amb.lnce.	—	—	—	—	—	—	14
139th. "	—	—	—	—	—	—	13
140th. "	—	—	—	—	—	—	1
52nd.Mot.Vet Sect.	—	—	—	—	—	—	
Total for Division	7	20	—	82	380	21	846
Attached Troops.							
189th.Brig.R.A.	—	1	—	—	—	—	26
54th.Battery R.F.A.	—	—	—	—	—	—	1
216th.A.Troops Co.	—	—	—	1	—	—	2
1st Can.Tunn Co.	—	—	—	—	—	—	1
A.O.Corps.	—	—	—	—	—	—	
Total.	7	21	—	83	380	21	876

STATEMENT SHOWING COURTS MARTIAL FOR THE MONTH OF FEBRUARY 1917.

Unit.	No.	Particulars of Charge.	Sentence.
12th. E.Surrey.	2	(1)Leaving his Post without permission.	2 years Imp H.L (18 months remitted)
		(2)Drunkenness.	Reduced to Ranks. (6 mths H.L.remitted)
11th. R.W.Kents.	1	Desertion (since killed)	6 months H.L.
20th. D.L.I.	3	(1)Manslaughter.	56 days F.P.1.
		(2)Drunkenness.	28 days F.P.1. fined 10/-
		(3)Disobeying Lawful Command.	40 days F.P.1.
23rd Middlesex	2	(1)Drunkenness.	Not Guilty
		(2)Stealing Goods.	Reduced to Ranks
11th. Queens	2	(1)Absent from Front Line.	35 days F.P.1. (30 days remitd)
		(2) ditto	30 days F.P.2.
10th. R.W.Kents	1	Disobeying Lawful Command.	Not Guilty
26th. R.Fusiliers	6	(1)Sleeping on his Post.	1 year I.H.L.
		(2)Drunkenness.	14 days F.P.1. fined £1.
		(3)Drunkenness.	14 days F.P.1. fined £1.1.
		(4)Wounding Comrade.	56 days detention remitd to 28 days F.P.1.
		(5)Disobeying Lawful Command.	6 mths H.L.
		(6)Asleep on Post.	Not Guilty
32nd R.Fusiliers	2	(1)Disobeying Lawful Command.	42 days F.P.2.
		(2)a.Failing to appear on Parade	28 days F.P.1.
		b.Malingering.	Not Guilty.
187th. Brig.R.F.A.	1	Conduct to the predudice of good order and Mil.Disc.	28 days F.P.1.
189th. Brig.R.F.A.	1	Knowingly making a false statement.	Not Guilty
190th. Brig.R.F.A.	1	Using threatening language.	56 days F.P.1.
10th. Corps Cyclists	1	Disrespectful langiage to N.C.O.	90 days F.P.1. 52 days remitd.
124th M.G.Co.	1	Striking two soldiers.	Reduced to Ranks
122nd M.G.Co.	1	Leaving his Post.	1 year I.H.L.

Vol XI

Confidential

War Diary

of

H.Q. 41st Div (A+Q)

For Month of March 1917

Army Form C. 2118

WAR DIARY
or
INTELLIGENCE SUMMARY

41st. Division,
"A" and "Q".

(Erase heading not required.)

Instructions regarding War Diaries and Intelligence Summaries are contained in F. S. Regs., Part II. and the Staff Manual respectively. Title Pages will be prepared in manuscript.

Place	Date	Hour	Summary of Events and Information	Remarks and references to Appendices
RENINGHELST.	March 1917.		A statement showing Casualties and Sick evacuations for the month is attached.	
			A statement showing Drafts, and Reinforcements, and Weekly Strength is attached.	
			A statement showing Courts Martial for the month is attached.	
			April 2nd. 1917.	
			[signature]	
			Major, D. A. A. G. 41st. Division.	

1875 Wt. W593/826 1,000,000 4/15 J.B.C. & A. A.D.S.S./Forms/C. 2118.

STATEMENT SHOWING COURTS MARTIAL

FOR THE MONTH OF MARCH 1917.

Unit.	No.	Particulars of Charge.	Sentence.
15th.Hants.	1	Talking to Sentry on duty in Guard Room.	Reduced to ranks.
11th.R.W.Kents.	3.	(1) Wounding an officer careless handling of rifle.	35 days F.P.1.
		(2) Insubordinate language to superior Officer.	56 days F.P.1.
		(3) Leaving post.	2 Years I.H.L.
20th.D.L.I.	2.	(1) Carelessly discharging rifle and injuring comrade.	56 days F.P.1.
		(2) Stealing goods.	90 days F.P.1.
23rd.Middlesex.	1.	Disobeying an order.	Not Guilty.
11th.Queens.	2.	(1) Breach of Censorship.	Reduced to ranks.
		(2) Absenting himself and insubordinate language.	75 days F.P.1.
10th.R.W.Kents.	1.	Carelessly discharging rifle and wounding comrade.	20 days F.P.2.
26th.R.Fusiliers.	1.	Sleeping on Post.	91 days F.P.1.
32nd. - do -	1.	Assaulting a Belgian.	7 days F.P.1.
10th.Queens.	1.	Absenting himself from trenches.	12 months I.H.L.
19th.Middlesex.	4.	(1) Drunkenness.	28 days F.P.1.& Fined 10/-.
		(2) - do -	41 days F.P.1.& Fined 10/-.
		(3) - do -	28 days F.P.1.& Fined £1.
		(4) - do -	56 days F.P.1.
125 M.G.Coy.	1.	Stealing Goods.	90 days F.P.1. Quashed.(2nd.Army C.M.13712 19/3/17).

STATEMENT SHOWING REINFORCEMENTS AND WEEKLY STRENGTH.

MARCH 1917.

UNIT.	Reinforcements Officers.	O.R.	Weekly Strength Other Ranks. Mar.1st.	Mar.3rd.	Mar.10th.	Mar.17th.	Mar.24th.	Mar.31st.
12th.East Surrey Regt.	5	43	1078	1082	1080	1057	1041	1043
15th.Hampshire.Regt.	6	85	891	909	893	882	884	908
11th.R.W.Kent Regt.	5	91	937	937	958	974	981	984
18th.K.R.R.Corps.	1	86	915	874	863	853	855	898
122nd.M.Gun Coy.	2	7	169	161	155	174	170	170
11th.R.W.Surrey Regt.	4	79	1062	1058	1048	1045	1027	1022
10th.R.W.Kent Regt.	6	38	986	995	990	983	968	980
23rd.Middlesex.Regt.	4	35	941	950	945	935	913	914
20th.D.L.I.	6	23	951	930	938	941	929	928
123rd.M.Gun Coy.	4	21	156	163	172	173	171	174
10th.R.W.Surrey Regt.	2	113	891	890	916	904	930	971
26th.R.Fusiliers.	7	20	924	862	845	845	831	824
32nd.R.Fusiliers.	1	8	932	937	927	917	912	908
21st.K.R.R.Corps.	1	69	912	899	881	881	884	933
124th.M.Gun Coy.	-	1	175	174	175	174	171	171
19th.Middlesex Regt.	-	3	941	955	951	943	938	933

UNIT.	OFFICERS.			OTHER RANKS.			EVACUATED SICK&
	Killed	Wounded	Missing	Killed	Wounded	Missing	
Total for Division. (Brought Forward).	2	6	—	31	195	2	464
Attached Troops.							
216th.Tun.Coy.	—	—	—	—	—	—	4
189th.Brigade.R.A.	—	—	—	1	1	—	13
Irish Fusiliers(Tra.Con)	—	—	—	—	—	—	3
N.Irish Horse. do.	—	—	—	—	—	—	1
R.Irish Rifles. do.	—	—	—	—	—	—	2
Scottish do do.	—	—	—	—	—	—	1
2nd.Can.Tun.Coy.	—	—	—	—	—	—	5
28th.R.W.Surrey Regt.	—	—	—	—	—	—	5
10th.Rly.Constn.Coy.	—	—	—	—	—	—	2
French Interpreters.	—	1	—	1	1	—	1
Wireless R.E.	—	—	—	—	—	—	—
1st.Can.Tun.Coy.	—	—	—	—	—	—	—
TOTAL.	2	7	—	33	197	2	501

CONFIDENTIAL.

The following Table shows numbers killed, wounded, missing, and evacuated sick during the month of March 1917 (to 12 noon 31st).

UNIT.	OFFICERS.			OTHER RANKS.			EVACUATED
	Killed	Wounded	Missing	Killed	Wounded	Missing	Sick.
Divisional H.Q.	-	-	-	-	-	-	3
122nd.M.Gun Coy.	-	-	-	-	1	-	6
12th.E.Surrey Regt.	1	-	-	4	19	-	31
15th.Hampshire Regt.	-	-	-	4	16	-	39
11th.R.W.Kent Regt.	-	2	-	4	52	-	24
18th.K.R.R.Corps.	-	-	-	3	27	-	33
123rd.M.Gun Coy.	-	-	-	-	1	-	16
11.Queens.	-	-	-	-	12	-	27
10th.R.W.Kent Regt.	1	1	-	4	9	2	31
23rd.Middlesex.	-	1	-	1	8	-	22
20th.Durham.L.I.	-	-	-	4	14	-	24
124th.M.Gun Coy.	-	-	-	-	-	-	5
10th.Queens.	-	-	-	1	4	-	30
26th.R.Fusiliers.	-	-	-	-	7	-	29
32nd.R.Fusiliers.	-	-	-	-	5	-	22
21st.K.R.R.Corps.	-	-	-	-	4	-	31
19th.Middlesex.	-	1	-	5	3	-	19
187th.Brigade R.A.	-	-	-	1	4	-	9
190th.Brigade R.A.	-	-	-	-	-	-	21
41st.Divn.A.C.	-	-	-	2	3	-	10
41st.T.M.Batteries.	-	-	-	-	3	-	12
228th.Field Coy R.E.	-	-	-	-	2	-	8
233rd.Field Coy R.E.	-	-	-	-	1	-	3
237th.Field Coy R.E.	-	-	-	-	2	-	-
41st.Divn.Sig.Coy.	-	-	-	-	-	-	3
41st.Divn.Train.	-	-	-	-	-	-	3
R.A.M.C.	-	1	-	-	-	-	-
138th.Field Ambince.	-	-	-	-	-	-	8
139th.Field Ambince.	-	-	-	-	-	-	7
140th.Field Ambince.	-	-	-	-	-	-	9
84th.Sanitary Section.	-	-	-	-	-	-	1
Total for Division. (Carried Forward)	2	6	1	31	195	2	464

Army Form C. 2118

WAR DIARY
or
INTELLIGENCE SUMMARY

41st. Division,
"A" and "Q".

(Erase heading not required.)

Instructions regarding War Diaries and Intelligence Summaries are contained in F. S. Regs., Part II. and the Staff Manual respectively. Title Pages will be prepared in manuscript.

Place	Date	Hour	Summary of Events and Information	Remarks and references to Appendices
RENINGHELST.	March 1917.		A statement showing Casualties and Sick evacuations for the month is attached.	
			A statement showing Drafts, and Reinforcements, and Weekly Strength is attached.	
			A statement showing Courts Martial for the month is attached.	
			April 2nd.1917.	
			[signature]	
			Major,	
			D. A. A. G.	
			41st. Division.	

STATEMENT SHOWING COURTS MARTIAL

FOR THE MONTH OF MARCH 1917.

Unit.	No.	Particulars of Charge.	Sentence.
15th.Hants.	1	Talking to Sentry on duty in Guard Room.	Reduced to ranks.
11th.R.W.Kents.	3.	(1) Wounding an officer carelessly handling of rifle.	35 days F.P.1.
		(2) Insubordinate language to superior Officer.	56 days F.P.1.
		(3) Leaving post.	2 Years I.H.L.
20th.D.L.I.	2.	(1) Carelessly discharging rifle and injuring comrade.	56 days F.P.1.
		(2) Stealing goods.	90 days F.P.1.
23rd.Middlesex.	1.	Disobeying an order.	Not Guilty.
11th.Queens.	2.	(1) Breach of Censorship.	Reduced to ranks.
		(2) Absenting himself and insubordinate language.	75 days F.P.1.
10th.R.W.Kents.	1.	Carelessly discharging rifle and wounding comrade.	20 days F.P.2.
26th.R.Fusiliers.	1.	Sleeping on Post.	91 days F.P.1.
32nd. - do -	1.	Assaulting a Belgian.	7 days F.P.1.
10th.Queens.	1.	Absenting himself from trenches.	12 months I.H.L.
19th.Middlesex.	4.	(1) Drunkenness.	28 days F.P.1.& Fined 10/-.
		(2) - do -	41 days F.P.1.& Fined 10/-.
		(3) - do -	28 days F.P.1.& Fined £1.
		(4) - do -	56 days F.P.1.
193 M.G.Coy.	1.	Stealing Goods.	90 days F.P.1. Quashed.(2nd.Army C.M.13712 19/3/17).

CONFIDENTIAL.

The following Table shows numbers killed, wounded, missing, and evacuated sick during the month of March 1917 (to 12 noon 31st).

UNIT.	OFFICERS.			OTHER RANKS.			EVACUATED
	Killed	Wounded	Missing.	Killed	Wounded	Missing.	Sick.
Divisional H.Q.	-	-	-	-	-	-	3
122nd.M.Gun Coy.	-	-	-	-	1	-	6
12th.E.Surrey Regt.	1	-	-	4	19	-	31
15th.Hampshire Regt.	-	-	-	4	16	-	39
11th.R.W.Kent Regt.	-	2	-	4	52	-	24
18th.K.R.R.Corps.	-	-	-	3	27	-	33
123rd.M.Gun Coy.	-	-	-	-	1	-	6
11.Queens.	-	1	-	4	12	2	27
10th.R.W.Kent Regt.	-	-	-	1	9	-	31
23rd.Middlesex.	-	-	-	4	8	-	22
20th.Durham L.I.	-	1	-	1	14	-	24
124th.M.Gun Coy.	-	-	-	-	-	-	5
10th.Queens.	-	-	-	-	4	-	30
35th.R.Fusiliers.	1	-	-	2	7	-	29
32nd.R.Fusiliers.	2	-	-	1	5	-	22
31st.K.R.R.Corps.	-	1	-	-	4	-	31
19th.Middlesex.	-	-	-	-	3	-	18
187th.Brigade R.A.	-	-	-	2	4	-	9
190th.Brigade R.A.	-	1	-	-	-	-	21
41st.Divn.A.C.	-	-	-	2	3	-	10
41st.T.M.Batteries.	-	-	-	-	-	-	8
228th.Field Coy R.E.	-	-	-	2	9	-	8
233rd.Field Coy R.E.	-	-	-	1	2	-	3
237th.Field Coy R.E.	-	-	-	-	1	-	3
41st.Divn.Sig.Coy.	-	-	-	-	-	-	18
41st.Divn.Train.	-	1	-	-	-	-	7
R.A.M.C.	-	-	-	-	-	-	9
138th.Field Amb.Incs.	-	-	-	-	-	-	9
139th.Field Amb.Incs.	-	-	-	-	-	-	1
140th.Field Amb.Incs.	-	-	-	-	-	-	-
84th.Sanitary Section.	-	-	-	-	-	-	1
Total for Division. (Carried Forward)	6	6	-	31	195	2	464

UNIT.	OFFICERS. Killed	OFFICERS. Wounded	OFFICERS. Missing.	OTHER RANKS. Killed	OTHER RANKS. Wounded	OTHER RANKS. Missing.	EVACUATED SICK&.
Total for Division. (Brought Forward).	2	6	-	31	195	2	464
Attached Troops.							
216th.Tun.Coy.	-	-	-	-	-	-	4
189th.Brigade.R.A.	-	-	-	1	1	-	13
Irish Fusiliers(Tra.Con)-	-	-	-	-	-	-	3
N.Irish Horse. do.	-	-	-	-	-	-	1
R.Irish Rifles. do.	-	-	-	-	-	-	2
Scottish do do.	-	-	-	-	-	-	1
2nd.Can.Tun.Coy.	-	-	-	-	-	-	5
28th.R.W.Surrey Regt.	-	-	-	-	-	-	5
10th.Rly.Constn.Coy.	-	-	-	-	-	-	2
French Interpreters.	-	-	-	-	-	-	1
Wireless R.E.	-	-	-	-	-	-	1
1st.Can.Tun.Coy.	-	1	-	1	1	-	1
TOTAL.	2	7	-	33	197	2	501

STATEMENT SHOWING REINFORCEMENTS AND WEEKLY STRENGTH.
MARCH 1917.

UNIT.	Reinforcements Officers.	Reinforcements O.R.	Weekly Strength Other Ranks. Mar.1st.	Mar.3rd.	Mar.10th.	Mar.17th.	Mar.24th.	Mar.31st.
12th.East Surrey Regt.	5	45	1078	1089	1080	1057	1041	1043
15th.Hampshire. Regt.	6	85	891	909	893	862	884	908
11th.R.W.Kent Regt.	5	91	937	937	958	974	991	964
18th.K.R.R.Corps.	1	86	915	874	863	855	855	898
122nd.M.Gun Coy.	2	7	169	181	165	174	170	170
11th.R.W.Surrey Regt.	4	79	1062	1058	1048	1045	1027	1022
10th.R.W.Kent Regt.	6	32	986	995	990	983	968	980
23rd.Middlesex. Regt.	4	55	941	950	945	935	913	914
20th.D.L.I.	6	23	951	930	938	941	929	928
123rd.M.Gun Coy.	4	21	156	165	172	173	171	174
10th.R.W.Surrey Regt.	2	113	891	890	916	904	930	971
26th.R.Fusiliers.	7	20	924	862	845	845	831	824
32nd.R.Fusiliers.	1	8	938	937	927	917	912	902
21st.K.R.R.Corps.	1	69	912	899	881	881	884	935
124th.M.Gun Coy.	—	1	175	174	175	174	171	171
19th.Middlesex Regt.	—	3	941	955	951	945	938	933

Army Form C. 2118

WAR DIARY
or
INTELLIGENCE SUMMARY

41st. Division.
"A" and "Q".

(Erase heading not required.)

Instructions regarding War Diaries and Intelligence Summaries are contained in F. S. Regs., Part II. and the Staff Manual respectively. Title Pages will be prepared in manuscript.

Place	Date	Hour	Summary of Events and Information	Remarks and references to Appendices
RENINGHELST.	April 1917.		A statement showing Casualties and Sick Wastage for the month is attached.	
			A statement showing Weekly Strength and Reinforcements received during the month is attached.	
			A statement showing Courts Martial for the month is attached.	

Lieut.Colonel,
A.A. &. Q.M.G.
41st.Division.

STATEMENT SHOWING COURTS MARTIAL

FOR THE MONTH OF   APRIL 1917.

Unit.	No.	Particulars of Charge.	Sentence.
12th.E.Surreys.	3.	(1) Sleeping on Post.	Death. Commuted to 10.Years P.S.
		(2) Leaving Post without orders.	- do -
		(3) Absence from Trenches without leave.	Reduced to Ranks. & 2.yrs.I.H.L.
18th.K.R.R.C.	1.	Drunkenness.	21 days F.P.1.
11th.R.W.Kents.	1.	- do -	14 days F.P.1.
20th.D.L.I.	1.	- do -	56 days F.P.1 & Find £1.
11th.R.W.Surreys.	3.	(1).Injuring man with Lewis Gun during instruction.	Not Guilty.
		(2).Disobeying Command & using bad language.	56 days F.P.1.
		(3).Drunkenness.	- do -
10th.R.W.Kents.	2.	(1).Wounding Comrade carelessly discharging rifle.	90 days F.P.1.
		(2).Using insub.language.	2 Years I.H.L.
26th.R.Fusiliers.	2.	(1).Disobeying order.	30 days F.P.1.
		(2).Breach of Censorship.	30 days F.P.2.
32 nd. " "	2.	(1).a. Absenting himself without leave.	)
		b. Disobeying Command.	)Find 30 days pay.
		c. Using insub.language.	)
		(2).a.Cowardice.	Not Guilty.
		b.Leaving patrol without orders.	2 Years I.H.L.
21st.K.R.R.C.	1.	Drunkenness.	28 days F.P.1.
No.1 Section. 41st.D.A.C.	2.	(1).Stealing Money.	6 months I.H.L.
		(2).Receiving Stolen Money.	- do -
237th.Fld.Coy.R.E.	1.	Drunkenness.	90 days F.P.1.
1st.Canadian Tun. Company.	5.	(1).Absenting himself from Trenches.	9 months I.H.L.
		(2) - do -	- do -
		(3).Drunkenness & escaping from Guard Room.	2 Years I.H.L.
		(4).Escaping escort.	- do -
		(5).Desertion.	- do -

CONFIDENTIAL.

The following table shows numbers killed, wounded, missing, and evacuated sick during the month of April 1917. (to 12 noon 31st).

UNIT.	OFFICERS. Killed	Wounded	Missing.	OTHER RANKS. Killed	Wounded	Missing.	EVACUATED Sick.
12th.E.Surrey Regt.	-	-	-	11	13	-	16
15th.Hampshire Regt.	-	1	-	6	35	-	43
11th.R.W.Kent Regt.	1	2	-	16	43	8	28
18th.K.R.R.Corps.	1	1	-	7	23	-	38
122nd.M.Gun Coy.	-	-	-	1	1	-	5
11th.R.W.Surrey Regt.	-	2	-	1	5	-	40
10th.R.W.Kent Regt.	1	-	-	5	5	-	32
23rd.Middlesex Regt.	1	-	-	3	7	-	27
20th.Durham L.I.	-	-	-	-	-	-	24
123rd.M.Gun Coy.	-	-	-	-	-	-	10
10th.R.W.Surrey Regt.	-	2	-	2	6	-	47
26th.R.Fusiliers.	-	1	-	6	7	-	23
32nd.R.Fusiliers.	-	1	-	-	11	-	29
21st.K.R.R.Corps.	-	-	-	2	2	-	24
124th.M.Gun Coy.	-	-	-	-	4	-	5
19th.Middlesex Regt.	-	1	-	2	13	-	12
Hdqrs. R.A.	-	-	-	-	-	-	1
187th.Bde.R.A.	-	1	-	6	6	-	23
190th.Bde.R.A.	-	-	-	2	1	-	10
41st. D.A.C.	-	-	-	-	4	-	13
41st.T.M.Batteries.	-	-	-	-	3	-	3
228th.Field Coy.R.E.	-	-	-	2	11	-	9
233rd.Field Coy.R.E.	-	-	-	2	10	-	4
237th.Field Coy.R.E.	-	-	-	-	5	-	5
41st.Div.Sig.Coy.	-	-	-	-	1	-	3
138th.Field Amb.nce.	-	-	-	-	-	-	3
139th.Field Amb.nce.	-	-	-	-	2	-	5
140th.Field Amb.nce.	-	-	-	-	-	-	3
41st.Divn.Train.	-	1	-	-	1	-	4
Total for Division.	4	13	-	72	209	8	489

/over.

UNIT.	Officers Missing.	Officers Killed.	Officers Wounded.	Officers Missing.	Other Ranks Killed.	Other Ranks Wounded.	Other Ranks Missing.	Evacuated Sick.
Attached Troops.								
189th.Bde.R.A.	-	-	-	-	-	-	-	7
1st.Can.Tunnelling Coy.	1	-	-	-	5	3	-	1
2nd. - do -	-	-	-	-	-	-	-	7
28th.R.W.Surrey (Labour Coy).	-	-	-	-	-	-	-	11
10th.R.O.Coy.	-	-	-	-	-	-	-	2
3rd.Devons.	-	-	-	-	-	-	-	1
Total.	1	-	-	-	5	3	-	29

STATEMENT SHOWING REINFORCEMENTS AND WEEKLY STRENGTH.
APRIL 1917.

Unit.	Reinforcements		Weekly Strength Other Ranks.				
	Officers.	O.Rks.	April 1st.	April 7th.	April 14th.	April 21st.	April 28th.
12th.E.Surrey Regt.	2	22	1043	1038	1029	1027	1020
15th.Hampshire Regt.	1	88	908	910	960	954	930
11th.R.W.Kent Regt.	3	18	964	956	941	911	918
18th.K.R.R.Corps.	1	51	898	917	886	882	879
122nd.M.Gun Coy.	-	8	170	175	173	173	171
11th.R.W.SurreyRegt.	1	12	1022	1013	1004	1000	991
10th.R.W.Kent Regt.	6	21	980	977	981	981	977
23rd.Middlesex Regt.	2	15	914	911	922	918	918
20th.Durham L.I.	3	13	928	913	918	901	899
123rd.M.Gun Coy.	-	5	174	172	176	175	175
10th.R.W.Surrey Regt.	-	29	971	970	975	965	941
26th.R.Fusiliers.	7	36	824	810	810	819	803
32nd.R.Fusiliers.	-	17	902	900	910	899	889
21st.K.R.R.Corps.	4	30	933	942	942	925	919
124th.M.Gun Coy.	-	8	171	169	170	172	171
19th.Middlesex Regt.	1	21	953	924	921	918	924

MAP C

Part of Sheet 5A (Belgium). SECOND ARMY AREA. (Showing Traffic Circuits dated 20-4-17.

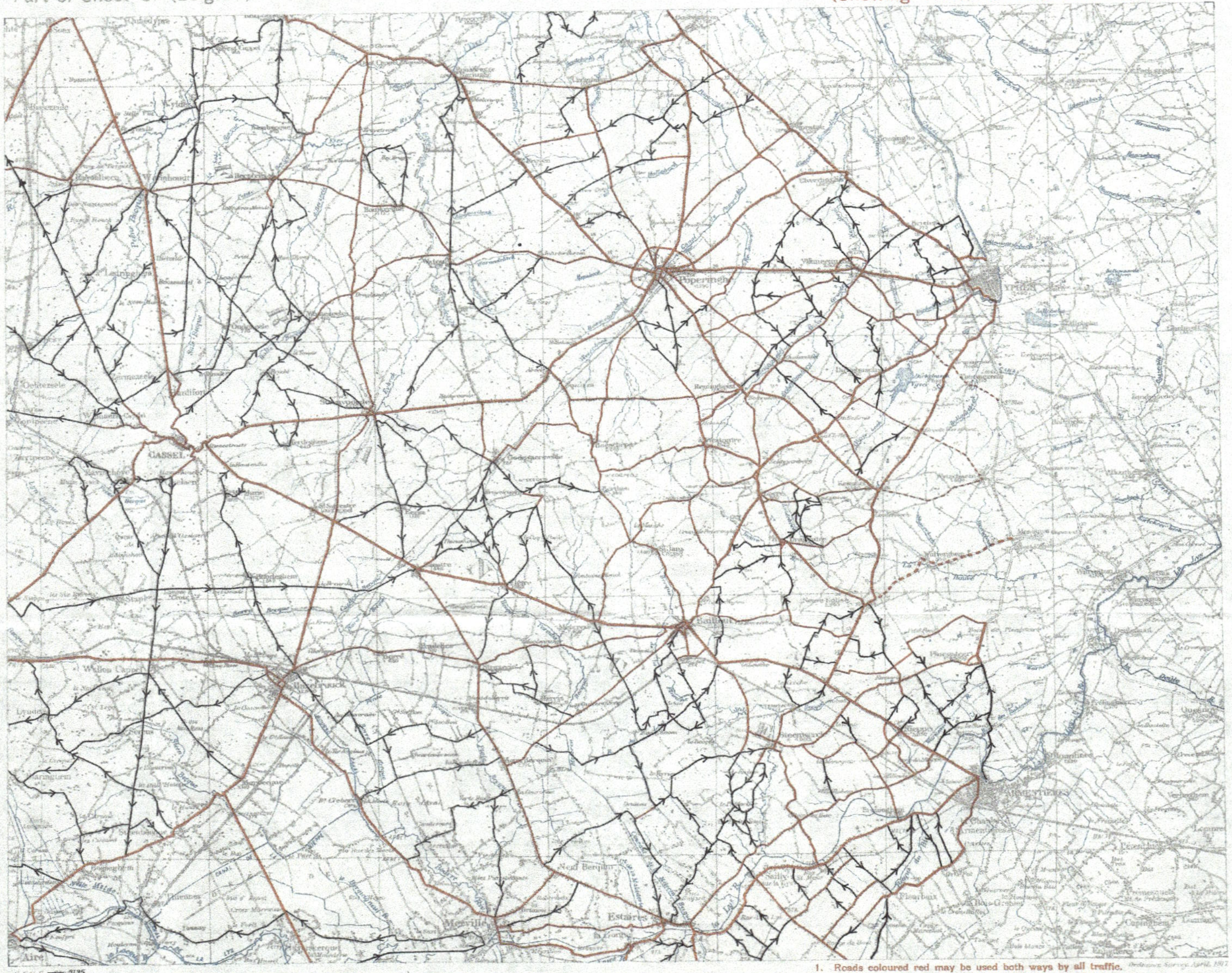

Scale 100,000 or 1 Inch to 1·58 Miles

1 Centimetre to 1 Kilometre

1. Roads coloured red may be used both ways by all traffic.
2. Roads coloured black must be used in the direction of the arrows by all motor lorries, motor busses, and steam tractors.
3. No restrictions are placed on the movements of motor cycles and motor cars, except that for their own safety they are advised to follow the arrows as much as possible.
4. Roads not coloured red or black must not be used by motor lorries, motor busses and steam tractors.

Extract from circular memo. issued with G.R.O., 692:—
"Empty vehicles must give way to loaded convoys, and when necessary, halt to allow the latter to pass."

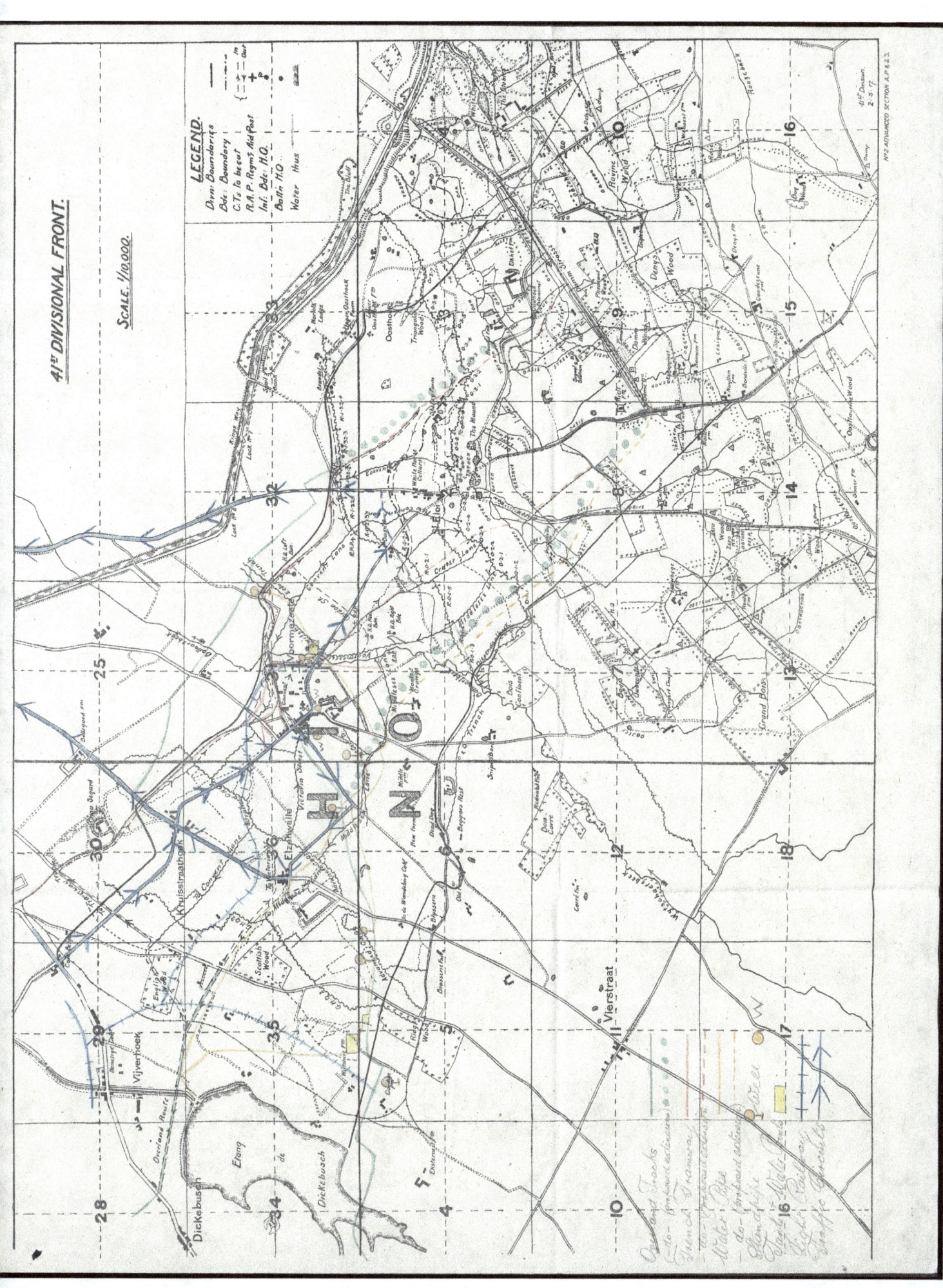

W. 15517—M. 141. 250,000. 1/16. L.S.&Co. Forms/W 3091/2.   Army Form W. 3091.

Cover for Documents.

Nature of Enclosures.

Notes, or Letters written.

Copies for
War Diary

Army Form C. 2118

WAR DIARY
or
INTELLIGENCE SUMMARY
(Erase heading not required.)

41st. Division
"A" and "Q".

Instructions regarding War Diaries and Intelligence Summaries are contained in F. S. Regs., Part II. and the Staff Manual respectively. Title Pages will be prepared in manuscript.

Place	Date	Hour	Summary of Events and Information	Remarks and references to Appendices
RENINGHELST.	May 31st.		A statement showing casualties for the month is attached.	
			A statement showing Courts Martial for the month is attached	
			A statement showing reinforcements and weekly strength for the month is attached,.	
	May 25th		Supply Railhead changed from WIPPENHOEK to RENINGHELST.	
	May 31st.		Supply Railhead changed from RENINGHELST to OUDERDOM.	

June 10th.1917.

Lieut Colonel,
A.A. &. Q.M.G.
41st.Division.

STATEMENT SHOWING COURTS MARTIAL

FOR THE MONTH OF MAY 1917.

Unit.	No.	Particulars of Charge.	Sentence.
18th.K.R.R.C.	1.	Drunkenness.	14 days. F.P.1.
11th.R.W.Kents.	2.	(1)a. Insub.language to Superior Officer.	a. Not Guilty.
		b. Disobedience.	b. 56 days.F.P.1.
		(2). Insub.language to Superior Officer.	28 days F.P.1.
10th.R.W.Kents.	2.	(1) Wounding Comrade.	42 days F.P.1.
		(2) Wounding himself.	90 days F.P.1.
26th.R.Fusiliers.	1.	Leaving Front Line.	9 months I.H.L.
32nd. - do -	1.	(a) Using insub.language to Superior Officer.	Not Guilty.
		(b) Conduct to the prejudice of discipline.	Fined 42 days pay.
190th.Brigade R.F.A.	2.	(1) Sleeping on Post.	3 months F.P.1.
		(2) In possession of pair of stirrup irons.	28 days F.P.1.
41st.Divl.Train.	2.	(1) Drunkenness.	28 days F.P.2.
		(2) a. Desertion.	90 F.P.1.
		b. Loss of kit.	Refund £2"0"8d

The following table shows numbers killed, wounded, missing, and evacuated sick during the month of May 1917. (to 12 noon 31st).

UNIT.	OFFICERS.			OTHER RANKS.			EVACUATED Sick.
	Killed.	Wounded.	Missing.	Killed.	Wounded.	Missing.	
Divl.Headquarters.	-	-	-	-	-	-	-
12th. E.Surrey Regt.	-	1	-	-	1	-	40
15th. Hampshire Regt.	-	-	-	-	11	-	49
11th. R.W.Kent Regt.	-	-	-	4	9	-	51
18th. K.R.R.Corps.	-	-	-	11	26	-	57
122nd. M. Gun Coy.	-	-	-	-	25	2	13
123rd. Brigade Hqrs.	-	-	-	-	1	-	-
11th. R.W.Surrey Regt.	-	-	-	6	15	-	40
10th. R.W.Kent Regt.	-	1	-	5	34	-	26
23rd. Middlesex Regt.	-	-	-	8	19	-	36
20th. Durham L.I.	-	2	-	3	29	-	32
123rd. M.Gun Coy.	-	-	-	1	6	-	11
10th. R.W.Surrey Regt.	-	-	-	1	2	-	25
26th. R. Fusiliers.	-	-	-	1	6	-	30
32nd. R. Fusiliers.	-	-	-	1	2	-	28
21st. K.R.R.Corps.	-	-	-	-	8	-	24
124th. M.Gun Coy.	-	2	-	5	-	-	6
19th. Middlesex Regt.	-	2	-	-	19	-	15
Hqrs. 41st.Divl.Artillory.	-	1	-	6	31	-	-
187th.Brigade R.A.	-	-	-	2	13	-	16
190th.Brigade R.A.	-	1	-	1	4	-	13
41st. D.A.C.	-	-	-	-	2	-	13
41st. T.M.Batteries.	-	-	-	-	6	-	5
228th.Field Coy. R.E.	-	1	-	-	10	-	8
233rd.Field Coy. R.E.	-	-	-	-	1	-	9
237th.Field Coy. R.E.	-	-	-	-	-	-	5
41st. Signal Coy.	-	-	-	-	10	-	2
138th.Field Amblnce.	-	-	-	-	3	-	4
139th.Field Amblnce.	-	-	-	1	1	-	6
140th.Field Amblnce.	-	-	-	1	3	-	6
41st.Divl.Train.	-	-	-	-	-	-	1
Total for Division.	1	15	1	56	298	2	571

/over.

UNITS	OFFICERS			OTHER RANKS			EVACUATED
	Killed	Wounded	Missing	Killed	Wounded	Missing	Sick
Attached Troops.							
1st. Can. Tunnelling Co.	-	1	-	-	1	-	-
45th. A.F.A. Brigade.	-	-	-	-	1	-	-
25th. A.F.A. Brigade.	-	-	-	1	14	-	-
1st. D.A.C.	-	-	-	-	-	-	-
65th. A.F.A. Brigade.	-	1	-	-	2	-	-
Canadian A.S.C.	-	-	-	-	1	-	-
2nd. Canadian Battn.	1	-	-	2	3	-	-
1st. T.M. Batteries.	-	-	-	1	-	-	-
"Z" Coy. R.E.	-	-	-	-	-	-	-
26th. A.F.A. Brigade.	-	1	-	1	1	-	-
Mil. Foot Police.	-	-	-	-	2	-	-
39th. Brigade R.A.	-	1	-	2	1	-	-
52nd. A.F.A. Brigade.	-	2	-	5	27	-	-
72nd. A.F.A. Brigade.	-	1	-	-	9	-	-
					4		
Total.	1	8		12	66		1

STATEMENT SHOWING REINFORCEMENTS AND WEEKLY STRENGTH.

MAY 1917.

Unit.	Reinforcements. Officers.	Reinforcements. O. Ranks.	Weekly Strength other Ranks. May 5th	May 12th	May 19th	May 26th
13th. E.Surrey Regt.	1	13	1027	1017	1018	1021
15th. Hants Regt.	1	8	931	919	919	921
11th. R.W.Kent Regt.	1	77	914	901	885	939
18th. K.R.R.Corps.	2	121	890	875	945	922
122nd. M.Gun Coy.	1	6	171	173	175 (3)	167
11th. R.W.Surrey Regt.	1	14	983	930	964	946
10th. R.W.Kent Regt.	—	34	982	956	932	929
23rd. Middlesex Regt.	—	120	901	890	877	951
20th. D.L. Infantry.	2	121	897	886	939	959
123rd. M. Gun Coy.	—	10	175	175	170	168
10th. R.W. Surrey Regt.	2	51	949	947	954	950
26th. R. Fusiliers	4	187	795	798	935	933
32nd. R. Fusiliers	—	122	872	866	861	905
21st. K.R.R.Corps.	5	65	918	914	972	971
124th. M. Gun Coy.	1	4	174	175	173	172
19th. Middlesex Regt.	1	58	918	915	907	935

SECRET.

41st. Division No. Q/335/S.

41st. DIVISION.

ADMINISTRATIVE INSTRUCTIONS IN CONNECTION WITH FORTHCOMING OPERATIONS.

To obviate having to issue long orders AND instructions at one time, and to enable units to digest them by degrees, the Administrative Instructions in connection with forthcoming operations, will be issued from time to time under various headings.

An index will be published with the last heading sent out, and units should then bind the whole together into one complete volume.

The following headings are now forwarded :-

(I). Personnel.

(II). Reinforcements.

(III). Prisoners of War.

(IV) Battle Stragglers

[signature]

Lieut. Colonel,
A.A. & Q.M.G.
41st. Division.

May 19th. 1917.

DESTRIBUTION :-

122nd. Brigade.	7 copies.	A.D.M.S.	4 copies.
123rd. Brigade.	7 copies.	A.D.V.S.	1 copy.
124th. Brigade.	7 copies.	A.P.M.	1 copy.
R.A.	6. "	D.A.D.O.S.	1 copy.
R.E.	4. "	Salvage Officer.	1 copy.
Signals.	1. "	Area Comm'dt.	1 copy.
Pioneers.	1. "	" G "	1 copy.
10th. Corps Q.	1 "	Reserve Division	1 copy.
47th. Division.	1 "	19th. Division.	1 copy.
Divl. Train.	1 "	S.S.O.	1 copy.
War Diary.	2 copies.	Spare.	11 copies.

I N D E X

to

41st. DIVISIONAL ADMINISTRATIVE ARRANGEMENTS.

Part (I). PERSONNEL.
" (II). REINFORCEMENTS.
" (III). PRISONERS OF WAR.
" (IV). BATTLE STRAGGLERS.
" (V). RATIONS.
" (VI). WATER.
" (VII). MEDICAL ARRANGEMENTS.
" (VIII). ORDNANCE.
" (IX). AMMUNITION.
" (X). BURIALS.
" (XI). VETERINARY.
" (XII). COMMUNICATIONS.
" (XIII). TRAFFIC CONTROL.
" (XIV). TRENCH TRAMWAY TRAFFIC.
" (XV). FIRST LINE TRANSPORT.
" (XVI). SANITATION.
" (XVII). SALVAGE.
" (XVIII). BATHS AND LAUNDRY.
" (XIX). RECREATION.
" (XX). R.E. STORES.
" (XXI). REPORTS AND RETURNS.

A P P E N D I C E S.

"A". Xth Corps instructions for collection of wounded
"B". Ammunition - Amount in Dumps.
"C". Ammunition Carriers - allotment of
"D". Burial Instructions Xth Corps.
"E". Trench Strength Return - Pro forma.

M A P S.

"A". Communications.
"B". Battle circuits.
"C". Second Army Traffic Map.

I. PERSONNEL.

(1). The number of Officers, N.C.Os and men to take part in the attack will be as laid down in S.S.135. Section .X.X.X. except that (i) only 17 Officers (excluding the Medical Officer) will accompany battalions (ii) Understudies for appointment of Adjutant will be left behind.

    Details left behind will be accomodated at the Reinforcement Camp.

(2). Nominal Rolls of Officers to be left behind will be forwarded to Divisional H.Qtrs when called for.

II. REINFORCEMENT CAMP.

    A Divisional Reinforcement Camp will be formed at the Brigade School at M.4.b.4.4. at which all details left behind by battalions and all reinforcements will be accomodated.

    This Camp will be arranged in Brigade Sections.

Headquarters.	No.	Found by.
Commandant.	1.	122nd.I.Bde.
Act.Adjutant.	1.	123rd.I.Bde.
Act.Qr.Mr.	1.	124th.I.Bde.
Act.Sgt.Major.	1.	122nd.I.Bde.
Act.Qr.Mr.Sgt.	1.	123rd.I.Bde.
Clerks.	1.	124th.I.Bde.

Per Brigade Section.		
O.C.Brigade Details.	1.	Each Brigade.
Act Adjt.&.Qr.Mr.	1.	- do -
Act.C.S.Major.	1.	- do -
Act. C.Q.M.Sgt.	1.	- do -
Regimental Police.	2.	- do -
Clerks.	1.	- do -
Sanitary Men.	2.	- do -
Travelling Cookers.	2.	

2.   The Divisional Train will deliver rations direct to the Camp.

    The Commandant will render A.B. B55 direct to Officer Commanding Divisional Train.

3.   Permanant Staff laid down above for the Headquarters will not be called up by Brigades for reinforcing without reference to this office.

4. The Commandant will render a return daily at 12.noon to Divisional Headquarters on the attached pro-forma.

Names of Officers sent up to Battalions will be entered on back.

III. PRISONERS OF WAR.

(1). Brigades will forward all Prisoners of War under escort (usual strength 10% of the number of prisoners,) to the Divisional Cage at MICMAC, and will be responsible for them until a receipt has been obtained from the Officer in Charge of the Cage.

(2). The 123rd.Infantry Brigade will detail a guard of 1 Sergeant, 1 Corporal and 24 men for the Cage. This Guard will report there at 10.a.m. on "Y" day.

(3). The evacuation of Prisoners from the Divisional to the Corps Cage at G.27.a.4.9. will be carried out by the A.P.M. 41st.Division. A Troop of Xth Corps Cavalry will be available for this purpose.

(4). The A.D.M.S. will detail a Medical Officer with orderly and material for duty at the Corps Cage.

Any prisoners requiring medical attention at the Divisional Cage will be sent to the Field Ambulance at OUDERDOM.

IV. BATTLE STRAGGLERS.

(1). Brigades, of which any portion is East of the BOLLART BEEK, will post Regimental Police along the Line of the BEEK to prevent straggling.

(2). Divisional Battle Straggler Posts, strength 2 M.M.P. and 1 N.C.O. and 3 Infantrymen will be detailed as under :-

Position.	Map Reference.	Found by.
MIDDLESEX LANE.	N.6.b.4½.9½.	124 Brigade
ELZENWALLE.	H.36.a.6.0.	122 "
CONVENT LANE.	H.36.a.9.5.	122 "
KRUISSTRAATHOEK.	H.30.d.5.3.	123 "

/ (3).

(3).

3.   The Divisional Collecting Station will be at
Billet NO.14. DICKEBUSCH (H.33.b.7.5½.) strength as under :-
   One Officer to be found by the 122. Infantry Brigade.
   Two M.M.P.
   One N.C.O. and 4 men from each Brigade, for
escort duties.

4.   The whole of the Infantry required in paras 2
and 3 above will report at the Divisional Collecting
Station on receipt of orders from this office and
will be posted under orders of the A.P.M.

5.   Detailed instructions have been issued to the
A.P.M.

RETURN OF PERSONNEL AT REINFORCEMENT CAMP.

Battalion.	Details left behind by battalion.		Reinforcements who have not been out before.		Reinforcements who have been out before.		Sent up to join Units.		Remarks.
	Offrs.	O.Ranks.	Offrs.	O.Ranks.	Offrs.	O.Ranks.	Offrs.	O.Ranks.	

Commandant,
Division 1 Reinforcement Camp.

V. RATIONS.

The system of dumping of rations and water has already been explained in this office No. Q/335/S dated 17th.April and 19th.May 1917. By this system it will be unnecessary to send up any food or water by road from after "U"/"V" night until "Z"/"A" night for any troops East of DICKEBUSCH.

The supply of rations on "Z"/"A" night for "A" day may present considerable difficulty. It is therefore all important that every man should be in possession of a serviceable ration on "Z" day in the event of its having to be consumed on "A" day.

Units must make arrangements to collect the iron rations of all casualties to act as an emergency reserve.

All units will indent on the S.S.O. for a supply of chewing gum for consumption on Zero day. This chewing gum has been used with great success during the recent operations in the South. It is found that if taken about half an hour before Zero hour, it greatly helps to alleviate hunger and thirst. It would perhaps be as well for units to warn their men that there is nothing in it in the nature of a drug and its sole object is to stay off hunger and thirst.

The supply of rations to Transport Lines and Units West of DICKEBUSCH during operations will continue under normal conditions.

VI. WATER.

(1). The scheme for dumping of water for all troops East of DICKEBUSCH for use during the bombardment were published under this office No. Q/335/S dated 17/4/17 and 19/5/17.

(2). The sources of water supply are as follows :-

(i). A 2 inch pipe-line running from DICKEBUSCH LAKE via RIDGEWOOD and MIDDLESEX LANE to O.1.a.1.8.
Standpipes at the following points :-
(a) N.6.b.4.9.
(b) O.1.a.1.8.

(ii). A branch from (i) at O.1.a.2.7. running N.E. to I.31.d.5.9. supplying :-

(a). Water Point at I.31.d.5.9. (where the VOORMEZEELE - BUS HOUSE - ST ELOI Road crosses the BOLLART BEEK.). At this point there will be standpipes for filling petrol tins, storage barrels, and two 160-gallon tanks, with a diversion road for filling water carts.

(b). Point I.31.d.5.9. where there will be standpipes for filling petrol tins, four 100-gallon tanks, and storage barrels

Further sources of supply :-

(iii). Two wells in VOORMEZEELE :-

(a). Brewery Well at I.31.c.$3\frac{1}{2}$.$5\frac{1}{2}$.

(b). Well in the village square I.31.c.6.4.

Both these supplies are plentiful. 2 scoops of of chlorinated lime required.
Each of these wells is being cleaned out and fitted with a windlass, rope, and bucket.

(c). A spring supply in OLD FRENCH TRENCH at I.32.d.$7\frac{1}{2}$.$2\frac{1}{2}$., liable to run dry in summer.

In the event of all the above supplies failing, water would have to be brought up in petrol tins on First Line Transport in the normal way, empty tins being exchanged for full at the unloading point.

(3). Xth Corps are also running a 4" Main from DICKEBUSCH LAKE via MIDDLESEX LANE (O.1.a.$2\frac{1}{2}$.8.) to MOATED GRANGE (O.1.a.6.4.). There will be a connection between this pipe and the 2" Main mentioned in para (2), giving an alternative supply to the latter in the event of the 2" pipe being broken between RIDGEWOOD and MIDDLESEX LANE.
As soon as circumstances permit, the 4" pipe will be pushed forward via PICCADILLY FARM (O.8.a.) to the neighbourhood of DOME HOUSE (O.8.d.$9\frac{1}{2}$.$6\frac{1}{2}$.) Tanks will be established under the embankment of the DAMM STRASSE near the latter point.

/ (4).

(4). WASHING WATER.

The POLLART BEEK. Not fit for drinking, as it is liable to contamination from a branch stream which runs into it from the German Lines.

(5). Brigades will arrange for all ground gained by them to be searched for wells, or other sources of water supply, and for the discovery of such to be reported at once to this office, in order that arrangements may be made to test the water which must on no account be used until declared fit to drink by the Medical authorities.

(6). WATER IN THE BACK AREA.

Water Points for filling Water Carts.

(1). G.34.c.5½.1.
(2). G.29.d.75.50,   (In 47th.Divl.Area.)
(3). G.36.c.2.0.   (Not yet completed - May 20th).
(4). M.6.d.7.6.   (- do -   - do -)
(5). H.28.d.2.1½.
(6). M.9.a.2.9½.

Horse Water Points.

(1). M.4.a.6.0.   (100^x of troughing,
                    1000 horses per hour.)
(2). M.6.b.4.0.   (30^x troughing -
                    300 horses per hour.)
(3). G.36.c.4.2. (in 47th.Divl.Area 100^x
                    troughing- 1000 horses per hour).
(4). N.1.a.6.8½. (1000 horses per hour.)
(5). H.31.b.5½.3.(300   "   "   ")
(6). M.6.a.6.3.   (300 horses per hour.)
(7). M.5.b.8.3½. (1000   "   "   ).

No. 6. and 7. not yet constructed -(May 20th.)

Pipe water supply is also being run direct into all horse lines in the camp on the ZEVECOTEN - LA CLYTTE - Road.

Instructions with regard to watering programmes for animals will be published shortly.

VII. MEDICAL.

(1).   Regimental Aid Posts :-

    No.1.   I.32.d.1.1½. } For 123rd Inf. Brigade.
    No.2.   I.32.c.5.½.

    No.3.   O.1.b.5.9.   } For 124th Inf. Brigade.
    No.4.   O.1.b.2.6.

As soon as the situation permits Regimental Aid Posts will be pushed forward, in order to facilitate the collection of wounded, and relieve the pressure on regimental stretcher bearers.

Divisional Collecting Post for wounded at VOORMEZEELE (I.31.c.4.7½.)

Advanced Dressing Station DICKEBUSCH, H.27.d.4.1.

Walking wounded by down communication trenches to Collecting Post at VOORMEZEELE, thence to DICKEBUSCH Advanced Dressing Station.

Captain J.La.T.LAUDER, R.A.M.C., D.S.O., M.C., will be in charge of Advanced Bearers. His Headquarters will be at the Collecting Post at VOORMEZEELE.

Requests for assistance will be addressed to him. If he is unable to furnish assistance, Divisional Headquarters "A" should be communicated with.

(2).   The A.P.M. will station police at the Collecting Post at VOORMEZEELE and the Advanced Dressing Station, at DICKEBUSCH.

    (a) To take the names of all lightly wounded men coming in without their arms and equipment.

    (b) To take over as stragglers men coming in as wounded or gassed, who, in the opinion of the medical Officer are not justified in doing so.

(3).   Xth Corps letter No.570 A. dated 28/12/16 on the responsibility for collection of wounded is attached vide Appendix "A".

(VIII). ORDNANCE.

(1). Divisional Ordnance Stores remain as at present at G.34.d.3½.3½.

(2). The normal procedure of supply of Ordnance material will continue.

(3). All captured war material will be sent back at once to Divisional Ordnance whence it will be despatched as soon as practicable to Railhead under arrangements to be made by D.A.D.O.S.

Attention is drawn to instructions with regard to captured war material which individual units may wish to claim. (Second Army Routine Orders No.617 and 618 dated 26/2/17 and Q.M.G's No. Q/2798/O.S.5/1090 dated 24/6/16, republished in D.R.O. No.1765 dated 21/5/17).

(IX). AMMUNITION.

(1). The Main Divisional Dump (Field Artillery Ammunition, Grenades, etc, etc,) is at G.24.d.8.7. on the OUDEZEELE - VLAMERTINGHE Road.

(2). Advanced Brigade Dumps :-

    (i). Right Brigade   I.31.d.2.3½.

    (ii). Left Brigade.   (I.31.d.5.9.
                           (I.32.d.2½.2½.

If necessary the Reserve Brigade will draw from these Brigade Dumps.

(3). The amounts of various natures of ammunition to be kept at Divisional and Brigade Dumps are shown in Appendix "B".

Each Brigade will detail an Officer for their Advanced Brigade Dump who will be responsible to the Staff Captain that the amounts of different natures of ammunition are maintained.

(4). Supply of ammunition from Divisional Dump to Brigade Dumps will be by First Line Transport of units to VOORMEZEELE, thence by tramway to Dumps.

(5). On and after the first day of bombardment the present Brigade Dump at DICKEBUSCH (H.34.a.7.9.) can be drawn on by either of the Brigades in Front Line to replenish their Forward Brigade Dumps or to provide the extra ammunition to be carried by every man on going into action (vide 41st.Division No.G.285/99/9 dated 17/4/17 - Instruction No.3. - Fighting Kit.)

(6). Ammunition now distributed in Strong Points and in Front Line system under the Divisional Defence Scheme will be left in situ until further orders as to salvage are received from this office.

(7). Special steps must be taken at all dumps to deal with a possible outbreak of fire.

Artillery Ammunition.

(8). The following amounts will be dumped at guns :-

Each	18 Pr.	1300 rounds.
"	4.5".	1000 rounds.
"	2" T.M.	500 rounds.
"	9.45" T.M.	100 rounds.

(9). In the event of batteries in action moving forward, arrangements must be made for Dumps at guns either to accompany guns at once or to be collected and forwarded later.

(10). Appendix "C" shows scale of ammunition carriers.

(11). Divisional Reserves for Artillery ammunition are at the A.R.P. at G.24.d.8.7.

(12). Supply from A.R.P. to batteries is direct by Light Railway or by ammunition wagons according to the positions of batteries.

(13). All ammunition echelons (Artillery and Infantry) are to be replenished as soon as empty.

(X). BURIALS.

(1). The Xth Corps Burial Scheme is attached vide Appendix "D".

(2). Units should indent on the Divisional Burial Officer, (c/o "A" Branch Divisional Headquarters), for a small supply of the discs and wire rods to enable them to bury any of their own dead who they may wish to.
Units burying any of their own dead must strictly comply with these instructions, account for every disc received by them, and forward rolls, discs, and packets of effects etc., to the Divisional Burial Officer.

(3). Any discs not used must be returned to the Divisional Burial Officer.

(4). The Divisional Burial Officer will notify Brigades the sites selected for burial grounds and battalions must use these as far as possible.

(XI). VETERINARY.

(1). The Mobile Veterinary Section will remain at its present position at G.33.c.0.1½.

(2). An advanced veterinary dressing station for the reception of all sick and wounded animals will be established in the stable of the farm at M.6.b.1½.9. (Sheet 28). from the First day of bombardment.("V" day).

(3). Evacuation from the Advanced Veterinary Dressing Station to the Mobile Vet. Section will be carried out under arrangements to be made by the A.D.V.S.

(XII). COMMUNICATIONS.

(vide Map "A" attached.)

(1). Light Railways.
The Light Railway extension from ENGLISH WOOD (H.29.d.) to VOORMEZEELE will be available for the carrying to VOORMEZEELE (later to SHELLEY DUMP) of R.E. material, stone, a certain amount of ammunition, and, (possibly, later on) rations.
This line will be extended by laying 16 lb. rails over the route of the existing trench tramway to SHELLEY DUMP (I.32.d.2.3.) when it will be possible to run through light railway trucks drawn by petrol tractors to the latter point.

(2). Trench Tramways.

(a). CAFE BELGE to VOORMEZEELE at the disposal of R.E. R.A., and Tunnelling Companies only.
(b). Continuation of (a)
  (i) to SHELLEY DUMP I.32.d.2.3. (vide para.1.)
  (ii) to OXFORD STREET O.1.b.9.5.
These lines will be at the disposal of the Left and Right Brigades respectively.
(c). A branch from (b) (ii) to MOATED GRANGE (O.1.b.2.5.) for conveyance of R.E. material and for evacuation of wounded from the R.A.P. to A.D.S. at VOORMEZEELE.

(3). As soon after zero as circumstances permit, the Trench Tramway system will be pushed forward with all speed to join the German System, the SHELLEY DUMP track via EAST of SHELLEY FARM to RUINED FARM (O.3.c.central) and later, depending on the tactical situation, the OXFORD STREET track via the WEST of the CRATERS in O.2.d. to the neighbourhood of PICCADILLY FARM (O.8.a.).

(4). Road Communications.
The CAFE BELGE - KRUISSTRAATHOEK - VOORMEZEELE road is being improved to take lorry traffic in both directions and the bridge over the BOLLART BEEK at I.31.d.2.4½. strengthened to carry all natures of traffic.
As soon as possible after zero, this road will be pushed on to ST ELOI and it is hoped a few days after zero to have a lorry circuit CAFE BELGE - VOORMEZEELE - ST ELOI - BEDFORD HOUSE (Square I.28.a.).

(5). To avoid the use of the CAFE BELGE - VOORMEZEELE - ST ELOI road, and to avoid VOORMEZEELE in the event of the latter being heavily shelled, an overland track fit for wheels (lightly loaded wagons only) is being prepared from the neighbourhood of BELLEGOED FARM (H.30.d.9.8½.) to SHELLEY DUMP (I.32.d.2.3.) and passing to the EAST of VOORMEZEELE.
This track will normally be at the disposal of the Left Brigade in the Line. As soon as possible after zero this track will be extended via SHELLEY FARM to the German Front Line System in the vicinity of RUINED FARM.

(6). A similar overland track for the Right Brigade has been prepared running from HALLEBAST CORNER (H.33.c.2.7.) across the S.W.corner of DICKEBUSCH LAKE - GORDON FARM (N.5.a.2.7.) - crossing VIERSTRAAT - ELZENWALLE road at N.6.a.3.8. - thence direct across country to VOORMEZEELE.

In wet weather traffic on reaching the YPRES - VIERSTRAAT road at N.6.a.3.8. will have to complete the journey to VOORMEZEELE by road via ELZENWALLE.

As soon as possible after zero this track will be pushed forward via MOATED GRANGE (O.1.a.central) to the neighbourhood of PICCADILLY FARM (O.8.a.).

(7). In dry weather all return traffic from VOORMEZEELE will use the track N.6.a.3.8. - GORDON FARM - S.W.corner of DICKEBUSCH LAKE.

In wet weather however this track must only be used by pack transport, and all return traffic from VOORMEZEELE will then use the circuit VOORMEZEELE - KRUISSTRAATHOEK - N.E. up the YPRES - VIERSTRAAT road, and then N.W. by the new switch road running to the EAST of SWAN CHATEAU (I.19.c.) and home by the YPRES - DICKEBUSCH road.

(8). Back Area.

The overland tracks in the back area are shewn on map "B". (vide sub-heading (XIII) Traffic Control).

(XIII). TRAFFIC CONTROL.

(1).   The battle traffic circuit affecting this Division is shewn on the attached sketch (Map "B") by arrows.

Traffic on all other roads will follow the Second Army Traffic Map issued herewith. (Map "C").

(2.).(a). Troops and traffic may use the roads most convenient to them provided the above circuits and traffic routes are adhered to.

(b). Infantry on the march may use any road in either direction but the transport must follow the circuit routes

(c). Motor and Ambulance cars have right of way in either direction on all roads but must follow traffic circuits as much as possible.

(d). When the cross country tracks are passable the following classes of traffic must make use of them :
Civilian Carts.
Empty Horse Transport.
Small parties of pedestrians and
  mounted men.
Infantry whenever possible.

(3).   When the road is dry enough, ammunition wagons and infantry transport from camps in Square M.4. proceeding to the Divisional Dump at OUDERDOM will use the track M.5.a.3.2. - G.35.c.7.5.- G.35.a.8.2. in the direction named, i.e. Northwards, to avoid congestion at the road junction at ZEVECOTEN.

(4).   The traffic circuit for vehicles going to VOORMEZEELE will be CAFE BELGE - KRUISSTRAATHOEK - VOORMEZEELE - South Westwards to Point H.36.d.5.½. - ELZENWALLE - KRUISSTRAATHOEK - North East to WITHUIS CABARET - and then by the new switch road running North East round SWAN CHATEAU to the main road.

(5).   In dry weather all traffic returning from VOORMEZEELE will proceed by the new overland track via the North end of RIDGEWOOD and the South end of DICKEBUSCH LAKE.

(6).   The overland track to DICKEBUSCH is shown on Map "B" by a dotted black line.

(XIV). TRENCH TRAMWAY TRAFFIC.

(N.B. These instructions will take effect from mid-day on May 26th. 1917.).

(1). Rolling Stock.
Trucks are distributed as required to units who are entirely responsible for their care and upkeep.

(2). Any truck requiring repairs which cannot be carried out by the unit, must be returned to the Traffic Superintendant at the Tramway Depot at VOORMEZEELE when a new truck will be given in exchange.

(3). There is a great shortage of trucks and it is therefore imperative that units should return to the Traffic Superintendant any trucks not required for immediate use. On no account must trucks, even though damaged, be left thrown about.

(4). A reserve of trucks will be kept at the Tramway Depot at VOORMEZEELE.

(5). Traffic.
2/Lieut.H.B.HACKNEY, 19th.Bn.Middlesex, is appointed Traffic Superintendant, Divisional Trench Tramways, with Headquarters at VOORMEZEELE (old M.G.Coys. house at I.31.c.2.5.). He will regulate all traffic on Divisional Lines and be responsible for accounting for all trucks.

(6). 2/Lieut.W.E.CARDEW, 15th.Hampshires attached 19th.Bn.Middlesex Regt., will be the Maintenance Officer and will be responsible for the upkeep and maintenance of all trench tramways, gangers for this purpose being placed at his disposal. His Headquarters will be at VOORMEZEELE with the Traffic Superintendant.

(7). The Traffic Superintendant and Maintenance Officer will be in communication by telephone with Brigades etc.

(8). It is imperative that any damage done to the track by shell fire or otherwise should be reported at once to the Maintenance Officer to enable him to effect repairs without delay, and thus ensure traffic being interfered with as little as possible.

(9) It is entirely in the interests of units themselves to prevent the trench tramway being damaged through men walking on the track.

(10). The Traffic Superintendant and Maintenance Officer will receive their orders direct from Divisional Headquarters, the latter officer keeping in close touch with the O.C. of the Company of the Pioneer Battalion which has been specially told off for Tramway Construction work.

(XV). FIRST LINE TRANSPORT.

(1). First Line Transport will remain in its positions ready to move at two hours notice.

(2). As soon as Brigades go up into the Line each Brigade will detail one cyclist to report at, and remain at "Q" office, to enable direct communications to be maintained between Brigade Transport Officers and "Q" Branch Divisional Headquarters.

(XVI). SANITATION.

(1). The greatest care must be paid to sanitation. All troops whether situated in the firing line or in rear must invariably make provision for latrines, no matter how short their stay in a particular site may be

(2). The indiscriminate fouling of the ground by using shell holes as latrines, as was done on the captured area last year on the SOMME, must be carefully guarded against. Regimental Police must be used to prevent this practice.

(3). All manure in horse lines must be disposed of by burning or, where this cannot be done, by building it into compact heaps well away from camps, and covering it with earth.

(4). In view of the lack of water in the district it is of the utmost importance that all sources of water should be carefully conserved. Special care must be taken to prevent soapy water from ablution trenches filtering into streams.

(5). In every unit special steps must be taken to protect all food from flies and rats.

(XVII). S A L V A G E.

(1).   All parties and individual men returning from the Front Line must carry back some salvaged article with them.

(2).   Salvaged articles will first be collected by units in numerous small dumps distributed throughout the trench area, whence they will be cleared by means of the Trench Tramway to Brigade Salvage Dumps at the loading sidings in VOORMEZEELE.

(3).   From VOORMEZEELE salvaged articles will be conveyed in the First Line Transport of units to an Advanced Divisional Dump at the Windmill at MICMAC H.32.c.8.4½. This advanced Divisional Dump will be established on "V" day.

(4).   Material salvaged from the back area will be brought in to the Main Divisional Dump at RENINGHELST (G.34.d.6.5.).

(5).   Brigades will each detail an Officer as Brigade Salvage Officer and supply him with any available personnel for salving all ground in the areas occupied by them.

(6).   Brigades must be prepared to salve all ammunition, bombs, etc., distributed in the trench area in connection with the Divisional Defence Scheme on receipt of instructions from this office that this is to be done.

(XVIII) BATHS AND LAUNDRY,

Baths and Laundry will be carried on during operations as usual.

Units requiring the use of the baths will apply to the officer in charge Baths, RENINGHELST stating numbers to be bathed and the most convenient hour. As much warning as possible should be given.

(XIX) R E C R E A T I O N, Etc.

(a). Soldiers Club, RENINGHELST (G.34.d.6½.3½.) Canteen, Theatre, Reading Room, and Tea and Supper Room.

(b). Y.M.C.A., RENINGHELST, (opposite Soldiers Club)

(c). Church Army Hut at CHIPPEWA CAMP. (M.6.a.5½.8.)

(d). Y.M.C.A. Hut at N.1.c.1½.2½.

(e). Y.M.C.A. Coffee Bar and Dry Canteen in DICKEBUSCH. (H.34.a.0.7.)

(XX) R. E. STORES.

(1). Up to "Z" Day arrangements for the supply of R.E. Stores will continue as at present.

(2). Hutting Dump.

OUDERDOM. G.29.d.8.3. R. E. Workshops and dump of material to be dealt with in the workshops. Material for back area, hutting material etc., and special stores, such as pumps, trench stores etc.

Divisional Dumps.

DICKEBUSCH, H.27.d.0.3. Divisional Dump for Forward area.
CAFE BELGE, H.24.c.3.0. Advanced Divisional Dump. Junction of Light Railway with Trench tramway.

Advanced Dumps. (for troops in line).

VOORMEZEELE, I.31.a.3.0. Field Coy. Dump for Support Battalion.
MOATED GRANGE, O.1.b.25.45. Field Coy. Dump for Right battalion sector.
SHELLEY LANE. I.32.d.2.3. Field Coy. Dump for left battalion sector.

(3.) R. E. stores are conveyed by road and tramway to the advanced dumps at VOORMEZEELE, MOATED GRANGE, and SHELLEY LANE, under arrangements made by the R.E.

(4). Method of Indenting for stores.

Units in the line may draw stores on an indent countersigned by a R.E. Officer of the Field Company working in their area, from that Field Company's forward dump.
    OUDERDOM, DICKEBUSCH, and CAFE BELGE dumps are under the immediate control of the C.R.E. Field Companies may draw from these dumps on their own authority, except for certain stores.
    The 19th Middlesex Pioneers may draw on their own authority certain stores from DICKEBUSCH Dump.
    All other units must obtain the authorisation of the C.R.E. before drawing stores from any R.E. Dump.
    Hutting material is an exception to the foregoing remarks. All indents for this must be countersigned by the officer in charge Hutting, before issue is made from OUDERDOM Dump, where all hutting material is kept.

(5). Prior to "Z" Day, all dumps will be stocked up to the establishments necessary for the commencement of offensive operations.
    From "Z" day inclusive:-
    (i) DICKEBUSCH DUMP will continue to be the main Divisional Dump.
    (ii) CAFE BELGE DUMP will cease to exist.
    (iii) VOORMEZEELE will be the Advanced Divisional Dump.
    (iv). Forward dumps will be as now, MOATED GRANGE DUMP, and SHELLEY LANE DUMP, with probably 2 dumps within the present German lines situated one on each of the two main pack routes.

(v) VOORMEZEELE DUMP to be supplied from DICKEBUSCH Dump by lorry and G.S.Wagon and also by Light Railway. MOATED GRANGE and SHELLEY LANE Dumps will be supplied by tram line from VOORMEZEELE Dump and by G.S.Wagon by way of the pack routes. Stores will be taken up to the line from VOORMEZEELE by way of the Pack routes either on pack animals or by men. When the pack routes have been made passable for wagons, wagons will be used to take stores up as far as may be possible and to form a forward dump of material at a suitable spot on the line of each pack route.

(vi) From "Z" Day inclusive, stores may be drawn from all dumps by any unit and no indent or authority will be necessary. Storemen i/c Dumps may however receive orders to reserve certain stores for certain units, but subject to this provision, stores will be issued on demand if available.

(XXI). REPORTS AND RETURNS.

The following are required :-

(i).   Trench Strength Return to be rendered on
       the attached pro-forma, (Appendix "E").
       on the day before battalions move up
       into the Line.

(ii). Estimated Casualty wires as soon as any
       battalion has suffered 50 casualties
       or a Machine Gun Company over 8 casualties
       in accordance with instructions already issued.

(iii). Special casualty wires in the event of any
       Commanding or Staff Officer becoming a
       casualty - the name of the Officer assuming
       his duties temporarily to be stated.

(iv). Reports of any localities where it is known
       there are dead or wounded left on the Field
       or large quantities of salvage.

(v).   The return required from the Reinforcement
       Camp vide Section (II) (REINFORCEMENTS).

(vi). The Officer in charge Ammunition refilling
       Point will wire Divisional Headquarters "Q"
       the amount of Artillery ammunition (including
       T.M.Ammunition) issued. These returns are to
       be made up to 12 noon and 8.p.m. daily and
       punctuality in rendering is far more important
       than absolute accuracy.

(vii). Statement of Artillery and T.M.Ammunition
       demanded to be sent by C.R.A. to D.H.Q."Q"
       every evening as soon as requirements are known.

41st.Divn.No.G/335/S.

The attached additional Section (No.XXII,PACKS AND SURPLUS BAGGAGE) is added to 41st.Division Administrative Instructions in connection with Forthcoming Operations.

Maps B & C are also enclosed.

[signature]
Major,
D. A. A. G.
41st.Division.

May 25th,1917.

(XXIII). PACKS AND SURPLUS BAGGAGE.

1. Packs and surplus baggage will be stored at RENINGHELST in the barn at G.34.d.6½.8.

2. The 123rd. Infantry Brigade will detail one Officer to take charge.

3. Each Infantry Brigade will detail one N.C.O. per Brigade and one man per battalion as storemen.
    Other units using the store will detail storemen in proportion.

4. Units other than those of Infantry Brigades who will require to use the store will inform this office as early as possible stating roughly the estimated cubic space they will require.

Appendix A

Xth. Corps No. 570.A.
41st. Division No. A.29/115.

---

1. Attention is drawn to F.S.R. Part 11 Chapter 11 Section 90, "General System for Dealing with Casualties in Action".

2. The form of fighting which we have experienced of late and which we may again anticipate does not permit of the procedure laid down being carried out in its entirety as the regulations quoted deal principally with an advance on some considerable scale. At the same time the general principals are still applicable.

3. The chief factors in the present type of Warfare that have to be considered are :-

   (a). A large number of casualties occur in a very short time, especially at the commencement of an attack.

   (b). The progress made is comparatively limited; therefore the casualties remain in the zone of actual hostilities, and, owing to hostile fire, removal is normally only possible at night, when casualties are difficult to locate.

   (c). The battle continues in the same area for may days. This fact prevents the systematic clearance of the battlefield by troops from the rear specially detailed.

   (d). The task of clearing the wounded from the fighting line must therefore devolve on the troops on the line actually engaged in the operations, aided by such assistance as it is possible to send up from the rear.

4. The attention of all Commanders is therefore directed to the following points, which show the procedure to be adopted.

   (a). The duty of rendering first aid to the wounded and bringing them back from the trench to the Regimental Aid Post lies principally with the Unit concerned, i.e. the Unit to which the wounded belong.

   (b). This duty is carried out by the Regimental Stretcher Bearers. Experience shows that the number of Regimental Stretcher Bearers is inadequate for the task. It will therefore usually be advisable for the O.C.Unit before the action starts, to detail a party to assist the Regimental Stretcher Bearers. The size of the party will depend upon the operations to be undertaken and the casualties which may be expected.

   (c). During the action when casualties have occurred, it is the duty of the Brigade Staff to allot to Units the areas to be searched by the Regimental Stretcher Bearers. The area allotted to each Unit will usually correspond with the frontage upon which the unit has been operating. Where one unit has supported another unit upon the same front, the area may be allotted for search and clearance to both Units, the Regimental Stretcher Parties working together.

   (d). If it is found during the action that the Regimental

Stretcher Bearer Party augmented as in (b) is still inadequate to deal with the casualties which have occurred in any area, application must be made by the Unit or Units concerned to Brigade Headquarters. Brigade Headquarters will detail such assistance as may be possible, and if unable with the resources at its disposal to cope with the situation, will apply to Divisional Headquarters for further assistance.

(e) The duty of allotting the areas as required the parties sent up by Brigade and Divisional Headquarters rests with the Brigade Staff, who are also responsible for guiding each party so allotted from Brigade Headquarters to the Regimental Aid Post of the area to which it has been allotted.

(f) Where troops are thus allotted to assist any Unit in collecting wounded from its area, it is essential that the Unit for whose assistance they are allotted, should provide guides who know the ground and can point out where the wounded lie or are likely to be found. These guides will usually be detailed from the Regimental Stretcher Party and will be stationed at the Regtl. Aid Post. Similarly, when a Unit in the front line is relieved before all its wounded have been collected, guides must be left at the Regimental Aid Post to show the incoming parties the direction in which the work of searching for wounded in the area should be continued.

5. The duty of the Bearer Divisions detailed at the A.D. Station and Aid Posts is to collect the wounded from the Regtl. Aid Posts and transfer them, either to the A.D.Station or direct to Ambulance vehicles.

Under the conditions contained in paras. 2 & 3, it will seldom be practicable to allot personnel of the Bearer Divns. to assist the Regtl. Stretcher Parties in searching for bringing in wounded to the Regtl. Aid Posts and O.Cs Units have not the right of demanding their assistance. In an emergency the O.C. a Unit or formation may ask for the assistance of the nearest Bearer Division, but must address his request for the same to the O.C. Bearer Divn. The latter is responsible for deciding whether he can or cannot spare any portion of his command from its duties as specified above in order to give the assistance required.

(Signed) C C C C C

Headquarters,
Xth. Corps.
28/12/16.

Brig. General,
D.A. & Q.M.G.
Xth. Corps.

APPENDIX "B".

	Divisional Dump.	Each Brigade Dump.
S. A. A.	1,000,000.	250,000.
Grenades Mills No.5.	30,000.	7,500.
Grenades Rifle)	5,000.	2,000.
Blank S.A.A.)		
Stokes Shells.	5,000.	2,000. ∅
Stokes cartridges Red.)	5,000.)*	2,000.)*
" " Green.)	5,000.)	2,000.)
Very Lights White 1".	4,000.	1,000.
" " " 1½".	1,500.	500.
Webley Pistol S. A. A.	10,000.	1,000.
"P" Grenades.	2,000.	250.
S.O.S. Signals.)		
Flares.)	As available from Army,	
Rockets.)	quantities depend largely	
Coloured Very Lights.)	on tactical considerations.	
Smoke Candles.)		

∅ . Majority of T.M. ammunition required to be dumped at or near guns before operations commence.

* . Or equivalent number all green with "Rings".

APPENDIX "C".

AMMUNITION CARRIERS.

8 per 18 pr. gun.   )   For all Divisional and Army Field
10 per 4. 5" How.   )   Artillery Brigades allotted.
)   Authority Q.O.C./299 dated 5/5/17.

The above will allow of :-

64 rounds per 18 pr. being carried in one journey.
40   "   " 4.5".   "   "   "   "

APPENDIX. 'D'.

X... CORPS BURIAL INSTRUCTIONS.

1. In the event of heavy fighting, the burial of the dead of 23rd, 24th, 41st, and 47th, Divisions will be done on Divisional Area basis.
2. Captain H.S.FUSSELL, 9th.S.Staff. Regt has been appointed Corps Burial Officer.

   Divisional Burial Officers have been detailed as follows :-

   23rd.Division. - 2/Lt. F.MASON. 9th.S.Staff Regt.
   24th.Division. - 2/Lt. H.L.BARKER. 12th.Sherwood.Fors.(P).
   41st.Division. - 2/Lt. S.E.BENNETT. 12th.East Surrey Regt.
   47th.Division. - Capt. J.W.PACE. 1/24th.London Regt.

3. Burying parties from the 4th.Canadian Labour Battalion will be detailed to each Division.

4. Divisional Burial Officers must thoroughly understand the procedure in connection with burials and must be capable of organising for this purpose the burial parties detailed to them.

MARKING OF GRAVES AND EFFECTS.

1. Graves will be marked with a disc hung on a wire rod which will be stuck in the ground at the head of the grave :-

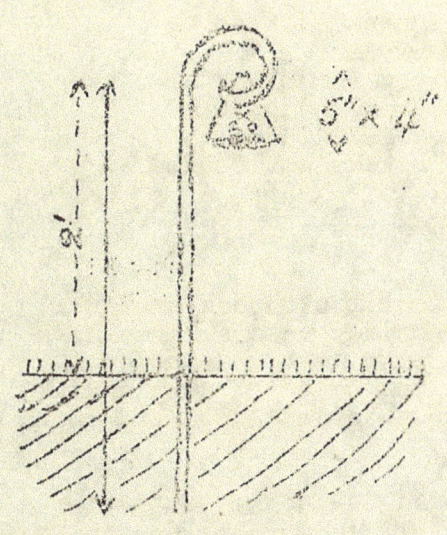 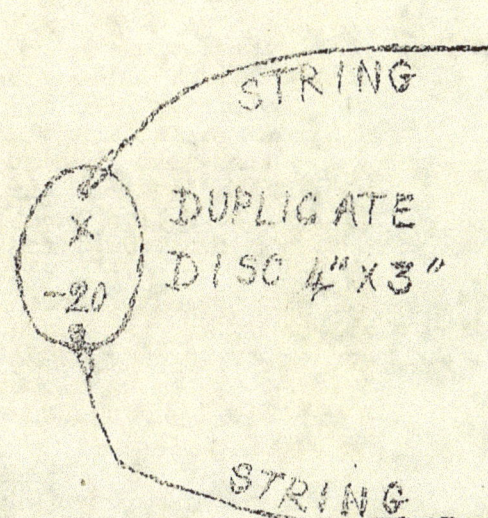

2. A duplicate disc bearing the same number as the disc over the grave will be tied to each ;-
   (a). Packet of effects (if only one body is buried in the grave.).
   (b). Sandbag of packets of effects (if more bodies than one are buried in the grave.)

3. A number of these rods and discs (in duplicate) will be issued to the Divisional Burial Officers, who will be held responsible that every disc not returned is accounted for on a roll vide pro forma below.

   Discs and rods will be supplied by Corps Burial Officer.

4. Divisional Burial Officers will draw from Corps Burial Officer ration bags for packing the effects of the dead.

SYSTEM OF BURIAL.

1. Divisional Burial Officers will be held responsible that burials are carried out in accordance with these instructions.

2. Burial parties will be divided into :—
  (a). Bearer Sections provided with stretchers for collecting the dead and bringing them to the grave.
      These stretchers will be drawn by Divisional Burial Officers from the Corps Burial Officer.

[Diagram of stretcher: 6' 6" long by 2' wide]

  (b). Sandbag parties to :—
 (i) Remove boots, greatcoat and equipment, and place them on one side. FOR SALVAGE
 (ii) Collect all personal effects and the RED identity disc and place them in a ration bag or packet and tie it up. The GREEN identity disc will be left on the man's body and buried with it.
(iii) Sort ration bags into sandbags.
 (iv) Lower body into grave.

3. Wherever possible Divisional Burial Officers should select sites for graves and have them dug before operations commence, if heavy fighting is imminent. Graves to hold 50 bodies should be 30 yards long by 4' 6" deep and 6' 6" wide, and should be dug as near to due north and south as possible.

4. Burying parties must observe the following routine:—
 (a) Remove nothing from the dead till ready to place in the grave.
 (b) Bury British, French and German separately.
 (c) Bury Officers with men, except General Officers, whose bodies will be disposed of as directed by the Senior Staff Officer on the ground.
 (d) Sandbag parties (See system of burial 2.b.).
 (e) Mark each grave (whether containing one or more bodies) with a wire rod and disc; the duplicate disc will be tied to the single packet of effects or to the sandbag of packets of effects (according to whether one or more bodies are buried in the same grave).
 (f) Retain sandbags containing effects of British and dispose of them as in 5.a.

/(g)

- 3 -

(g). Mark sandbags containing effects of French
   "C.S.O." and send to Corps Salvage Officer.
(h). Mark sandbags containing effects of Germans
   "Xth Corps "G"" and send it at once to Xth Corps G.S."I".

5.a. The Officer in charge of a burial party on completion
of his work will make a nominal roll in the following form :-

Xth Corps Graves Map Reference.	Regtl Number.	Rank.	Name.	Regiment.	Religion.
X /20. N.3?.d.4.2.	100.	Pte.	T. Jones.	1st. D.L.I.	C of E.

He will sign and date the roll and print his own name and regiment.
   He will send the sandbags and rolls to his Divisional
Burial Officer who will forward them to the Corps Burial Officer.
(b) The Corps Burial Officer will send
   (i) The Sandbags to the Corps Salvage Officer who will be
       responsible for despatching such effects to the D.A.G.,
       Base, and obtaining receipts from the R.T.O. which will
       be forwarded to   Division "A".
  (ii) The rolls to   Division "A".

FRENCH and GERMAN DEAD.

1.   Reference 4.g. the Corps Salvage Officer will make a roll
of the contents of the sandbags thus received and send it to the
French Mission Xth Corps.

2.   Reference 4.h. the Corps Intelligence Officer will make
a roll of the contents of sandbags thus received and send it to
Intelligence, Second Army.

PERSONNEL AVAILABLE.

1.   The 4th Canadian Labour Battalion is allotted for the
clearing of the Battlefield and burial of the dead of the Xth
Corps.
   They will be detailed by the Corps Burial Officer to
Divisions by whom they will be rationed and accommodated if
necessary.

2.   When the 4th Canadian Labour Battalion is employed under
the Corps Burial Officer to clear a certain area, the D.A.C.G.,
and D.A.P.S., will detail one C. of E., one R.C., and one
Nonconformist Chaplain for duty with the Battalion.
   Divisions will detail Chaplains to accompany the
Divisional Burial Officer.

3.   Chaplains will not render their returns of burials to
the Corps Burial Officer, but as laid down in para.1 of
"Instructions to Chaplains" page 27 "Extracts from G.R.O.
Part 1 dated 1/1/17".

CORPS HEAVY ARTILLERY & UNITS OF CORPS TROOPS.

These will be responsible for carrying out their own burials
and forwarding all rolls as laid down in para.5 System of
Burials to Xth Corps "A" and effects to the Corps Burial Officer.

APPENDIX ('E').

-- Regiment.

Total Strength ....Officers...............Other Ranks.

Trench Strength. ....Officers...............Other Ranks.

Difference....................Officers...............Other Ranks.

Explanation of above difference.

Detail.	Officers.	Other Ranks.
Transport Personnel.		
Q.M. Stores personnel.		
Unfits.		
Orderly Room personnel.		
Officers left behind.		
N.C.Os. left behind.		
Bombers left behind.		
Lewis Gunners left behind.		
Signallers left behind.		
Reinforcements not yet absorbed in Companies. (Date of arrival to be shown on reverse).		
Cooks.		
Shoemakers.		
Tailors.		
Pioneers.		
Armourer Sergeant.		
Post Sergeant.		
Sanitary personnel.		
Water personnel.		
Company Quartermaster Sergeants.		
Company Clerks.		
Army Employ.		
Corps employ.		
Divisional employ.		
Brigade employ.		
Total to agree with "Difference Shown above".		

Date, ...

Nominal Roll of Officers left behind to be given on reverse.

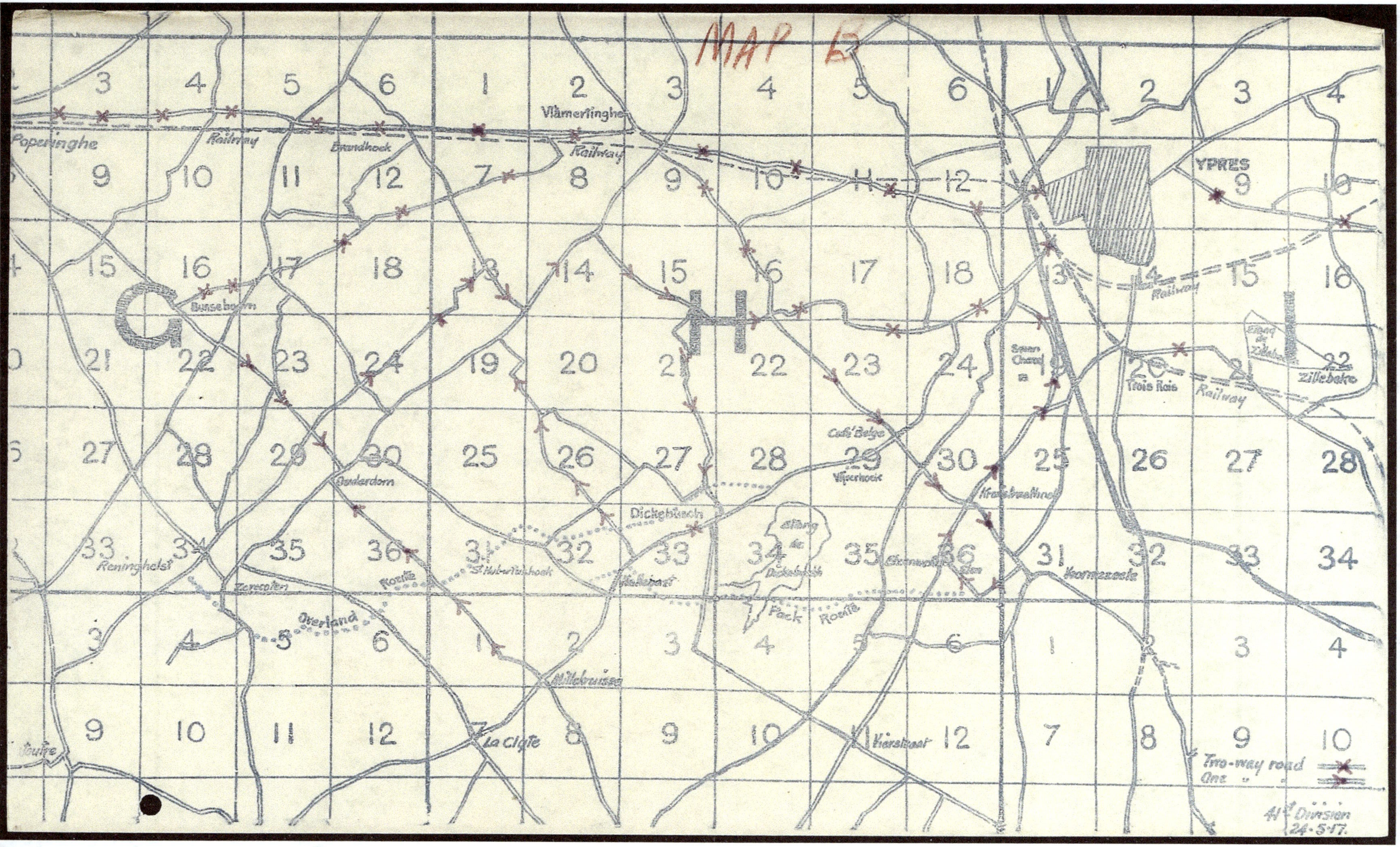

MAP B
Poperinghe
Railway
Brandhoek
Vlamertinghe
Railway
YPRES
Railway
Busseboom
Ouderdom
Reninghelst
Zevecoten
Overland
Route
Dickebusch
Café Belge
Vijverhoek
Kruisstraathoek
Voormezeele
Trois Rois
Railway
Zillebeke
Pack Route
Millekruisse
La Clyte
Kierstraat
Two-way road
One
41st Division
24.5.17.

Secret

Q335/S/7

122nd Infantry Brigade.	A. D. M. S.
123rd Infantry Brigade.	A. D. V. S.
124th Infantry Brigade.	A. P. M.
R. A.	D. A. D. O. S.
R. E.	Salvage Officer.
Signal Company.	Area Commandant.
19th Middlesex.	"G".
Xth Corps "Q".	Reserve Division.
47th Division "Q".	19th Division "Q".
Divisional Train.	S. S. O.
War Diary.	

Herewith addenda to "Administrative Instructions" issued under this office No. Q/335/S dated 19/5/17 etc. This should be inserted at the end of heading XV — FIRST LINE TRANSPORT.

[signature]

Lieut. Colonel,
A. A. & Q. M. G.,
41st Division.

28th May 1917.

ADVANCE OF WAGON AND TRANSPORT LINES.
(Addenda to XV First Line Transport)

1. On the capture of the final objective, it is proposed to move forward certain wagon and transport lines as under :-

   (a). **Artillery.**

	From.	To.
1st Divisional Artillery, (less D.A.C.).	M.4.c.	Area W. of DICKEBUSCH LAKE, enclosed by points -
Two Batteries, 65th A.F.A. Brigade.	M.4.c.	H.33.b.8.7.-
187th Brigade R.F.A.	G.34.c.	H.33.d.7½.0.-
	M.4.a.	H.33.c.2.7.
	G.35.d.	
277th A.F.A. Brigade, (3 Batteries)	M.4.c.	

   (b). **Infantry.**

123rd Inf. Brigade Trnsprt.	RENINGHELST -LOCRE ROAD.	Field between DICKEBUSCH - YPRES ROAD & N.W. end of DICKEBUSCH LAKE i.e. about Point H.34.a.8.8.

2. Arrangements are being made by the C.R.E. to send up water troughs and pumps, and to establish water points at the edge of DICKEBUSCH LAKE.

3. Should circumstances allow, later, of the Supply Railhead and Ammunition Refilling Points being advanced to the neighbourhood of DICKEBUSCH, the following will also be pushed forward :-

Transport of 124th Inf.Bde.	To area selected for 122nd Infantry Brigade Transport (v.para.1 (b).
3 Field Companies, R.E.	
All Artillery Wagon Lines, Less D.A.C's.	Part to area selected for Artillery in para.1 (a) remainder to sites around DICKEBUSCH LAKE dependant on the position of heavy guns at the time.
Divisional Train.	Vicinity of DICKEBUSCH LAKE dependant on position of guns.

4. On the moves taking place D.A.C's will be pushed forward to take over camps vacated by the units that have moved forward.

5. Units on moving up will take with them all tents and shelters and camp stores now held by them.

SECRET.

41st Div.
Q/335/S/7.

122nd Infantry Brigade.
123rd Infantry Brigade.
124th Infantry Brigade.
R. A.
R. E.
Signal Company.
19th Middlesex.
Xth Corps "Q".
47th Division. "Q".
Divisional Train.
War Diary.

A. D. M. S.
A. D. V. S.
A. P. M.
D. A. D. O. S.
Salvage Officer.
Area Commandant.
"G".
Reserve Division.
19th Division "Q".
S. S. O.

Reference this office No.Q/335/S/7 dated 28/5/17; &
para. 3 of memorandum forwarded therewith - Advance of
Wagon and Transport Lines -
    for "To area selected for <u>122nd</u> Infantry Brigade"
read "To area selected for <u>123rd</u> Infantry Brigade".

[signature]

Lieut.Colonel,
A.A. & Q.M.G.,
41st Division.

29th May 1917.

SECRET.   41st.Division No.Q/335/S.

_____

       Reference 41st.Division Administrative Instruction in connection with forthcoming Operations, herewith Map "A".

                                                                  Major,
                                                  D. A. A. G.
May 29th.1917.   41st.Division.

War Diary

AMENDMENT TO 41st. DIVISIONAL ADMINISTRATIVE
INSTRUCTIONS IN CONNECTION WITH FORTHCOMING OPERATIONS.

(VI). W A T E R.

Para. 2. (ii.a.) for I.31.d.5.9. read I.31.d.2.5.

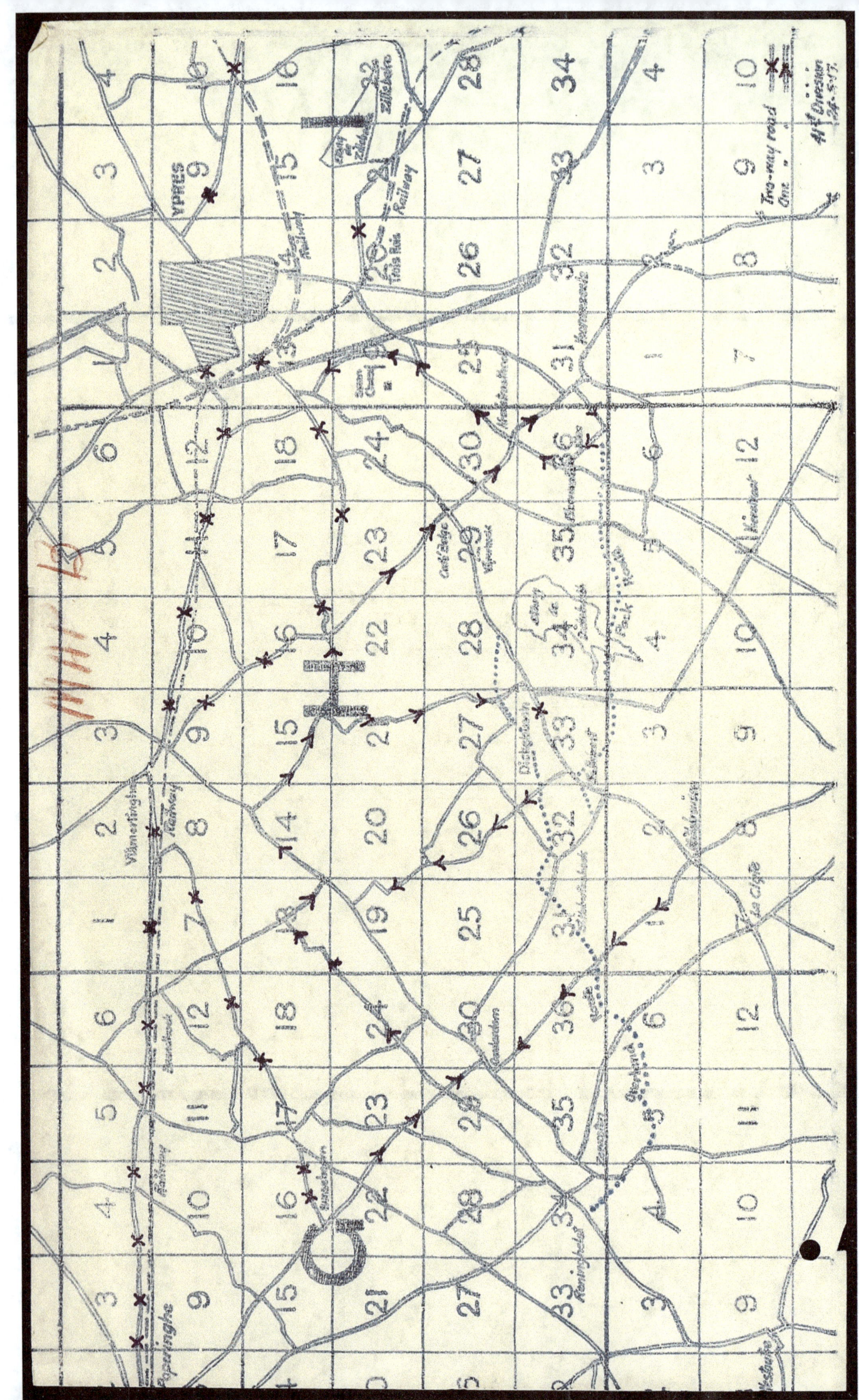

Secret

Q335/S/7

122nd Infantry Brigade.	A. D. M. S.
123rd Infantry Brigade.	A. D. V. S.
124th Infantry Brigade.	A. P. M.
R. A.	D. A. D. O. S.
R. E.	Salvage Officer.
Signal Company.	Area Commandant.
19th Middlesex.	"G".
Xth Corps "Q".	Reserve Division.
47th Division "Q".	19th Division "Q".
Divisional Train.	S. S. O.
War Diary.	

Herewith addenda to "Administrative Instructions" issued under this office No. Q/335/S dated 19/5/17 etc. This should be inserted at the end of heading XV – FIRST LINE TRANSPORT.

28th May 1917.

Lieut.-Colonel,
A.A. & Q.M.G.,
41st Division.

ADVANCE OF WAGON AND TRANSPORT LINES.
(Addenda to XV First Line Transport)

1. On the capture of the final objective, it is proposed to move forward certain wagon and transport lines as under :-

   (a). Artillery.

	From.	To.
1st Divisional Artillery, (less D.A.C.).	M.4.c.	Area W. of DICKEBUSCH LAKE, enclosed by points - H.33.D.8.7.- H.33.c.7½.0.- H.33.c.8.7.
Two Batteries, 65th A.F.A. Brigade.	M.4.c.	
187th Brigade R.F.A.	G.34.c.) M.4.a.) G.35.d.)	
277th A.F.A. Brigade, (3 Batteries)	M.4.c.	

   (b). Infantry.

123rd Inf. Brigade Trnsprt.	RENINGHELST -LOCRE ROAD.	Field between DICKEBUSCH - YPRES ROAD & N.W. end of DICKEBUSCH LAKE i.e. about Point H.34.a.3.8.

2. Arrangements are being made by the C.R.E. to send up Water troughs and pumps, and to establish water points at the edge of DICKEBUSCH LAKE.

3. Should circumstances allow, later, of the Supply Railhead and Ammunition Refilling Points being advanced to the neighbourhood of DICKEBUSCH, the following will also be pushed forward :-

Transport of 124th Inf.Bde.	To area selected for 122nd Infantry Brigade Transport (v.para.1 (b).
3 Field Companies, R.E.	
All Artillery Wagon Lines, Less D.A.C's.	Part to area selected for Artillery in para.1 (a) remainder to sites around DICKEBUSCH LAKE dependant on the position of heavy guns at the time.
Divisional Train.	Vicinity of DICKEBUSCH LAKE dependant on positions of guns.

4. On the moves taking place D.A.C's will be pushed forward to take over camps vacated by the units that have moved forward.

5. Units on moving up will take with them all tents and shelters and camp stores now held by them.

S E C R E T.					41st Div.
-----------					Q/335/S/7.

122nd Infantry Brigade.			A. D. M. S.
123rd Infantry Brigade.			A. D. V. S.
124th Infantry Brigade.			A. P. M.
R. A.							D. A. D. O. S.
R. E.							Salvage Officer.
Signal Company.					Area Commandant,
19th Middlesex.					"G".
Xth Corps "Q".					Reserve Division.
47th Division. "Q".				19th Division "Q".
Divisional Train.				S. S. O.
War Diary.

  Reference this office No.Q/335/S/7 dated 28/5/17; 4 para. 3 of memorandum forwarded therewith - Advance of Wagon and Transport Lines -

  for "To area selected for 122nd Infantry Brigade"

  read "To area selected for 123rd Infantry Brigade".

						Lieut.Colonel,
						A.A. & Q.M.G.,
29th May 1917.				41st Division.

S E C R E T.　　　　　　　　　　　　　　41st.Division No.Q/335/S.

_____

      Reference 41st.Division Administrative Instructions in connection with forthcoming Operations, herewith Map "A".

                                             Major,
                                          D. A. A. G.
May 29th.1917.   41st.Division.

SECRET

41st Division Administrative Instructions
AMENDMENT

Administrative Instructions, section XXI "Reports and Returns" para vi first paragraph delete " The Officer in charge Ammunition refilling point will wire Divisional Headquarters "Q" the amount of Artillery ammunition (including T.M.Ammunition) issued". and substitute "C. R. A. and Brigades will wire to D.H.Q. "Q" the quantities of Artillery and T.M.Ammunition expended".

[signature]

1st.June 1917.

Captain,
D. A. Q. H. G.
41st.Division.

Copies to :-
122nd Infantry Brigade.
123rd Infantry Brigade.
124th Infantry Brigade.
R.A.
R.E.
Signals.
Pioneers
Xth.Corps Q.
47th Division.
Divisional Train
War Diary

A. D. H. S.
A. D. V. S.
A. P. M.
D. A. D. O. S.
Salvage Officer
Area Comm'dt.
"G"
Reserve Division.
19th Division.
S.S.O.
Spare.

41st.Divn.No.Q/335/S.

AMENDMENT TO 41st.DIVISION ADMINISTRATIVE INSTRUCTIONS IN CONNECTION WITH FORTHCOMING OPERATIONS.

Add to Section (VIII) a new subsection (4) as under :-

(4). Attention is drawn to the necessity of preventing revolvers, field glasses, wire cutters, compasses, watches, etc., from disappearing with wounded.

These must accompany wounded to the Divisional Collecting Station at VOORMEZEELE or Advanced Dressing Station at DICKEBUSCH and on no account be evacuated further.

D.A.D.O.S. will arrange to collect them periodically from the above places.

Captain,
D. A. Q. M. G.
41st. Division.

June 3rd.1917.

Copies to :-
122nd.Inf.Brigade.	A.D.M.S.
123rd.Inf.Brigade.	A.D.V.S.
124th.Inf.Brigade.	A.P.M.
R.A.	D.A.D.O.S.
R.E.	Salvage Officer
Signals.	Area Commandant.
Pioneers.	"G".
Xth Corps Q.	24th.Division.
47th.Division.	19th.Division.
Divisional Train.	S.S.O.
War Diary.	Spare.

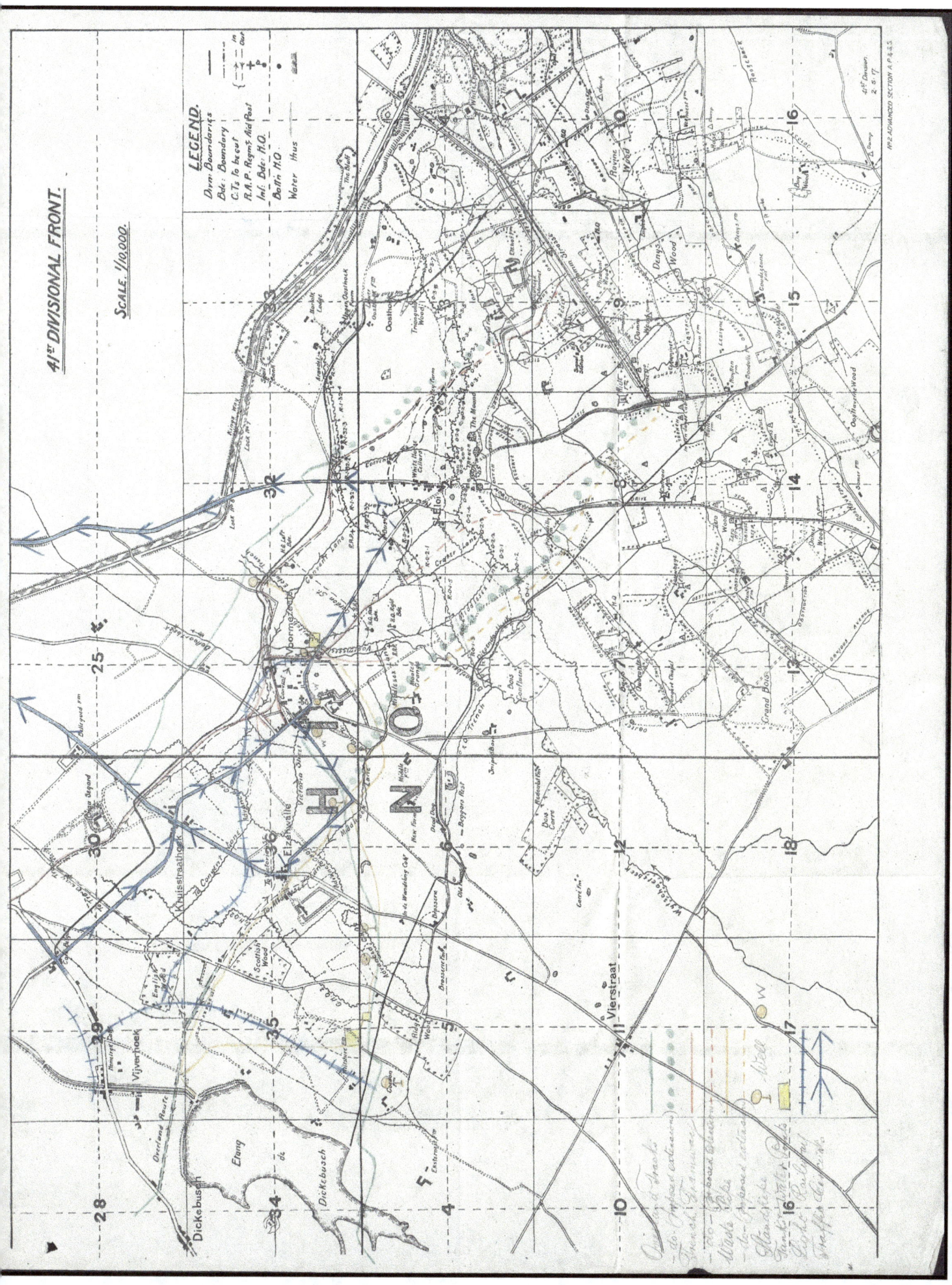

War Diary

AMENDMENT TO 41st. DIVISIONAL ADMINISTRATIVE
INSTRUCTIONS IN CONNECTION WITH FORTHCOMING OPERATIONS.

(VI). W A T E R.

Para. 2. (ii.a.) for I.31.d.5.9. read I.31.d.2.5.

I N D E X

to

41st. DIVISIONAL ADMINISTRATIVE ARRANGEMENTS.

Part	(I).	PERSONNEL.
"	(II).	REINFORCEMENTS.
"	(III).	PRISONERS OF WAR.
"	(IV).	BATTLE STRAGGLERS.
"	(V).	RATIONS.
"	(VI).	WATER.
"	(VII).	MEDICAL ARRANGEMENTS.
"	(VIII).	ORDNANCE.
"	(IX).	AMMUNITION.
"	(X).	BURIALS.
"	(XI).	VETERINARY.
"	(XII).	COMMUNICATIONS.
"	(XIII).	TRAFFIC CONTROL.
"	(XIV).	TRENCH TRAMWAY TRAFFIC.
"	(XV).	FIRST LINE TRANSPORT.
"	(XVI).	SANITATION.
"	(XVII).	SALVAGE.
"	(XVIII).	BATHS AND LAUNDRY.
"	(XIX).	RECREATION.
"	(XX).	R.E. STORES.
"	(XXI).	REPORTS AND RETURNS.

A P P E N D I C E S.

"A". Xth Corps instructions for collection of wounded
"B". Ammunition - Amount in Dumps.
"C". Ammunition Carriers - allotment of
"D". Burial Instructions Xth Corps.
"E". Trench Strength Return - Pro forma.

M A P S.

"A". Communications.
"B". Battle circuits.
"C". Second Army Traffic Map.

SECRET.

41st. Division No. Q/335/S.

41st. DIVISION.

ADMINISTRATIVE INSTRUCTIONS IN CONNECTION WITH FORTHCOMING OPERATIONS.

To obviate having to issue long orders AND instructions at one time, and to enable units to digest them by degrees, the <u>Administrative Instructions</u> in connection with forthcoming operations, will be issued from time to time under various headings.

An index will be published with the last heading sent out, and units should then bind the whole together into one complete volume.

The following headings are now forwarded :-

(i). Personnel.

(II). Reinforcements.

(III). Prisoners of War.

(IV) Battle Stragglers

[signature]

Lieut.Colonel,
A.A. & Q.M.G.
41st.Division.

May 19th.1917.

DESTRIBUTION :-

122nd.Brigade.	7 copies.	A.D.M.S.	4 copies.
123rd.Brigade.	7 copies.	A.D.V.S.	1 copy.
124th.Brigade.	7 copies.	A.P.M.	1 copy.
R.A.	6. "	D.A.D.O.S.	1 copy.
R.E.	4. "	Salvage Officer.	1 copy.
Signals.	1. "	Area Comm'dt.	1 copy.
Pioneers.	1. "	"G"	1 copy.
10th.Corps Q.	1 "	Reserve Division	1 copy.
47th.Division.	1 "	19th.Division.	1 copy.
Divl.Train.	1 "	S.S.O.	1 copy.
War Diary.	2 copies.	Spare.	11 copies.

I. PERSONNEL.

(1). The number of Officers, N.C.Os and men to take part in the attack will be as laid down in S.S.135. Section .X.X.X. except that (i) only 17 Officers (excluding the Medical Officer) will accompany battalions (ii) Understudies for appointment of Adjutant will be left behind.

Details left behind will be accomodated at the Reinforcement Camp.

(2). Nominal Rolls of Officers to be left behind will be forwarded to Divisional H.Qtrs when called for.

II. REINFORCEMENT CAMP.

A Divisional Reinforcement Camp will be formed at the Brigade School at M.4.b.4.4. at which all details left behind by battalions and all reinforcements will be accomodated.

This Camp will be arranged in Brigade Sections.

Headquarters.	No.	Found by.
Commandant.	1.	122nd.I.Bde.
Act.Adjutant.	1.	123rd.I.Bde.
Act.Qr.Mr.	1.	124th.I.Bde.
Act.Sgt.Major.	1.	122nd.I.Bde.
Act.Qr.Mr.Sgt.	1.	123rd.I.Bde.
Clerks.	1.	124th.I.Bde.

Per Brigade Section.		
O.C.Brigade Details.	1.	Each Brigade.
Act Adjt.& Qr.Mr.	1.	- do -
Act.C.S.Major.	1.	- do -
Act. C.Q.M.Sgt.	1.	- do -
Regimental Police.	2.	- do -
Clerks.	1.	- do -
Sanitary Men.	2.	- do -
Travelling Cookers.	2.	

2. The Divisional Train will deliver rations direct to the Camp.

The Commandant will render A.B. B55 direct to Officer Commanding Divisional Train.

3. Permanant Staff laid down above for the Headquarters will not be called up by Brigades for reinforcing without reference to this office.

/ (4).

4. The Commandant will render a return daily at 12.noon to Divisional Headquarters on the attached pro-forma.

Names of Officers sent up to Battalions will be entered on back.

III. PRISONERS OF WAR.

(1). Brigades will forward all Prisoners of War under escort (usual strength 10% of the number of prisoners,) to the Divisional Cage at MICMAC, and will be responsible for them until a receipt has been obtained from the Officer in Charge of the Cage.

(2). The 123rd.Infantry Brigade will detail a guard of 1 Sergeant, 1 Corporal and 24 men for the Cage. This Guard will report there at 10.a.m. on "Y" day.

(3). The evacuation of Prisoners from the Divisional to the Corps Cage at G.27.a.4.9. will be carried out by the A.P.M. 41st.Division. A Troop of Xth Corps Cavalry will be available for this purpose.

(4). The A.D.M.S. will detail a Medical Officer with orderly and material for duty at the Corps Cage.

Any prisoners requiring medical attention at the Divisional Cage will be sent to the Field Ambulance at OUDERDOM.

IV. BATTLE STRAGGLERS.

(1). Brigades, of which any portion is East of the BOLLART BEEK, will post Regimental Police along the Line of the BEEK to prevent straggling.

(2). Divisional Battle Straggler Posts, strength 2 M.M.P. and 1 N.C.O. and 3 Infantrymen will be detailed as under :-

Position.	Map Reference.	Found by.
MIDDLESEX LANE.	H.6.b.4½.9½.	121 Brigade
ELZENWALLE.	H.36.a.6.0.	122
CONVENT LANE.	H.36.a.9.5.	122
KRUISSTRAATHOEK.	H.30.d.5.3.	123

/ (3).

(3).

3.   The Divisional Collecting Station will be at Billet No.14. DICKEBUSCH (H.33.b.7.5½.) strength as under :-
One Officer to be found by the /22. Infantry Brigade.
Two M.M.P.
One N.C.O. and 4 men from each Brigade, for escort duties.

4.   The whole of the Infantry required in paras 2 and 3 above will report at the Divisional Collecting Station on receipt of orders from this office and will be posted under orders of the A.P.M.

5.   Detailed instructions have been issued to the A.P.M.

RETURN OF PERSONNEL AT REINFORCEMENT CAMP.

Battalion.	Details left behind by battalion.		Reinforcements who have not been out before.		Reinforcements who have been out before.		Sent up to join Units.		Remarks.
	Offrs.	O.Ranks.	Offrs.	O.Ranks.	Offrs.	O.Ranks.	Offrs.	O.Ranks.	

Commandant,
Division 1 Reinforcement Camp.

V. RATIONS.

The system of dumping of rations and water has already been explained in this office No. Q/335/S dated 17th.April and 19th.May 1917. By this system it will be unnecessary to send up any food or water by road from after "U"/"V" night until "Z"/"A" night for any troops East of DICKEBUSCH.

The supply of rations on "Z"/"A" night for "A" day may present considerable difficulty. It is therefore all important that every man should be in possession of a serviceable FROM ration on "Z" day in the event of its having to be consumed on "A" day.

Units must make arrangements to collect the iron rations of all casualties to act as an emergency reserve.

All units will indent on the S.S.O. for a supply of chewing gum for consumption on Zero day. This chewing gum has been used with great success during the recent operations in the South. It is found that if taken about half an hour before Zero hour, it greatly helps to alleviate hunger and thirst. It would perhaps be as well for units to warn their men that there is nothing in it in the nature of a drug and its sole object is to stay off hunger and thirst.

The supply of rations to Transport Lines and Units West of DICKEBUSCH during operations will continue under normal conditions.

VI. WATER.

(1). The scheme for dumping of water for all troops East of DICKEBUSCH for use during the bombardment were published under this office No. Q/335/S dated 17/4/17 and 19/5/17.

(2). The sources of water supply are as follows :-

(i). A 2 inch pipe-line running from DICKEBUSCH LAKE via RIDGEWOOD and MIDDLESEX LANE to O.1.a.1.8.

Standpipes at the following points :-
    (a) N.6.b.4.9.
    (b) O.1.a.1.8.

(ii). A branch from (i) at O.1.a.2.7. running N.E. to I.31.d.5.9. supplying :-

(a). Water Point at I.31.d.5.9. (where the VOORMEZEELE - BUS HOUSE - ST ELOI Road crosses the BOLLART BEEK.). At this point there will be standpipes for filling petrol tins, storage barrels, and two 160-gallon tanks, with a diversion road for filling water carts.

(b). Point I.31.d.5.9, where there will be standpipes for filling petrol tins, four 100-gallon tanks, and storage barrels

Further sources of supply :-

(iii). Two wells in VOORMEZEELE :-

(a). Brewery Well at I.31.c.$3\frac{1}{2}$.$5\frac{1}{2}$.

(b). Well in the village square I.31.c.6.4.

Both these supplies are plentiful. 2 scoops of of chlorinated lime required.
Each of these wells is being cleaned out and fitted with a windlass, rope, and bucket.

(c). A spring supply in OLD FRENCH TRENCH at I.32.d.$7\frac{1}{2}$.$2\frac{1}{2}$., liable to run dry in summer.

In the event of all the above supplies failing, water would have to be brought up in petrol tins on First Line Transport in the normal way, empty tins being exchanged for full at the unloading point.

(3). Xth Corps are also running a 4" Main from DICKEBUSCH LAKE via MIDDLESEX LANE (O.1.a.$2\frac{1}{2}$.8.) to MOATED GRANGE (O.4.a.6.4.). There will be a connection between this pipe and the 2" Main mentioned in para (2), giving an alternative supply to the latter in the event of the 2" pipe being broken between RIDGEWOOD and MIDDLESEX LANE.
As soon as circumstances permit, the 4" pipe will be pushed forward via PICCADILLY FARM (O.8.a.) to the neighbourhood of DOME HOUSE (O.8.d.$9\frac{1}{2}$.$6\frac{1}{2}$.) Tanks will be established under the embankment of the DALM STRASSE near the latter point.

/ (4).

(4). WASHING WATER.

The BOLLART BEEK. Not fit for drinking, as it is liable to contamination from a branch stream which runs into it from the German Lines.

(5). Brigades will arrange for all ground gained by them to be searched for wells, or other sources of water supply, and for the discovery of such to be reported at once to this office, in order that arrangements may be made to test the water which must on no account be used until declared fit to drink by the Medical authorities.

(6). WATER IN THE BACK AREA.

Water Points for filling Water Carts.

(1). G.34.c.5½.1.
(2). G.29.d.75.50.   (In 47th.Divl.Area.)
(3). G.36.c.2.0.   (Not yet completed - May 20th).
(4). M.6.d.7.6.   (- do -   - do -)
(5). H.28.d.2.1½.
(6). M.9.a.2.9½.

Horse Water Points.

(1). H.4.a.6.0.   (100X of troughing,
                    1000 horses per hour.) or more
(2). M.6.b.4.0.   (30X troughing -
                    1000 ~~300~~ horses per hour.)
(3). G.30.b.4.2. (in 47th.Divl.Area 100X
                    troughing- ~~1000~~ horses per hour).
not finished (4). H.1.a.6.8½. (1000 horses per hour.) 500/750
(5). H.31.b.5½.3. (300   "   "   ")
(6). M.6.a.6.2.   (1000 ~~300~~ horses per hour.) or more
not finished (7). M.5.b.8.3½. (1000 ~~1080~~ "   ").

No. 4 ~~6~~ and 7. not yet constructed -(May 20th.)

Pipe water supply is also being run direct into all horse lines in the camp on the ZEVECOTEN - LA CLYTTE - Road.

Instructions with regard to watering programmes for animals will be published shortly.

VII. MEDICAL.

(1). Regimental Aid Posts :-

No.1. I.32.d.1.1½.) For 123rd Inf. Brigade.
No.2. I.32.c.5.½.   )

No.3. O.1.b.5.9.   ) For 124th Inf. Brigade.
No.4. O.1.b.2.6.   )

As soon as the situation permits Regimental Aid Posts will be pushed forward, in order to facilitate the collection of wounded, and relieve the pressure on regimental stretcher bearers.

Divisional Collecting Post for wounded at VOORMEZEELE (I.31.c.4.7½.)

Advanced Dressing Station DICKEBUSCH, H.27.d.4.1.

Walking wounded by down communication trenches to Collecting Post at VOORMEZEELE, thence to DICKEBUSCH Advanced Dressing Station.

Captain J.La.T.LAUDER, R.A.M.C., D.S.O., M.C., will be in charge of Advanced Bearers. His Headquarters will be at the Collecting Post at VOORMEZEELE.

Requests for assistance will be addressed to him. If he is unable to furnish assistance, Divisional Headquarters "A" should be communicated with.

(2). The A.P.M. will station police at the Collecting Post at VOORMEZEELE and the Advanced Dressing Station, at DICKEBUSCH.

    (a) To take the names of all lightly wounded men coming in without their arms and equipment.

    (b). To take over as stragglers men coming in as wounded or gassed, who, in the opinion of the medical Officer are not justified in doing so.

(3). Xth Corps letter No.570 A. dated 28/12/16 on the responsibility for collection of wounded is attached vide Appendix "A".

(VIII). O R D N A N C E.

(1). Divisional Ordnance Store remains as at present at G.34.d.9½.5½.

(2). The normal procedure of supply of Ordnance material will continue.

(3). All captured war material will be sent back at once to Divisional Ordnance whence it will be despatched as soon as practicable to Railhead under arrangements to be made by D.A.D.O.S.

Attention is drawn to instructions with regard to captured war material which individual units may wish to claim. (Second Army Routine Orders No.617 and 618 dated 26/2/17 and Q.M.G's No. Q/2798/O.S.B/1090 dated 24/6/16, republished in D.R.O. No.1765 dated 21/5/17).

(IX). A M M U N I T I O N.

(1). The Main Divisional Dump (Field Artillery Ammunition, Grenades, etc, etc,) is at G.24.d.8.7. on the OUDERDOM - VLAMERTINGHE Road.

(2). Advanced Brigade Dumps :-

    (i). Right Brigade   I.31.d.2.3½.

    (ii).Left Brigade. (I.31.d.5.2.
                         (I.32.d.2½.2½.

If necessary the Reserve Brigade will draw from these Brigade Dumps.

(3). The amounts of various natures of ammunition to be kept at Divisional and Brigade Dumps are shown in Appendix "D".

Each Brigade will detail an Officer for their Advanced Brigade Dump who will be responsible to the Staff Captain that the amounts of different natures of ammunition are maintained.

/ (4)

(4). Supply of ammunition from Divisional Dump to Brigade Dumps will be by First Line Transport of units to VOORMEZEELE, thence by tramway to Dumps.

(5). On and after the first day of bombardment the present Brigade Dump at DICKEBUSCH (H.34.a.7.9.) can be drawn on by either of the Brigades in Front Line to replenish their Forward Brigade Dumps or to provide the extra ammunition to be carried by every man on going into action (vide 41st.Division No.G.285/99/9 dated 17/4/17 - Instruction No.3. - Fighting Kit.)

(6). Ammunition now distributed in Strong Points and in Front Line system under the Divisional Defence Scheme will be left in situ until further orders as to salvage are received from this office.

(7). Special steps must be taken at all dumps to deal with a possible outbreak of fire.

Artillery Ammunition.

(8). The following amounts will be dumped at guns :-

    Each 18 Pr.   1300 rounds.
    "   4. 5".   1000 rounds.
    "   2" T.M.   300 rounds.
    "   9. 45" T.M. 100 rounds.

(9). In the event of batteries in action moving forward, arrangements must be made for Dumps at guns either to accompany guns at once or to be collected and forwarded later.

(10). Appendix "C" shows scale of ammunition carriers.

(11). Divisional Reserves for Artillery ammunition are at the A.R.P. at G.24.d.8.7.

(12). Supply from A.R.P. to batteries is direct by Light Railway or by ammunition wagons according to the positions of batteries.

(13). All ammunition echelons (Artillery and Infantry) are to be replenished as soon as empty.

(X). B U R I A L S.

(1). The Xth Corps Burial Scheme is attached vide Appendix "D".

(2). Units should indent on the Divisional Burial Officer, (c/o "A" Branch Divisional Headquarters), for a small supply of the discs and wire rods to enable them to bury any of their own dead who they may wish to.
Units burying any of their own dead must strictly comply with these instructions, account for every disc received by them, and forward rolls, discs, and packets of effects etc., to the Divisional Burial Officer.

(3). Any discs not used must be returned to the Divisional Burial Officer.

(4). The Divisional Burial Officer will notify Brigades the sites selected for burial grounds and battalions must use these as far as possible.

(XI). V E T E R I N A R Y.

(1). The Mobile Veterinary Section will remain at its present position at G.33.c.0.1½.

(2). An advanced veterinary dressing station for the reception of all sick and wounded animals will be established in the stable of the farm at M.6.b.1½.9. (Sheet 28). from the First day of bombardment.("V" day).

(3). Evacuation from the Advanced Veterinary Dressing Station to the Mobile Vet. Section will be carried out under arrangements to be made by the A.D.V.S.

(XII). COMMUNICATIONS.

(vide Map "A" attached.)

(1). Light Railways.
The Light Railway extension from ENGLISH WOOD (H.29.d.) to VOORMEZEELE will be available for the carrying to VOORMEZEELE (later to SHELLEY DUMP) of R.E. material, stone, a certain amount of ammunition, and, (possibly, later on) rations.
This line will be extended by laying 18 lb. rails over the route of the existing trench tramway to SHELLEY DUMP (I.32.d.2.3.) when it will be possible to run through light railway trucks drawn by petrol tractors to the latter point.

(2). Trench Tramways.

(a). CAFE BELGE to VOORMEZEELE at the disposal of R.E. R.A., and Tunnelling Companies only.
(b). Continuation of (a)
(i) to SHELLEY DUMP I.32.d.2.3. (vide para.1.)
(ii) to OXFORD STREET O.1.b.9.5.
These lines will be at the disposal of the Left and Right Brigades respectively.
(c). A branch from (b) (ii) to MOATED GRANGE (O.1.b.2.5.) for conveyance of R.E. material and for evacuation of wounded from the R.A.P. to A.D.S. at VOORMEZEELE.

(3). As soon after zero as circumstances permit, the Trench Tramway system will be pushed forward with all speed to join the German System, the SHELLEY DUMP track via EAST of SHELLEY FARM to RUINED FARM (O.3.c.central) and later, depending on the tactical situation, the OXFORD STREET track via the WEST of the CRATERS in O.2.d. to the neighbourhood of PICCADILLY FARM (O.8.a.).

(4). Road Communications.
The CAFE BELGE - KRUISSTRAATHOEK - VOORMEZEELE road is being improved to take lorry traffic in both directions and the bridge over the BOLLART BEEK at I.31.d.2.4½. strengthened to carry all natures of traffic.
As soon as possible after zero, this road will be pushed on to ST ELOI and it is hoped a few days after zero to have a lorry circuit CAFE BELGE - VOORMEZEELE - ST ELOI - BEDFORD HOUSE (Square I.26.a.).

(5). To avoid the use of the CAFE BELGE - VOORMEZEELE - ST ELOI road, and to avoid VOORMEZEELE in the event of the latter being heavily shelled, an overland track fit for wheels (lightly loaded wagons only) is being prepared from the neighbourhood of BELLEGOED FARM (H.30.d.9.8½.) to SHELLEY DUMP (I.32.d.2.3.) and passing to the EAST of VOORMEZEELE.
This track will normally be at the disposal of the Left Brigade in the Line. As soon as possible after zero this track will be extended via SHELLEY FARM to the German Front Line System in the vicinity of RUINED FARM.

(6). A similar overland track for the Right Brigade has been prepared running from HALLEBAST CORNER (H.33.c.2.7.) across the S.W.corner of DICKEBUSCH LAKE - GORDON FARM (N.5.a.2.7.) - crossing VIERSTRAAT - ELZENWALLE road at N.6.a.3.8. - thence direct across country to VOORMEZEELE.

In wet weather traffic on reaching the YPRES - VIERSTRAAT road at N.6.a.3.8. will have to complete the journey to VOORMEZEELE by road via ELZENWALLE.

As soon as possible after zero this track will be pushed forward via MOATED GRANGE (O.1.a.central.) to the neighbourhood of PICCADILLY FARM (O.8.a.).

(7). In dry weather all return traffic from VOORMEZEELE will use the track N.6.a.3.8. - GORDON FARM - S.W.corner of DICKEBUSCH LAKE.

In wet weather however this track must only be used by pack transport, and all return traffic from VOORMEZEELE will then use the circuit VOORMEZEELE - KRUISSTRAATHOEK - N.E. up the YPRES - VIERSTRAAT road, and then N.W. by the new switch road running to the EAST of SWAN CHATEAU (I.19.c.) and home by the YPRES - DICKEBUSCH road.

(8). <u>Back Area.</u>

The overland tracks in the back area are shewn on map "B". (vide sub-heading (XIII) Traffic Control).

(XIII). TRAFFIC CONTROL.

(1). The battle traffic circuit affecting this Division is shewn on the attached sketch (Map "B") by arrows.
Traffic on all other roads will follow the Second Army Traffic Map issued herewith. (Map "C").

(2).(a). Troops and traffic may use the roads most convenient to them provided the above circuits and traffic routes are adhered to.

(b). Infantry on the march may use any road in either direction but the transport must follow the circuit routes

(c). Motor and Ambulance cars have right of way in either direction on all roads but must follow traffic circuits as much as possible.

(d). When the cross country tracks are passable the following classes of traffic must make use of them :-
    Civilian Carts.
    Empty Horse Transport.
    Small parties of pedestrians and
        mounted men.
    Infantry whenever possible.

(3). When the road is dry enough, ammunition wagons and infantry transport from camps in Square M.4. proceeding to the Divisional Dump at OUDERDOM will use the track M.5.a.3.2. - G.35.c.7.5.- G.35.a.8.2. in the direction named, i.e. Northwards, to avoid congestion at the road junction at ZEVECOTEN.

(4). The traffic circuit for vehicles going to VOORMEZEELE will be CAFE BELGE - KRUISSTRAATHOEK - VOORMEZEELE - South Westwards to Point H.36.d.5.½. - ELZENWALLE - KRUISSTRAATHOEK - North East to WITHUIS CABARET - and then by the new switch road running North East round SWAN CHATEAU to the main road.

(5). In dry weather all traffic returning from VOORMEZEELE will proceed by the new overland track via the North end of RIDGEWOOD and the South end of DICKEBUSCH LAKE.

(6). The overland track to DICKEBUSCH is shown on Map "B" by a dotted black line.

(XIV). TRENCH TRAMWAY TRAFFIC.

(N.B. These instructions will take effect from mid-day on May 26th. 1917.).

(1). <u>Rolling Stock</u>.
Trucks are distributed as required to units who are entirely responsible for their care and upkeep.

(2). Any truck requiring repairs which cannot be carried out by the unit, must be returned to the Traffic Superintendant at the Tramway Depot at VOORMEZEELE when a new truck will be given in exchange.

(3). There is a great shortage of trucks and it is therefore imperative that units should return to the Traffic Superintendant any trucks not required for immediate use. On no account must trucks, even though damaged, be left thrown about.

(4). A reserve of trucks will be kept at the Tramway Depot at VOORMEZEELE.

(5). <u>Traffic</u>.
2/Lieut.H.B.HACKNEY, 19th.Bn.Middlesex, is appointed Traffic Superintendant, Divisional Trench Tramways, with Headquarters at VOORMEZEELE (old M.G.Coys. house at I.31.c.2.5.). He will regulate all traffic on Divisional Lines and be responsible for accounting for all trucks.

(6). 2/Lieut.W.E.CARDEW, 15th.Hampshires attached 19th.Bn.Middlesex Regt., will be the Maintenance Officer and will be responsible for the upkeep and maintenance of all trench tramways, gangers for this purpose being placed at his disposal. His Headquarters will be at VOORMEZEELE with the Traffic Superintendant.

(7). The Traffic Superintendant and Maintenance Officer will be in communication by telephone with Brigades etc.

(8). It is imperative that any damage done to the track by shell fire or otherwise should be reported <u>at once</u> to the Maintenance Officer to enable him to effect repairs without delay, and thus ensure traffic being interfered with as little as possible.

(9) It is entirely in the interests of units themselves to prevent the trench tramway being damaged through men walking on the track.

(10). The Traffic Superintendant and Maintenance Officer will receive their orders direct from Divisional Headquarters, the latter officer keeping in close touch with the O.C. of the Company of the Pioneer Battalion which has been specially told off for Tramway Construction work.

(XV). FIRST LINE TRANSPORT.

(1).   First Line Transport will remain in its positions ready to move at two hours notice.

(2).   As soon as Brigades go up into the Line each Brigade will detail one cyclist to report at, and remain at "Q" office, to enable direct communications to be maintained between Brigade Transport Officers and "Q" Branch Divisional Headquarters.

(XVI). SANITATION.

(1).   The greatest care must be paid to sanitation. All troops whether situated in the firing line or in rear must invariably make provision for latrines, no matter how short their stay in a particular site may be

(2).   The indiscriminate fouling of the ground by using shell holes as latrines, as was done on the captured area last year on the SOMME, must be carefully guarded against. Regimental Police must be used to prevent this practice.

(3).   All manure in horse lines must be disposed of by burning or, where this cannot be done, by building it into compact heaps <u>well away from camps</u>, and covering it with earth.

(4).   In view of the lack of water in the district it is of the utmost importance that all sources of water should be carefully conserved. Special care must be taken to prevent soapy water from ablution trenches filtering into streams.

(5).   In every unit special steps must be taken to protect all food from flies and rats.

(XVII). S A L V A G E.

(1).   All parties and individual men returning from the Front Line must carry back some salvaged article with them.

(2).   Salvaged articles will first be collected by units in numerous small dumps distributed throughout the trench area, whence they will be cleared by means of the Trench Tramway to Brigade Salvage Dumps at the loading sidings in VOORMEZEELE.

(3).   From VOORMEZEELE salvaged articles will be conveyed in the First Line Transport of units to an Advanced Divisional Dump at the Windmill at MICMAC H.32.c.8.4½. This advanced Divisional Dump will be established on "V" day.

(4).   Material salvaged from the back area will be brought in to the Main Divisional Dump at RENINGHELST (G.34.d.6.5.).

(5).   Brigades will each detail an Officer as Brigade Salvage Officer and supply him with any available personnel for salving all ground in the areas occupied by them.

(6).   Brigades must be prepared to salve all ammunition, bombs, etc., distributed in the trench area in connection with the Divisional Defence Scheme on receipt of instructions from this office that this is to be done.

(XVIII) BATHS AND LAUNDRY.

Baths and Laundry will be carried on during operations as usual.
Units requiring the use of the baths will apply to the officer in charge Baths, RENINGHELST stating numbers to be bathed and the most convenient hour. As much warning as possible should be given.

(XIX) RECREATION, Etc.

(a). Soldiers Club, RENINGHELST (G.34.d.6½.3½.) Canteen, Theatre, Reading Room, and Tea and Supper Room.

(b). Y.M.C.A., RENINGHELST, (opposite Soldiers Club)

(c). Church Army Hut at CHIPPEWA CAMP. (M.6.a.5½.8.)

(d). Y.M.C.A. Hut at N.1.c.1½.2½.

(e). Y.M.C.A. Coffee Bar and Dry Canteen in DICKEBUSCH. (H.34.a.0.7.)

(XX) **R. E. STORES.**

(1). Up to "Z" Day arrangements for the supply of R.E. Stores will continue as at present.

(2). Hutting Dump.

OUDERDOM, G.29.d.8.3. R. E. Workshops and dump of material to be dealt with in the workshops. Material for back area, hutting material etc., and special stores, such as pumps, trench stores etc.

Divisional Dumps.

DICKEBUSCH, H.27.d.0.3. Divisional Dump for Forward area.
CAFE BELGE, H.24.c.3.0. Advanced Divisional Dump. Junction of Light Railway with Trench tramway.

Advanced Dumps. (for troops in line).

VOORMEZEELE, I.31.a.3.0. Field Coy. Dump for Support Battalion.
MOATED GRANGE, O.1.b.25.45. Field Coy. Dump for Right battalion sector.
SHELLEY LANE. I.32.d.2.3. Field Coy. Dump for left battalion sector.

(3.) R. E. stores are conveyed by road and tramway to the advanced dumps at VOORMEZEELE, MOATED GRANGE, and SHELLEY LANE, under arrangements made by the R.E.

(4). Method of Indenting for stores.

Units in the line may draw stores on an indent countersigned by a R.E. Officer of the Field Company working in their area, from that Field Company's forward dump.

OUDERDOM, DICKEBUSCH, and CAFE BELGE dumps are under the immediate control of the C.R.E. Field Companies may draw from these dumps on their own authority, except for certain stores.

The 19th Middlesex Pioneers may draw on their own authority certain stores from DICKEBUSCH Dump.

All other units must obtain the authorisation of the C.R.E. before drawing stores from any R.E.Dump.

Hutting material is an exception to the foregoing remarks. All indents for this must be countersigned by the officer in charge Hutting, before issue is made from OUDERDOM Dump, where all hutting material is kept.

(5). Prior to "Z" Day, all dumps will be stocked up to the establishments necessary for the commencement of offensive operations.
From "Z" day inclusive:-
(i) DICKEBUSCH DUMP will continue to be the main Divisional Dump.
(ii) CAFE BELGE DUMP will cease to exist.
(iii) VOORMEZEELE will be the Advanced Divisional Dump.
(iv). Forward dumps will be as now, MOATED GRANGE DUMP, and SHELLEY LANE DUMP, with probably 2 dumps within the present German lines situated one on each of the two main pack routes.

(v) VOORMEZEELE DUMP to be supplied from DICKEBUSCH Dump by lorry and G.S.Wagon and also by Light Railway. MOATED GRANGE and SHELLEY LANE Dumps will be supplied by tram line from VOORMEZEELE Dump and by G.S.Wagon by way of the pack routes. Stores will be taken up to the line from VOORMEZEELE by way of the Pack routes either on pack animals or by men. When the pack routes have been made passable for wagons, wagons will be used to take stores up as far as may be possible and to form a forward dump of material at a suitable spot on the line of each pack route.

(vi) From "Z" Day inclusive, stores may be drawn from all dumps by any unit and no indent or authority will be necessary. Storemen i/c Dumps may however receive orders to reserve certain stores for certain units, but subject to this provision, stores will be issued on demand if available.

(XXI). REPORTS AND RETURNS.

The following are required :-

(i). Trench Strength Return to be rendered on the attached pro-forma, (Appendix "E"), on the day before battalions move up into the Line.

(ii). Estimated Casualty wires as soon as any battalion has suffered 50 casualties or a Machine Gun Company over 8 casualties in accordance with instructions already issued.

(iii). Special casualty wires in the event of any Commanding or Staff Officer becoming a casualty - the name of the Officer assuming his duties temporarily to be stated.

(iv). Reports of any localities where it is known there are dead or wounded left on the Field or large quantities of salvage.

(v). The return required from the Reinforcement Camp vide Section (II) (REINFORCEMENTS).

(vi). The Officer in charge Ammunition refilling Point will wire Divisional Headquarters "Q" the amount of Artillery ammunition (including T.M.Ammunition) issued. These returns are to be made up to 12 noon and 8.p.m. daily and punctuality in rendering is far more important than absolute accuracy.

(vii). Statement of Artillery and T.M.Ammunition demanded to be sent by C.R.A. to D.H.Q."Q" every evening as soon as requirements are known.

(XXII). PACKS AND SURPLUS BAGGAGE.

1. Packs and surplus baggage will be stored at
RENINGHELST in the barn at G.34.d.6½.8.

2. The 123rd. Infantry Brigade will detail one Officer
to take charge.

3. Each Infantry Brigade will detail one N.C.O. per
Brigade and one man per battalion as storemen.
    Other units using the store will detail storemen
in proportion.

4. Units other than those of Infantry Brigades who
will require to use the store will inform this office as
early as possible stating roughly the estimated cubic
space they will require.

Appendix A

Xth. Corps No. 570.A.
41st. Division No. A.29/115.

----

1. Attention is drawn to F.S.R. Part II Chapter II Section 90, "General System for Dealing with Casualties in Action".

2. The form of fighting which we have experienced of late and which we may again anticipate does not permit of the procedure laid down being carried out in its entirety as the regulations quoted deal principally with an advance on some considerable scale. At the same time the general principals are still applicable.

3. The chief factors in the present type of Warfare that have to be considered are :-

   (a). A large number of casualties occur in a very short time, especially at the commencement of an attack.

   (b). The progress made is comparatively limited; therefore the casualties remain in the zone of actual hostilities, and, owing to hostile fire, removal is normally only possible at night, when casualties are difficult to locate.

   (c). The battle continues in the same area for may days. This fact prevents the systematic clearance of the battlefield by troops from the rear specially detailed.

   (d). The task of clearing the wounded from the fighting line must therefore devolve on the troops on the line actually engaged in the operations, aided by such assistance as it is possible to send up from the rear.

4. The attention of all Commanders is therefore directed to the following points, which show the procedure to be adopted.

   (a). The duty of rendering first aid to the wounded and bringing them back from the trench to the Regimental Aid Post lies principally with the Unit concerned, i.e. the Unit to which the wounded belong.

   (b). This duty is carried out by the Regimental Stretcher Bearers. Experience shows that the number of Regimental Stretcher Bearers is inadequate for the task. It will therefore usually be advisable for the O.C.Unit before the action starts, to detail a party to assist the Regimental Stretcher Bearers. The size of the party will depend upon the operations to be undertaken and the casualties which may be expected.

   (c). During the action when casualties have occurred, it is the duty of the Brigade Staff to allot to Units the areas to be searched by the Regimental Stretcher Bearers. The area allotted to each Unit will usually correspond with the frontage upon which the unit has been operating. Where one unit has supported another unit upon the same front, the area may be allotted for search and clearance to both Units, the Regimental Stretcher Parties working together.

   (d). If it is found during the action that the Regimental

Stretcher Bearer Party augmented as in (b) is still inadequate to deal with the casualties which have occurred in any area, application must be made by the Unit or Units concerned to Brigade Headquarters. Brigade Headquarters will detail such assistance as may be possible, and if unable with the resources at its disposal to cope with the situation, will apply to Divisional Headquarters for further assistance.

(e) The duty of allotting the areas as required the parties sent up by Brigade and Divisional Headquarters rests with the Brigade Staff, who are also responsible for guiding each party so allotted from Brigade Headquarters to the Regimental Aid Post of the area to which it has been allotted.

(f) Where troops are thus allotted to assist any Unit in collecting wounded from its area, it is essential that the Unit for whose assistance they are allotted, should provide guides who know the ground and can point out where the wounded lie or are likely to be found. These guides will usually be detailed from the Regimental Stretcher Party and will be stationed at the Regtl. Aid Post. Similarly, when a Unit in the front line is relieved before all its wounded have been collected, guides must be left at the Regimental Aid Post to show the incoming parties the direction in which the work of searching for wounded in the area should be continued.

5. The duty of the Bearer Divisions detailed at the A.D. Station and Aid Posts is to collect the wounded from the Regtl. Aid Posts and transfer them, either to the A.D. Station or direct to Ambulance vehicles.

Under the conditions contained in paras. 2 & 3, it will seldom be practicable to allot personnel of the Bearer Divns. to assist the Regtl. Stretcher Parties in searching for bringing in wounded to the Regtl. Aid Posts and O.Cs Units have not the right of demanding their assistance. In an emergency the O.C. a Unit or formation may ask for the assistance of the nearest Bearer Division, but must address his request for the same to the O.C. Bearer Divn. The latter is responsible for deciding whether he can or cannot spare any portion of his command from its duties as specified above in order to give the assistance required.

(signed) CCCCC

Headquarters,
Xth. Corps.
28/12/16.

Brig. General,
D.A. & Q.M.G.
Xth. Corps.

APPENDIX "B".

	Divisional Dump.	Each Brigade Dump.
S. A. A.	1,000,000.	250,000.
Grenades Mills No.5.	30,000.	7,500.
Grenades Rifle)	5,000.	2,000.
Blank S.A.A.)		
Stokes Shells.	5,000.	2,000. ∅
Stokes cartridges Red.)	5,000.)*	2,000.)*
" " Green.)	5,000.)	2,000.)
Very Lights White 1".	4,000.	1,000.
" " " 1½".	1,500.	500.
Webley Pistol S. A. A.	10,000.	1,000.
"P" Grenades.	2,000.	250.
S.O.S. Signals.)		
Flares.)	As available from Army.	
Rockets.)	quantities depend largely	
Coloured Very Lights.)	on tactical considerations.	
Smoke Candles.)		

∅ . Majority of T.M. ammunition required to be dumped at or near guns before operations commence.

* . Or equivalent number all green with "Rings".

APPENDIX "C".

AMMUNITION CARRIERS.

8 per 18 pr. gun.) For all Divisional and Army Field
10 per 4. 5" How.) Artillery Brigades allotted.
) Authority Q.O.C./299 dated 5/5/17.

The above will allow of :-

64 rounds per 18 pr. being carried in one journey.

40 " " 4. 5". " " " " "

APPENDIX 'D'.

Xth CORPS BURIAL INSTRUCTIONS.

1. In the event of heavy fighting, the burial of the dead of 23rd, 24th, 41st, and 47th, Divisions will be done on Divisional Area basis.

2. Captain H.S.FUSSELL, 9th.S.Staff. Regt has been appointed Corps Burial Officer.

Divisional Burial Officers have been detailed as follows :-

23rd.Division. - 2/Lt. F.MASON. 9th.S Staff Regt.
24th.Division. - 2/Lt. H.L.BARKER. 12th Sherwood.Fors.(P).
41st.Division. - 2/Lt. S.E.BENNETT 15th.East Surrey Regt.
47th.Division. - Capt. J.W.PACE. 1/24th.London Regt.

3. Burying parties from the 4th.Canadian Labour Battalion will be detailed to each Division.

4. Divisional Burial Officers must thoroughly understand the proceedure in connection with burials and must be capable of organising for this purpose the burial parties detailed to them.

MARKING OF GRAVES AND EFFECTS.

1. Graves will be marked with a disc hung on a wire rod which will be stuck in the ground at the head of the grave.

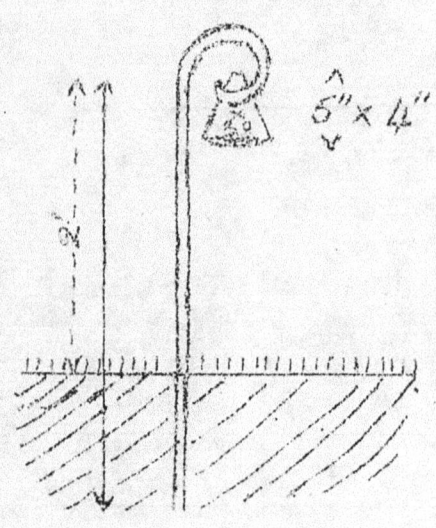
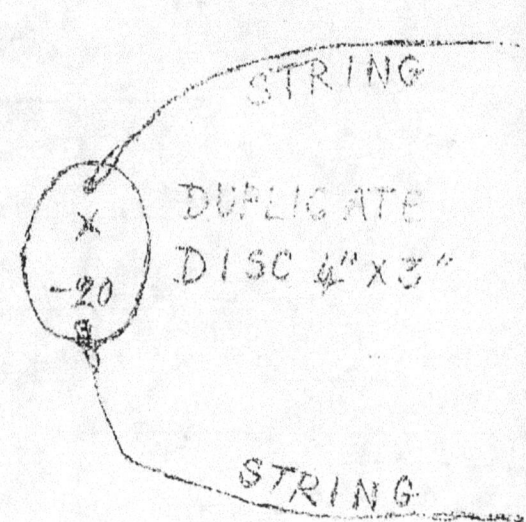

2. A duplicate disc bearing the same number as the disc over the grave will be tied to each :-
   (a).Packet of effects (if only one body is buried in the grave.).
   (b).Sandbag of packets of effects (if more bodies than one are buried in the grave.)

3. A number of these rods and discs (in duplicate) will be issued to the Divisional Burial Officers, who will be held responsible that every disc not returned is accounted for on a roll, vide pro forma below.

Discs and rods will be supplied by Corps Burial Officer.

\- 2 -

4. Divisional Burial Officers will draw from Corps Burial Officer ration bags for packing the effects of the dead.

SYSTEM OF BURIAL.

1. Divisional Burial Officers will be held responsible that burials are carried out in accordance with these instructions.

2. Burial parties will be divided into :-
 (a) Bearer Sections provided with stretchers for collecting the dead and bringing them to the grave.
   These stretchers will be drawn by Divisional Burial Officers from the Corps Burial Officer.

[Diagram of stretcher: 6' 6" long by 2' wide]

 (b) Sandbag parties to :-
 (i) Remove boots, greatcoat and equipment, and place them on one side. FOR SALVAGE
 (ii) Collect all personal effects and the RED identity disc and place them in a ration bag or packet and tie it up. The GREEN identity disc will be left on the man's body and buried with it.
 (iii) Sort ration bags into sandbags.
 (iv) Lower body into grave.

3. Wherever possible Divisional Burial Officers should select sites for graves and have them dug before operations commence, if heavy fighting is imminent.   Graves to hold 50 bodies should be 30 yards long by 4' 6" deep and 6' 6" wide, and should be dug as near to due north and south as possible.

4. Burying parties must observe the following routine:-
 (a) Remove nothing from the dead till ready to place in the grave.
 (b) Bury British, French and German separately.
 (c) Bury Officers with men, except General Officers, whose bodies will be disposed of as directed by the Senior Staff Officer on the ground.
 (d) Sandbag parties (See system of burial 2.b.).
 (e) Mark each grave (whether containing one or more bodies) with a wire rod and disc; the duplicate disc will be tied to the single packet of effects or to the sandbag of packets of effects (according to whether one or more bodies are buried in the same grave).
 (f) Retain sandbags containing effects of British and dispose of them as in 5.a.

/(g)

- 3 -

(g). Mark sandbags containing effects of French
  "C.S.O." and send to Corps Salvage Officer.
(h). Mark sandbags containing effects of Germans
  "Xth Corps "G" " and send it at once to Xth Corps G.S."I".

5.a. The Officer in charge of a burial party on completion of his work will make a nominal roll in the following form :-

Xth Corps Graves Map Reference.	Regtl Number.	Rank.	Name.	Regiment.	Religion.
X /20. E.5.d.4.2.	100.	Pte.	Jones.	1st. D.L.I.	C of E.

He will sign and date the **roll** and <u>print</u> his own name and regiment.

He will send the sandbags and rolls to his Divisional Burial Officer who will forward them to the Corps Burial Officer.

(b) The Corps Burial Officer will send
(i) The Sandbags to the Corps Salvage Officer who will be responsible for despatching such effects to the D.A.G., Base, and obtaining receipts from the R.T.O. which will be forwarded to Division "A".
(ii) The rolls to Division "A".

FRENCH and GERMAN DEAD.

1. Reference 4.g. the Corps Salvage Officer will make a roll of the contents of the sandbags thus received and send it to the French Mission Xth Corps.

2. Reference 4.h. the Corps Intelligence Officer will make a roll of the contents of sandbags thus received and send it to Intelligence, Second Army.

PERSONNEL AVAILABLE.

1. The 4th Canadian Labour Battalion is allotted for the clearing of the Battlefield and burial of the dead of the Xth Corps.
They will be detailed by the Corps Burial Officer to Divisions by whom they will be rationed and accommodated if necessary.

2. When the 4th Canadian Labour Battalion is employed under the Corps Burial Officer to clear a certain area, the D.A.C.G., and D.A.P.G., will detail one C. of E., one R.C., and one Nonconformist Chaplain for duty with the Battalion.
Divisions will detail Chaplains to accompany the Divisional Burial Officer.

3. Chaplains will not render their returns of burials to the Corps Burial Officer, but as laid down in para.1 of "Instructions to Chaplains" page 27 "Extracts from G.R.O. Part 1 dated 1/1/17".

CORPS HEAVY ARTILLERY & UNITS OF CORPS TROOPS.

These will be responsible for carrying out their own burials and forwarding all rolls as laid down in para.5 System of Burials to Xth Corps "A" and effects to the Corps Burial Officer.

A P P E N D I X   ('E').

.... Regiment.

Total Strength .... Officers .... Other Ranks.

Trench Strength. .... Officers .... Other Ranks.

Difference .... Officers .... Other Ranks.

Explanation of above difference.

Detail.	Officers.	Other Ranks.
Transport Personnel.		
Q.M. Stores personnel.		
Unfits.		
Orderly Room personnel.		
Officers left behind.		
N.C.Os. left behind.		
Bombers left behind.		
Lewis Gunners left behind.		
Signallers left behind.		
Reinforcements not yet absorbed in Companies. (Date of arrival to be shown on reverse).		
Cooks.		
Shoemakers.		
Tailors.		
Pioneers.		
Armourer Sergeant.		
Post Sergeant.		
Sanitary personnel.		
Water personnel.		
Company Quartermaster Sergeants.		
Company Clerks.		
Army Employ.		
Corps employ.		
Divisional employ.		
Brigade employ.		
Total to agree with "Difference Shown above".		

Date, ...

Nominal Roll of Officers left behind to be given on reverse.

WAR DIARY
INTELLIGENCE SUMMARY

Army Form C. 2118

JUNE 1917. H.Q. 2nd Aust. Pioneers

Jnr 14

Place	Date	Hour	Summary of Events and Information	Remarks and references to Appendices
RENINGHELST	7th	—	Attack by Second Army on MESSINES - WYTSCHAETE Ridge to eliminate salient. Orders in connection with the operation in Appx at I	Appx at I
WESTOUTRE	22nd		Owing to intermittent shelling of RENINGHELST by enemy H.V. gun, Civil P.O. were moved to WESTOUTRE	
"	30th		Supply Dumps was transferred to CTESIRE more. Battalion moved to the BERTHEN rest area	

1711

M. Stokes
aaron
H.st Pioneers

WAR DIARY
INTELLIGENCE SUMMARY

JUNE 1917. Army Form C. 2118 Copy

(Erase heading not required.)

Place	Date	Hour	Summary of Events and Information	Remarks and references to Appendices
RENINGHELST	7th	—	Attack by Second Army on NESSINES - WYTSCHAETE ridge - For administrative orders in connection with the operation v. Appendix I.	Appendix I
WESTOUTRE	22nd		Owing to intermittent shelling of RENINGHELST by enemy H.V. gun, Divl. H.Qrs. were moved to WESTOUTRE.	
"	30th		Supply railhead was transferred to CAESTRE on move of the Division to the BERTHEN rest area.	

1.7.17.

M. Stockdale
aveng
41st Division

WAR DIARY
or
INTELLIGENCE SUMMARY

(Erase heading not required.)

Army Form C. 2118

JUNE 1917

"A" & "Q" 41st. Division.

Instructions regarding War Diaries and Intelligence Summaries are contained in F. S. Regs., Part II. and the Staff Manual respectively. Title Pages will be prepared in manuscript.

Place	Date	Hour	Summary of Events and Information	Remarks and references to Appendices
			A statement showing reinforcements for the month of June.	
			A statement showing casualties for the month of June.	
			A statement showing courts martial for the month of June.	

Army Form C. 2118

WAR DIARY
or
INTELLIGENCE SUMMARY
(Erase heading not required.)

JUNE 1917 "A" & "Q" 41st. Division.

Instructions regarding War Diaries and Intelligence Summaries are contained in F.S. Regs., Part II. and the Staff Manual respectively. Title Pages will be prepared in manuscript.

Place	Date	Hour	Summary of Events and Information	Remarks and references to Appendices
			A statement showing reinforcements for the month of June.	
			A statement showing casualties for the month of June.	
			A statement showing courts martial for the month of June.	

STATEMENT SHOWING REINFORCEMENTS AND WEEKLY STRENGTH

DURING THE MONTH - JUNE 1917.

Unit.	Reinforcements. Other Ranks.	Weekly Strength Other Ranks.				
		June 2nd.	June 9th.	June 16th.	June 23rd.	June 30th.
12th.East Surrey Regt.	45	1017	843	795	764	760
15th.Hampshire Regt.	23	936	748	750	726	723
11th.R.W.Kent Regt.	22	912	784	704	686	677
18th.K.R.R.Corps.	40	914	871	748	729	750
122nd.M.Gun.Coy.	34	163	149	166	168	171
11th.R.W.Surrey Regt.	33	923	787	707	675	652
10th.R.W.Kent Regt.	31	925	844	691	687	860
23rd.Middlesex Regt.	15	963	812	726	693	662
20th.Durham L.I.	26	937	820	793	766	715
123rd.M.Gun Coy.	42	159	144	176	179	163
10th.R.W.Surrey Regt.	17	981	893	867	839	814
26th.R.Fusiliers.	24	943	749	741	665	626
32nd.R.Fusiliers.	26	955	783	784	773	737
21st.K.R.R.Corps.	10	963	887	827	776	749
124th.M.Gun Coy.	51	170	162	180	168	179
19th.Middlesex Regt.	7	942	930	921	918	911

STATEMENT SHOWING REINFORCEMENTS AND WEEKLY STRENGTH

DURING THE MONTH - JUNE 1917.

Unit.	Reinforcements. Other Ranks.	Weekly Strength Other Ranks.				
		June 2nd.	June 9th.	June 16th.	June 23rd.	June 30th.
12th.East Surrey Regt.	45	1017	843	795	784	760
15th.Hampshire Regt.	23	936	748	750	726	723
11th.R.W.Kent Regt.	22	912	784	704	686	677
18th.K.R.R.Corps.	40	914	871	748	729	750
122nd.M.Gun.Coy.	34	163	149	166	168	171
11th.R.W.Surrey Regt.	33	923	787	707	675	652
10th.R.W.Kent Regt.	31	925	844	691	687	860
23rd.Middlesex Regt.	15	965	812	726	693	662
20th.Durham L.I.	26	937	820	793	766	715
123rd.M.Gun Coy.	42	159	144	178	179	163
10th.R.W.Surrey Regt.	17	981	893	867	839	814
26th.R.Fusiliers.	24	943	749	741	665	626
32nd.R.Fusiliers.	26	955	785	784	773	737
21st.K.R.R.Corps.	10	963	887	827	776	749
124th.M.Gun Coy.	51	170	162	180	168	179
19th.Middlesex Regt.	7	942	930	921	918	911

The following table shows numbers killed, wounded, missing, and evacuated sick during the month of June 1917. (to 12 noon 30th).

UNIT.	OFFICERS. Killed.	Wounded.	Missing.	OTHER RANKS. Killed.	Wounded.	Missing.	EVACUATED SICK.
Divl.Headquarters.	-	-	-	1	1	-	1
122nd.Bde.H.Qrs.	-	1	-	-	-	-	-
12th.E.Surrey Regt.	-	8	-	33	184	10	33
15th.Hants Regt.	2	8 x	-	46	172	10	32
11th.R.W.Kent Regt.	2	8	-	30	216	2	37
18th.K.R.R.Corps.	3	3	-	44	139	10	46
122nd.M.G.Coy.	-	2	-	5	15	1	13
123rd.Bde.H.Qrs.	-	1	-	-	-	-	-
11th.Queens.	7	6	-	41	194	40	39
10th.R.W.Kent Regt.	5	7	-	37	223	10	29
23rd.Middlesex.	4	11	-	47	243	16	37
20th.Durham L.I.	2	6	-	37	180	15	42
123rd.M.G.Coy.	-	5	-	9	31	-	10
124th.Bde.H.Qrs.	-	1	-	1	-	-	-
10th.Queens.	1	6	-	27	112	13	29
26th.R.Fusiliers.	4	7	-	45	216	37	32
32nd.R.Fusiliers.	2	6	-	18	185	11	37
21st.K.R.R.Corps.	1	2	-	29	166	11	56
124th.M.G.Coy.	-	2	-	5	18	-	6
19th.Middlesex.	-	1	-	3	41	5	7
H.Qrs.41st.Artillery.	-	-	-	-	-	-	1
187th.Bde.R.F.A.	2	2	-	1	25	-	18
190th.Bde.R.F.A.	1	3	-	4	24	-	19
41st.D.A.C.	-	3	-	-	6	-	11
41st.T.M.B's.	-	-	-	-	10	-	6
228th.Fld.Coy.R.E.	1	2	-	11	17	-	12
233rd.Fld.Coy.R.E.	-	-	-	1	11	-	10
237th.Fld.Coy.R.E.	-	-	-	-	8	-	5
41st.Signal Coy.	-	-	-	-	5	-	2
138th.Fld.Ambulance.	-	2	-	2	6	-	7
139th.Fld.Ambulance.	-	-	-	-	-	-	7
140th.Fld.Ambulance.	-	-	-	1	5	-	4
Divl.Train.	-	-	-	-	3	-	3
Divl.Supply Column.	-	1	-	-	-	-	3
Total for Division.	38	104	-	469	2458	187	593

X Includes H.O.

/over.

UNITS.	OFFICERS.			Other Ranks.		
	Killed.	Wounded.	Missing.	Killed.	Wounded.	Missing.
Attached Troops.						
72nd.Bde.R.F.A.	-	6	-	5	32	1
39th.Bde.R.F.A.	-	3	-	1	13	-
1st.D.A.C.	-	1	-	2	8	-
26th.Bde.R.A.	-	2	-	2	10	-
52nd.Bde.R.A.	-	3	-	6	29	2
277th.Bde.R.A.	-	4	-	8	26	-
25th.Bde.R.A.	1	2	-	1	6	-
55th.Bde.R.A.	-	1	-	3	11	-
235th.Bde.R.A.	-	2	-	7	19	-
86th.Bde.R.A.	-	2	-	2	20	-
1st.Can.Tunn.Coy.	-	-	-	1	4	-
1st.Div.T.M.B's	-	-	1	1	1	-
504th.Batty.R.A.	-	-	-	-	5	-
14th.Bde.R.A.	-	-	-	-	3	-
236th.Bde.R.A.	-	-	-	-	3	-
119th.Bde.R.A.	-	-	-	-	3	-
TOTAL.	1	26	1	38	191	3

The following table shows numbers killed, wounded, missing, and evacuated sick during the month of June 1917. (to 12 noon 30th).

UNIT.	OFFICERS.			OTHER RANKS.			EVACUATED SICK.
	Killed.	Wounded.	Missing.	Killed.	Wounded.	Missing.	
Divl.Headquarters.	-	1	-	-	1	-	1
122nd.Bde.H.Qrs.	-	1	-	-	-	-	-
12th.E.Surrey Regt.	-	8	-	33	184	10	33
15th.Hants Regt.	2	8 ✗	-	46	172	10	32
11th.R.W.Kent Regt.	2	8	-	30	216	2	37
18th.K.R.R.Corps.	3	3	-	44	139	10	46
122nd.M.G.Coy.	-	2	-	5	15	1	13
123rd.Bde.H.Qrs.	1	1	-	-	-	-	-
11th.Queens.	7	6	-	41	194	40	39
10th.R.W.Kent Regt.	5	7	-	37	223	10	29
23rd.Middlesex.	4	11	-	47	243	16	37
20th.Durham L.I.	2	6	-	37	180	13	42
123rd.M.G.Coy.	-	5	-	9	31	-	10
124th.Bde.H.Qrs.	1	-	-	1	-	-	-
10th.Queens.	1	6	-	27	112	13	29
26th.R.Fusiliers.	4	7	-	45	216	37	32
32nd.R.Fusiliers.	2	6	-	18	185	11	37
21st.K.R.R.Corps.	1	2	-	29	166	11	56
124th.M.G.Coy.	-	1	-	5	18	3	6
19th.Middlesex.	-	-	-	3	41	-	7
H.Qrs.41st.Artillery.	-	-	-	1	-	-	-
187th.Bde.R.F.A.	2	2	-	1	25	-	18
190th.Bde.R.F.A.	1	3	-	4	24	-	19
41st.D.A.C.	-	3	-	-	6	-	11
41st.T.M.B's.	-	-	-	-	10	-	6
228th.Fld.Coy.R.E.	1	2	-	1	17	-	12
233rd.Fld.Coy.R.E.	-	-	-	1	11	-	10
257th.Fld.Coy.R.E.	-	-	-	-	8	-	5
41st.Signal Coy.	-	-	-	-	5	-	2
138th.Fld.Ambulance.	-	-	-	2	6	-	7
139th.Fld.Ambulance.	-	-	-	-	-	-	7
140th.Fld.Ambulance.	-	-	-	1	5	-	4
Divl.Train.	-	-	-	-	3	-	3
Divl.Supply Column.	-	-	-	-	-	-	3
Total for Division.	38	104	-	469	2458	187	593

✗ Includes M.O.

/over.

UNITS.	OFFICERS.			Other Ranks.		
	Killed.	Wounded.	Missing.	Killed.	Wounded.	Missing.
Attached Troops.						
72nd.Bde.R.F.A.	–	6	–	5	32	1
39th.Bde.R.F.A.	–	3	–	1	13	1
1st.D.A.C.	–	1	–	2	8	–
26th.Bde.R.A.	–	2	–	2	10	–
52nd.Bde.R.A.	–	3	–	6	29	2
277th.Bde.R.A.	–	4	–	8	26	–
25th.Bde.R.A.	1	2	–	1	6	–
65th.Bde.R.A.	–	1	–	3	11	–
235th.Bde.R.A.	–	2	–	7	19	–
86th.Bde.R.A.	–	2	–	2	20	–
1st.Can.Funn.Coy.	–	–	–	1	4	–
1st.Div.T.M.B's.	–	–	–	–	1	–
504th.Batty.R.A.	–	–	–	–	1	–
14th.Bde.R.A.	–	–	–	–	5	–
236th.Bde.R.A.	–	–	–	–	3	–
119th.Bde.R.A.	–	–	–	–	3	–
TOTAL.	1	26	–	38	191	3

STATEMENT SHOWING COURTS MARTIAL FOR THE MONTH OF

JUNE 1917.

Unit.	No.	Particulars of Charge.	Sentence.
11th.R.W.Kent Regt.	2.	(1). Disobeying lawful command.	2 years I.H.L.
		(2). Absence without leave.	6 months I.H.L.
20th.Durham L.I.	9.	(1). Disobeying lawful command.	6 months I.H.L.
		(2). Drunkenness.	42 days F.P.1.
		(3). - do -	Not Guilty.
		(4). Absence without leave.	90 days F.P.1.
		(5). - do -	28 days F.P.1.
		(6). - do -	56 days F.P.1.
		(7). - do -	Not Guilty.
		(8). - do -	56 days F.P.1.
		(9). - do -	56 days F.P.1.
12th.E.Surrey Regt.	1.	Desertion.	Death.
41st.D.A.C.	1.	Striking a soldier.	Reduced to ranks.
253rd.Field Coy R.E.	2.	(1). Drunkenness.	90 days F.P.1.
		(2). - do -	90 days F.P.1.

STATEMENT SHOWING COURTS MARTIAL FOR THE MONTH OF
JUNE 1917.

Unit.	No.	Particulars of Charge.	Sentence.
11th.R.W.Kent Regt.	2.	(1). Disobeying lawful command.	2 years I.H.L.
		(2). Absence without leave.	6 months I.H.L.
20th.Durham L.I.	9.	(1). Disobeying lawful command.	6 months I.H.L.
		(2). Drunkenness.	42 days F.P.1.
		(3). - do -	Not Guilty.
		(4). Absence without leave.	90 days F.P.1.
		(5). - do -	28 days F.P.1.
		(6). - do -	56 days F.P.1.
		(7). - do -	Not Guilty.
		(8). - do -	56 days F.P.1.
		(9). - do -	56 days F.P.1.
12th.E.Surrey Regt.	1.	Desertion.	Death.
41st.D.A.C.	1.	Striking a soldier.	Reduced to ranks.
233rd.Field Coy R.E.	2.	(1). Drunkenness.	90 days F.P.1.
		(2). - do -	90 days F.P.1.

"A" Form
MESSAGES AND SIGNALS.

Army Form C. 2121
(in Pads of 100).

TO War Diary

G.B. 283.   31st.

Traffic circuits laid down in 41st. Division

Administrative Instructions (41st.Div.Q/355/S.)

will come into force at 6.a.m. tomorrow aaa

From
Place   41st.Division.A.
Time

Army Form C. 2118

WAR DIARY
or
INTELLIGENCE SUMMARY

(Erase heading not required.)

41st Division "A" and "Q".

Instructions regarding War Diaries and Intelligence Summaries are contained in F.S. Regs., Part II. and the Staff Manual respectively. Title Pages will be prepared in manuscript.

Place	Date	Hour	Summary of Events and Information	Remarks and references to Appendices
BERTHEN	July 1st		D.H.Q. moved from WESTOUTRE to BERTHEN on the Division moving out of the Line to rest.	A
"	July		Administrative Instructions issued in connection with "G".	
"	July 17th		Divisional Machine Gun Co.(No.238) joined Division from Base	
"	July 18th		124th Infantry Brigade moved from METEREN area to WESTOUTRE area.	
"	July 18th		Divisional Horse Show.	
"	July 21st		123rd Infantry Brigade moved from BERTHEN area. (THIEUSHOEK) to WESTOUTRE area	
"	July 23rd		122nd Infantry Brigade moved from BERTHEN Area to WESTOUTRE area	
WESTOUTRE	July 25th		Divisional Headquarters moved to WESTOUTRE.	
	July 26th		Major R.E.Holmes a Court D.S.O., D.A.A.G., left to take up appointment of A.A.&.Q.M.G. 39th Divn.	
	July 27th		Captain E.G.Whately arrived to take up appointment of D.A.A.G.	
	July 30th		Leave allotment reduced to 12 per day (from 27th). 141 Infantry Brigade moved into RIDGEWOOD area. 19th Middlesex and 124th Infantry Brigade moving into assembly positions.	
	July 31st		Division attacked. By 11.a.m. about 120 stretcher cases and 230 walking wounded had passed through Field Ambulance and 113 prisoners through cage. Up to 6.p.m. 738 all ranks had passed through Dressing Stations. Of these 200 belong to units outside Division. The casualties for this action will be shown in the statement for August.	
			A statement showing Courts Martial for the month is attached.	
			A statement showing reinforcements for the month is attached.	
			A statement showing the casualties for the month is attached.	

Lieut Colonel,
A. A. &. Q. M. G.

Administrative Instructions

In connection 41st Div

O.O. 140

SECRET.

A

41st.Div.
Q/411/S.

Copies to :-

122nd Infantry Brigade.	123rd Infantry Brigade.
124th Infantry Brigade.	C.R.A.
Xth Corps Q.	C.R.E.
19th Middlesex Regt.	1st. Canadian Tunn. Coy.
41st. Signal Coy.	41st. Divl. Train.
"G"	A.D.M.S.
A.P.M.	D.A.D.V.S.
Divl. M.G. Officer.	Divl. Observation Officer.
File.	War Diary.
19th Division Q.	47th Division Q.
24th Division Q.	Spare.

Herewith Administrative Arrangements for Forthcoming Operations in connection with 41st. Divisional Operation Order No.140 dated 9th July 1917.

Please ACKNOWLEDGE.

Para 1. RATIONS AND WATER.
" 2. WATER.
" 3. S.A.A., GRENADES, L.T.M. AMMUNITION.
" 4. ARTILLERY AND T.M. AMMUNITION.
" 5. R.E. STORES.
" 6. MEDICAL.
" 7. PRISONERS OF WAR.
" 8. STRAGGLER POSTS.
" 9. REINFORCEMENT CAMP.
" 10. PACKS AND SURPLUS KIT.

Apendix "A" WATER.
Apendix "B" AMMUNITION.
Apendix "C" REINFORCEMENT RETURN.

[signature]
Lieut Colonel,
A.A. & Q.M.G.,
41st. Division.

14th July 1917.

SECRET.   41st. Division No. Q/411/9

ADMINISTRATIVE ARRANGEMENTS FOR FORTHCOMING OPERATIONS

REFERENCE 41st DIVISION OPERATION ORDER No. 140 of 9th instant
----

(1).   RATIONS AND WATER.

   In order to reduce wheeled traffic on roads and tracks on X and Y days, barrage rations as under will be dumped near forward limit of horse transport.

   2 days for 122 and 123 Brigade for consumption Y and Z day
   1 day for 2 battalions 124 Brigade for consumption Z day

   Positions of dumps to be selected by Brigades and marked with notice boards showing unit for which intended and date of consumption. Positions of dumps to be reported to Divisional Headquarters when selected.

   Battalions strength has been calculated at 700.
   One third galls of water per man per diem in petrol tins will be dumped with these rations.

   The method of drawing these rations and petrol tins will be issued later.
   Rations for consumption on Z plus 1 and subsequent days will be delivered as normally by pack or wheeled transport under Brigade arrangements ; it may be necessary for Division to allot times to each Brigade Transport.

(2).   WATER.

   Details of water supply in Forward Area are as shewn in Appendix "A".
   A reserve of water carts is being placed at the disposal of the Division, in the event of the pipe line being broken, these carts will be put forward to a convenient central point (probably near bridge I.33.d.3.6.) where water carrying parties can exchange empty for full petrol tins.

(3).   S.A.A., GRENADES, AND LIGHT TRENCH MORTAR AMMUNITION.

   Divisional Dump will be at N.4.c.5.2.
   Brigade Dumps will be established at
   Left Brigade   I.34.c.5.0.
   Right Brigade   O.4.a.4.7.

   These are being prepared and partially filled by 47th Division.
   In addition small battalion dumps will be formed in the neighbourhood of the Front Line, in recesses off the main forward communication trenches; these are being constructed by 47th Division and will be partially filled by them.
   Brigades will report the position of these and amounts placed in each as soon as fixed.
   Appendix "B" shows amounts allotted for operations at Divisional Dump and in Brigade and Forward Dumps. The distribution between the Brigade and the more forward dumps should normally be 50% of Brigade allotment in each.

(4). ARTILLERY AND T.M.AMMUNITION.

The following amounts of Artillery and T.M.ammunition are being dumped at the gun positions by the 47th Division :-

    18 pdr.   per gun   1300 rounds

    4.5" How " "   1100 rounds.

NEWTON TRENCH MORTARS.

Per gun   300 rounds.

Will be dumped under Divisional arrangements.

(5) R.E.STORES.

Divisional R.E.Dump will be at BRASSERIE N.6.a.1.1. Advanced R.E.Dumps are being formed at

    Right Sector   OAK DUMP   O.3.b.9.7.

    Left Sector   IMP DUMP   O.4.a.8.8.

(6) MEDICAL.

Regimental Aid Posts

    Right Brigade Sector.   O.3.d.6.8.
                              O.4.a.6.2.

    Left Brigade Sector.   O.4.b.2.9.
                              I.34.d.8.8.

Collecting Posts.

    Right Sector   SHELLY LANE   I.32.d.3.3.

    Left Sector   SPOIL BANK   I.33.d.3.2.

Advanced Dressing Station VOORMEZEELE I.31.c.4.6.
Collecting Station for walking wounded
                      BRASSERIE   N.6.a.2.2.
Main Dressing Station for seriously wounded
                      LA CLYTTE ROAD M.6.a.8.8.
Main Dressing Station for walking wounded
                      LA CLYTTE   N.7.c.4.5.

(7) PRISONERS OF WAR.

Escorts to Prisoners of War being sent back should not exceed 5% of the number of prisoners.
The Officer in Charge of the Cage will give a receipt to the escort for all prisoners handed over to him, and return escort to their units.
The position of the cage will be notified later.

(8) STRAGGLER POSTS.

A line of Divisional Straggler Posts will be established at

    O.2.a.4.6. (BUS HOUSE)
    I.32.d.4.4.
    I.33.a.2.3. (BRIDGE)

Brigades will arrange for posts, found from regimental police, on all main communication trenches in their area to be posted previous to zero hour.
Stragglers arrested by Divisional Posts will handed over to 1st Line Transport of unit and sent back at first opportuni

(9). **REINFORCEMENT CAMP.**

A Divisional Reinforcement Camp will not be formed, details left behind under G.S.135 will remain in their Battalion Transport Camp where any drafts arriving during the operations will be sent.

Brigades will place an officer in charge of all personnel with their transport and he will render return (Appendix "G") to Divisional Headquarters "A" and "Q" office by 4.p.m. daily.

No personnel is to be sent up to join their units without orders from Divisional Headquarters. Brigades who desire Officers or men to be sent up should wire Divisional Headquarters "A" and "Q" office.

(10). **PACKS AND SURPLUS KIT.**

Packs and surplus kit will be stored at RENINGHELST in the barn at C.34.d.65.80., the personnel now there will be maintained, no additional men may be sent by units.

In order to admit of great-coats being rapidly issued should opportunity occur these will be rolled in bundles separate from the packs.

Men should be warned to leave no private property in their great-coat pockets.

APPENDIX "A".

1. Water Cart refilling point - I.31.d.2.4.
2. Water Tanks and Stand Pipes   N.6.a.10.10.
    N.5.a.90.95.
    N.5.b.30.80.
    I.31.d.20.40.
    I.31.d.80.85.
    O.1.d.35.75.
    O.8.a.65.90.
    O.9.a.70.20.
    I.33.a.50.10. *
    I.33.c.80.70. *
    I.33.c.50.45. *
    I.33.d.30.50. *
    O.4.a.75.60. *

Tanks marked * mean supply unreliable.

3. Stand Pipes only -   N.6.a.2.9.
    N.6.b.4.9.

4. Wells.   I.31.c.40.60.)
    I.31.c.60.40.)
    O.2.a.60.70.) Notice Boards
    O.3.c.95.10.) erected show-
    I.33.c.80.85.) ing amount of
    I.32.d.85.20.) chlorination
    O.10.b.10.40.) required.
    O.9.d.35.25.)

APPENDIX "B".

	Divl. Dump. Minimum to be maintained.	Brigade and Battn. Dumps in each Sector, exclusive of existing defensive dumps.
S.A.A.	250,000	250,000
No.5.Mills Grenade.	5,000	5,000
Rifle Grenades blank S.A.A.	3,000	2,000
Stokes Ammn. with cartridges.	3,000	1,000
Very Lights 1".	1,000	1,000
Very Lights 1½".	500	500
Webley Pistol.	1,000	500
P Grenades.	1,000	500
S.O.S. Signals. Flares. Rockets. Colored Very Lights. Smoke Candles.	As allotted by Army. Quantities depend on tactical considerations.	

This does not include equipment of bombers and grenadiers, or any establishment on wheels.

APPENDIX "C".

RETURN OF PERSONNEL .... INFANTRY BRIGADE.

Battalion.	Details left behind by Brigades.		Reinforcements who have not been out before.		Reinforcements who have been out before.		Sent up to join Units.		Remarks.
	Offrs.	O.Rks.	Offrs.	O.Rks.	Offrs.	O.Rks.	Offrs.	O.Rks.	

Date ....

8 i/c Personnel .... Inf. Brigade.

SECRET.

41st Div.
Q/411/12.

122nd Infantry Brigade.
123rd Infantry Brigade.
124th Infantry Brigade.
Divisional Train.
S. S. O.
C. R. A.
47th Division "Q".

(i) With reference to this office Q/411/S of 14/7/17 - Administrative Instructions for Forthcoming Operations.
Para.1, Sub-paras. 1, 2, & 3 are cancelled and the following substituted.
One days (Z day) Barrage Rations will be dumped for the 10 Battalions in the Front Line, i.e. 4 Battalions South of the Canal and 6 Battalion North thereof.

(ii) Rations will be installed on the 18th instant as follows :-
2800 Rations in the immediate vicinity of OAK DUMP, O.4.a.1.7.
4200 Rations in the immediate vicinity of IMP DUMP, O.4.a.8.8.

(iii) These rations will be drawn from CAESTRE at 11.0.a.m. Those for IMP DUMP in three lorries to be provided by O.C. Divisional Train - Those for OAK DUMP by two lorries to be provided by S.M.T.O. Xth Corps.

(iv) O.C. Divisional Train will detail a Supply Officer to take over these rations at CAESTRE and supervise their conveyance to Cross Roads at N.6.a.1.1. where they should arrive at 3.0. p.m.

(v) 10 G.S. Wagons from party from 41st D.A.C. proceeding to forward area on 18th instant will meet the lorries at N.6.a.1.1. and will be organised into two convoys.
A. Convoy will convey 2800 rations direct to OAK DUMP.
B. Convoy will convey 4200 rations to the Bridge at NORFOLK LODGE.

(vi) Guides provided by 47th Division will be at N.6.a.1.1. at 3.0. p.m.

(vii) Convoy "B" will be met at the Bridge at NORFOLK LODGE about 4.0.p.m. by a carrying party to be provided from party of 123rd Infantry Brigade, who are proceeding to RIDGEWOOD on 18th, for work under C.R.E. they will man handle the rations to the situation selected near IMP DUMP.

/(ix)

(viii)   Carrying and Loading parties will be conveyed as follows:-
3 Lorries will pick up 100 men as detailed in para.(vi)
at 1.0.p.m. at THIEUSHOUK Cross Roads Q.35.b. whence
they will be taken to N.6.a.1.1. A representative of "Q"
Branch will be present at N.6.a.1.1. and will detach a
sufficient loading party. The remainder will proceed
by lorry to VOORMEZEELE and thence by march route to
NORFOLK LODGE Bridge (vide para.vii) and await arrival
of the wagons.

(ix)   On completion of the duty, parties and wagons will
proceed to their new billets at RIDGEWOOD and
MILLEKRUISSE and CHIPPAWA.

(x)   A representative of each Brigade concerned will take
over the rations at N.6.a.1.1. and will assume responsibility for dumping.

(xi)   After installation in the dumps, 47th Division have agreed
to guard the dump in each case until relieved by this
Division.

                                        (sd) Eric White,

                                        Major,
                                        D. A. Q. M. G.,
17th July 1917.   41st. Division.

SECRET.   41st Division No. Q/411/14.

FURTHER ADMINISTRATIVE ARRANGEMENTS FOR FORTHCOMING OPERATIONS.
IN CONTINUATION & AMENDMENT TO THOSE DATED 14/7/17.

BARRAGE RATIONS & WATER.

Barrage rations and water will be dumped for one day only - these are for consumption on "Z" day. Special allowance has not been made for Machine Gun Companies, Trench Mortar Batteries, and Brigade H.Q. and rations for these units will be taken from the surplus of the 200 rations dumped for each Battalion.

WATER.

Brigades will be issued with Petrol Tins at the scale of 100 per Battalion, with these mobile dumps of water will be formed as far forward in the trench system as possible.
Dump of Petrol Tins filled by reserve water carts, will be established at NORFOLK LODGE BRIDGE I.33.d.3.6.

AMMUNITION.

15000 red/aeroplane flares have been allotted to the Division and these have been re-allotted as follows :-

122 Infantry Brigade.	5000
123 Infantry Brigade.	5000
124 Infantry Brigade.	3000
Divisional Reserve.	2000
TOTAL	15,000

200 S.O.S. Rockets have been asked for and will be allotted as follows :-

122 Infantry Brigade.	50
123 Infantry Brigade.	50
124 Infantry Brigade.	25
Divisional Reserve.	75
TOTAL.	200

S.A.A., Grenades, flares etc., required to equip Battalions will be drawn under Brigade arrangements from Divisional Dump, on dates to be notified by Divl. Headquarters.

ARTILLERY & T.M. AMMUNITION.

Newton T.M.

Only 100 rounds per gun will be dumped.

PRISONERS OF WAR.

      Prisoners cage will be at N.3.a.central where all prisoners will be sent.

MAP.

      A revised map showing Tramways, Overland Tracks, Dumps etc., will be issued prior to operations.

                                          Lieut-Colonel,
                                          A.A.&.Q.M.G.,
19th July 1917.   41st.Division.

Copies to :-

122nd Infantry Brigade.	123rd Infantry Brigade.
124th Infantry Brigade.	C.R.A.
Xth Corps Q.	C.R.E.
19th Middlesex Regt.	1st Canadian Tunnelling Coy.
41st Signal Coy.	41st Divl. Train.
"G".	A.D.M.S.
A.P.M.	D.A.D.V.S.
Divl. M.G. Officer.	Divl. Observation Officer.
File.	War Diary.
19th Division Q.	47th Division Q.
24th Division Q.	Spare.

41st. Division No. Q/411/17.

122nd. Infantry Brigade.	123rd. Infantry Brigade.
124th Infantry Brigade.	C.R.A.
Xth Corps Q.	C.R.E.
19th Middlesex.	1st Canadian Tun. Co.
41st. Signal Co.	41st. Divisional Train.
"G".	A.D.M.S.
A.P.M.	D.A.D.V.S.
Divl M. Gun Officer.	Divisional Observation Offr.
File.	War Diary.
19th Division Q.	47th Division Q.
24th Division Q.	Spare.

The attached additional section, No.11. CLEARING THE BATTLEFIELD, and appendix "D", BURIAL INSTRUCTIONS, are forwarded in connection with "41st. Divisional Administrative Arrangements in connection with 41st. Divisional Operation Order No. 140 dated July 9th", forwarded under this office No. Q/411/S dated 14th July 1917.

[signature]
Major,
D.A.A.G.
41st. Division.

July 21st. 1917.

(11).   ## CLEARING THE BATTLEFIELD.

1. Owing to the shortness of the advance contemplated, salvage and burial operations will have to be carried out by the fighting troops under Brigade arrangements.

2. 2/Lieut S.E.BENNETT 12th East Surrey Regiment is appointed Divisional Burial Officer.
　　He will
　　(a). Issue discs, rods, forms for burial return, tags for effects to Brigades vide attached instructions.
　　(b). Units will send in their burial returns to him as soon as possible.
　　(c). Supervise burials at the Dressing Station at VOORMEZEELE and at the burial grounds at BUS HOUSE and O.3.b. 9½. 6½

3. Units will carry out the attached instructions as far as practicable, special care being taken to mark the graves at the time of burying or as soon after as possible.

4. A supply of notice boards will be issued to Brigades for marking sites selected for burying. Graves should be grouped to-gether as far as practicable.

5. The usual proceedure will be followed for Salvage. Battalions and Brigades will establish dumps at suitable places, which should be at points to which wheeled transport with rations comes up.
　　Salvage will be evacuated from these points to an advanced Divisional Dump in the neighbourhood of LA CLYTTE, (exact position will be notified later), by returning empty ration vehicles. In the event of these being unable to cope with the amount indents for transport will be sent into 41st.Division "Q".

APPENDIX "D".

BURIAL INSTRUCTIONS.

(1). **MARKING OF GRAVES AND EFFECTS.**

1. Graves will be marked with a disc hung on a wire rod which will be stuck in the ground at the head of the grave :-

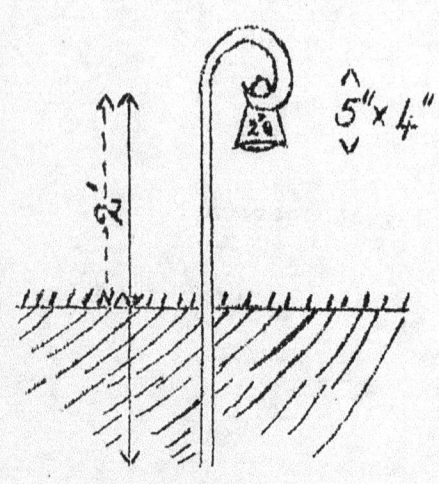
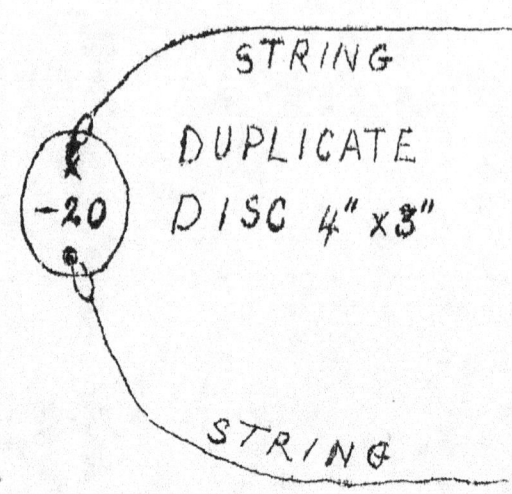

2. A duplicate disc bearing the same number as the disc over the grave will be tied to each :-
   (a) Packet of effects (if only one body is buried in the grave).
   (b) Sandbag of packets of effects (if more bodies than one are buried in the same grave).

3. A number of these rods and discs (in duplicate) will be issued to units, who will be held responsible that every disc not returned is accounted for on a roll (vide pro-forma below).
   Discs and rods will be supplied by the Divisional Burial Officer.

(2). **SYSTEM OF BURIAL.**

1. Burial Officers will be held responsible that burials are carried out in accordance with these instructions.

2. Burial Parties must observe the following routine :-
   (a). Remove nothing from the dead until ready to place into the grave.
   (b). Bury British, French, and German separately.
   (c). Bury Officers with men except General Officers.
   (d). Collect all personal effects and the RED identity disc and place them in a ration bag or packet, and tie it up. The GREEN identity disc will be left on the man's body and buried with it.
   (e). Mark each grave (whether containing one or more bodies) with wire rod and disc; the duplicate disc will then be tied to the single packet of effects, or to the sandbag of packets of effects (according to whether one or more bodies are buried in the grave).
   (f). Return sandbags containing effects of British and send them to the Divisional Burial Officer.
   (g). Mark sandbags containing effects of Germans "Xth Corps G and send it at once to Divisional Burial Officer.

(ii).

3. The Officer in charge of a Burial Party on completion of his work will make a nominal roll in the following form :-

Xth Corps Graves No. & Map Reference.	Regtl. No.	Rank.	Name.	Regt.	Religion.
X /20 E.36.d.4.2.	100.	Pte	T.JONES	1st D.L.I.	C of E.

He will sign and date the roll and <u>print</u> his own name and Regiment.

He will send the sandbags and rolls to his Divisional Burial Officer who will forward them to the Corps Burial Officer.

The Corps Burial Officer will send
  (a). The sandbags to the Corps Salvage Officer who will be responsible for dispatching such effects to the Base, and obtaining receipts from the R.T.O. which will be forwarded to Division "A".
  (b). The Rolls to Division "A".

SECRET.
                                                    41st Div.
                                                    Q/411/21.

            FURTHER ADMINISTRATIVE ARRANGEMENTS FOR FORTHCOMING
    OPERATIONS IN CONTINUATION AND AMENDMENT TO THOSE DATED 14/7/17.

(1).   RATIONS.

        The two Battalions 124th Infantry Brigade moving to
        BLUFF, SPOIL BANK area on Y/Z night will take rations
        for Z day with them and will not draw on the BARRAGE
        Rations dumped for them for use on that day.
        Those rations will be drawn by 124th Infantry Brigade
        on Z night for consumption by two of those battalions
        on Z plus 1 day.

(2)   WATER.

        2/Lieut. W. H. SAXELBY, 19th Middlesex, is appointed
        Divisional Water Officer, H.Q., H.36.d.9.4. (telegrams
        VOORMEZEELE DEEP DUG-OUT).
        A second forward dump of petrol tins will be made at
        O.4.a.8½.6. and filled from spring at that point.
        The pipe supply from DICKEBUSCH LAKE is being carried
        on N.E. down the DAMMSTRASSE from O.9.a.8.2. and
        tanks erected at O.4.c.2.2. and O.4.a.8.6.

(3)   TRAMWAYS.

        2/Lieut. CARPENTER, 19th Middlesex, is appointed
        Divisional Tramway Officer and will control all
        Tramway Traffic in the Divisional area.
        Application for trucks should be made to him at
        H.36.d.9.4. or by telegram to VOORMEZEELE DEEP DUG-OUT.
        Pushing parties must be provided by the Units using the
        line.

(4)   R. E. STORES.

        Dumps of material for consolidation will be formed at
        O.5.d.8.3. and O.5.b.6.6.

(5)   PRISONERS OF WAR.

        Paragraph (7) of 41st Division Q/411/S is modified as
        follows :-
        One troop of "D" squadron 4th Australian Light Horse
        will be stationed at the BRASSERIE N.6.a.1.1. for
        escort duties.
        All prisoners will be sent to the BRASSERIE by Brigades.
        Captain A. H. REID, 32nd Royal Fusiliers, will be
        posted there from Zero hour to superintend the transfer
        of prisoners from escorts provided by Brigades to the
        Australian Light Horse.   He will give receipts to
        escorts of Brigades and obtain them from the Australian
        Light Horse.

(6)   ACCOMMODATION OF BRIGADE DETAILS.

        (i) Brigade details of 122nd Infantry Brigade will be
        accommodated at WOOD CAMP from night 25th/26th instant.
        The night 24th/25th instant they will bivouac at their
        Brigade Transport Lines.

(ii) Brigade details, 123rd Infantry Brigade will be accommodated at MURRUMBIDGEE WEST CAMP on the night of the 26th/27th instant; the night of the 25th/26th they will bivouac at their Brigade Transport Lines.

(iii) The 124th Infantry Brigade must allot camps in the "A" Brigade area to allow _____ of the above

(iv). Details of 124th Infantry Brigade will remain at DEZON CAMP on move of their Brigade into the Forward area.

Eric White
Major.

Lieut.Colonel,
A.A. & Q.M.G.,
41st Division.

23rd July 1917.

Copies to -

122nd Infantry Brigade.	123rd Infantry Brigade.
124th Infantry Brigade.	C. R. A.
Xth Corps Q.	C. R. E.
19th Middlesex Regt.	1st Canadian Tunnelling Coy.
41st Signal Coy.	41st Divl. Train.
"G".	A. D. M. S.
A. P. M.	D. A. D. V. S.
Divl. Machine Gun Officer.	Divl. Observation Officer.
File.	War Diary.
19th Division Q.	47th Division Q.
24th Division Q.	Spare.

41st DIVISION.

STATEMENT SHOWING REINFORCEMENTS AND WEEKLY STRENGTH DURING JULY 1917.

Unit.	Reinforcements received during month.	Strength. Week endg. July 7th.	Strength Week endg July 14th.	Strength Week endg July 21st	Strength week endg July 28th
12th E.Surrey.	271	823	876	969	964
15th Hampshire Rgt.	300	852	959	959	943
11th R.W.Kents.	400	942	918	967	963
18th K.R.R.C.	227	893	944	935	935
122nd M.Gun Co.	2	161	162	176	173
11th R.W.Surrey.	339	821	963	941	942
10th R.W.Kent Rgt.	324	747	742	952	965
23rd Middlesex.	518	738	844	940	932
20th D.L.I.	357	1058	1043	1046	1013
123rd M.Gun Co.	29	172	173	176	178
10th R.W.Surrey.	200	815	825	946	942
26th R.Fusiliers.	497	731	910	1044	1036
32nd R.Fusiliers.	289	757	810	900	971
21st K.R.R.C.	221	752	929	906	904
124th M.Gun Co.	14	162	159	172	169
19th Middlesex.	77	909	907	967	963

The following table shows numbers killed, wounded, missing, and evacuated sick during the month of July 1917 (to noon 31st).

Unit.	OFFICERS Killed	OFFICERS Wounded	OFFICERS Missing	OTHER RANKS Killed	OTHER RANKS Wounded	OTHER RANKS Missing	Evacuated Sick.
D.H.Qtrs.	-	-	-	-	-	-	3
12th E.Surrey.	-	2	-	6	10	-	17
15th Hants.	1	-	-	14	34	2	13
11th R.W.Kents.	1	1	-	4	64	3	29
18th K.R.R.C.	1	2	-	1	32	-	25
122nd M.Gun Co.	-	-	-	-	6	-	6
123rd Bde H.Q.	2	-	-	-	-	-	-
11th Queen's.	-	1	-	12	38	-	28
10th R.W.Kents.	-	1	-	11	17	-	31
23rd Middlesex.	-	-	-	3	16	-	35
20th D.L.I.	1	-	-	13	109	5	40
123rd M.Gun Co.	-	-	-	4	11	-	4
10th Queen's.	7	-	-	5	12	-	21
23th R.Fusiliers.	-	1	-	1	5	-	20
32nd R.Fusiliers.	-	-	-	2	30	-	66
21st K.R.R.C.	-	-	-	2	3	-	31
124th M.Gun Co.	-	-	-	1	11	-	3
19th Middlesex.	-	1	-	3	20	-	12
Artillery H.Q.	-	-	-	-	-	-	1
187th Bde R.A.	1	-	-	5	13	-	12
190th Bde R.F.A.	-	-	-	-	15	-	31
41st D.A.C.	-	-	-	1	1	-	8
228th F.Co.R.E.	-	1	-	1	9	-	7
233rd F.Co.R.E.	1	1	-	2	11	-	5
237th F.Co.R.E.	-	-	-	1	3	-	4
Carried Forward.	7	11	-	89	470	10	450

| | OFFICERS | | | OTHER RANKS. | | | Evacuated |
Unit.	Killed	wounded	Missing.	Killed	Wounded	Missing	Sick.
Brt. Forward.	7	11	-	89	470	10	450
41st T.M.Bttys.	-	-	-	1	6	-	1
41st Signal Co.	-	-	-	-	4	-	3
138th Fld Amb.	-	-	-	3	2	-	5
139th Fld Amb.	-	-	-	-	-	-	6
140th Fld.Amb.	-	-	-	-	2	-	5
Divl Train.	-	-	-	-	-	-	-
52nd.M.V.Sectn.	-	-	-	-	-	-	1
Total.	7	11	-	93	484	10	470

Casualties incurred in the action of 31/7/17 to be included in statement of August. 1917.

41st DIVISION.

STATEMENT SHOWING COURTS MARTIAL HELD DURING JULY 1917.

Unit.	No of cases.	Charge.	Sentence.
12th E.Surrey.	1.	Absence without Leave.	56 days F.P.1.
15th Hants.	6.	2 Disobeying Law Commd.	28 days F.P. each.
		2 Civil Offence Forgery.	Each red.to ranks.
		1 Discharging Firearm.	14 days F.P.1.
		1 Drunkenness.	28 days F.P.1.
11th W.Kents.	1.	Desertion.	Death com.10 yrs.
18th K.R.R.	3.	1 Desertion	10 yrs P.S.
		1 Prej.Good order & M.D.	Reduced to ranks.
		1 Sleeping on post.	56 days F.P.1.
23rd Middlesex.	1	Absence without leave	56 days F.P.1.
11th Queen's.	1	Drunkenness	Red.to ranks.
10th W.Kents.	1	Absence without leave	90 days F.P.1.
10th Queen's.	7.	6 Desertion.	3 Not Guilty
			1-12 months I.H.L.
			1- 2 yrs I.H.L.
			1- Killed in action.
		1 Drunkenness.	Reduced to ranks.
26th R.Fusiliers.	1	Absence without leave	1 yr.com.28 days F.
32nd.R.Fusiliers.	6.	5 Desertion.	3-Not guilty
			1-6 months I.H.L.
			1-2 years I.H.L.
		1 Stealing.	90 days F.P.1.
21st K.R.R.C.	1	Forgery.	90 days (Quashed).
190th Bde R.F.A.	2.	1 Disobeying Law Commd.	90 days F.P.1.
		1 Drunkenness.	90 days fined £1.
19th Middlesex.	1	Insubordinate Language	21 days F.P.1.

Army Form C. 2118

WAR DIARY
or
INTELLIGENCE SUMMARY

41st. DIVISION "A" & "Q"

AUGUST 1917.

(Erase heading not required.)

Instructions regarding War Diaries and Intelligence Summaries are contained in F.S. Regs., Part II. and the Staff Manual respectively. Title Pages will be prepared in manuscript.

Place	Date	Hour	Summary of Events and Information	Remarks and references to Appendices
WESTOUTRE.	Aug 11th	—	Administrative Instructions issued for move to BERTHEN Area.	Appendix A.
BERTHEN	Aug 19th		Administrative Instructions issued for move from BERTHEN Area to Second Army Training Area.	Appendix B.
WIZERNES.	Aug 21st		Division Headquarters opened at WIZERNES.	Appendix C.
			A Statement showing Casualties & Sick wastage is attached.	
			A Statement showing Courts Martial for the month is attached.	Appendix D.

September 10th. 1917.

[signature]
Lieut.Colonel,
A.A.&.Q.M.G.
41st Division.

Appendix A

SECRET.
41st Div.
Q.64/185.

122nd Infantry Brigade.
123rd Infantry Brigade.
124th Infantry Brigade.
A.D.M.S.
19th Middlesex Regt.
C.R.E.
"G".

Reference 41st Division Operation Order No. 152 of 11/8/17.

The Units of the 41st Division will embus in accordance with attached table.

2. Maximum accommodation in each bus is 25 all ranks, beside the driver and mate. If numbers allow, 20, gives comfortable room.

3. Busses will be drawn up at the point of embussing close to the right hand side of the road, 15 yards to each bus.

4. Troops will be in position on left of road distributed along the stretch of road to be used for embussing, in parties of 25 for each 15 yards, ten minutes before arrival of convoy.

5. Embussing will only commence on receipt of orders from the Divisional Staff Officer in charge, when all the busses are clear of the troops of the 39th Division they have brought up.

6. Brigades will detail a Staff Officer to be present during the embussing of his Brigade.

7. All troops East of the LA CLYTTE - DICKEBUSCH Road will move to HALLEBAST CORNER via track of GORDON FARM - DICKEBUSCH LAKE-H.33.c.15.65., leaving the HALLEBAST CORNER - VIERSTRAAT ROAD clear for troops of 39th Division.

8. No baggage of any kind may be taken in the busses.

11th August 1917.

Lieut.Colonel,
A.A. & Q.M.G.,
41st Division.

War Diary

EMBUSSING TABLE.

Date.	Convoy.	No. of Busses.	Accommodation.	Units.	Time of Arrival.	Place.
12th.	A.	25	625	"A" Battalion.) 123rd Machine GunCoy.) Bde.	9.30.a.m.	Head of Convoy will be at K.2.h.65.60. facing North.
	B.	25	625	"B" Battalion.) 123rd H. M. Batty.) Bde.	10.0.a.m.	do.
	C.	25	625	"C" Battalion.) 123rd Bde. H.Q.) Bde.	10.30.a.m.	do.
	D.	25	625	"D" Battalion. "	11.0.a.m.	do.
13th.	A.	10	250.	228th Field Company.	5.15.p.m.	do.
	A.	25.	625.	"A" Battalion. 122nd Bde. 233rd Field Coy. 123rd M.G.Coy.	10.0.a.m.	do.
14th.	B.	25	625.	"B" Battn. 122nd Bde. ½ Coy. 19th Middx.	10.30.a.m.	do.
	C.	25	625.	"C" Battn. 122nd Bde. 237th Field Coy. 50 details.R.A.M.C.	11.0.a.m.	do.
	D.	25.	625.	"D" Battn.122nd Bde. ½ Coy. 19th Middx. 122nd Bde. H.Q. 50 details R.A.M.C.	11.30.a.m.	do.

Date.	Convoy.	No. of Busses.	Accommodation.	Units.	Time of Arrival.	Place.
	A.	25	625	"A" Battn. 124th Inf. Bde. 1 Coy. 19th Middlesex. H.Q. 19th Middlesex.	5.0.p.m.	Head of Convoy will be at N.2.c.65.60. facing N.
	B.	25.	625	"B" Battn. 124th Inf. Bde. 1 Coy. 19th Middlesex.	5.30.p.m.	do
15th.	C.	25	625	"C" Battn. 124th Inf. Bde. 1 Coy. 19th Middlesex. 20 Details R.A.M.C.	6.0.p.m.	do
	D.	25	625	"D" Battn. 124th Inf. Bde. 124th Bde. Headquarters. 124th Machine Gun Coy. 80. details R.A.M.C.	6.30.p.m.	do

ADMINISTRATIVE INSTRUCTIONS REFERENCE 41st DIVISION ORDER
NO. 152 of 11th AUGUST 1917.

41st Division No. Q.64/185/1.

I. SUPPLIES.

12th instant.

125nd Infantry Brigade, No.3 Coy. Divisional Train will draw from BRULOOZE as normally - march independently of 123rd Brigade to new area and will deliver rations on arrival.
122nd and 124th Brigades as at present.

13th instant.

123rd Infantry Brigade Rations; drawn by lorry from BRULOOZE and delivered to a Refilling Point to be selected by O.C. Divisional Train in new 123rd Infantry Brigade area.
122nd and 124th Brigades as at present.

14th instant.

122nd Infantry Brigade, No.2 Coy, Divisional Train, repeats procedure carried out by No.3 Coy. on 12th instant.
123rd Brigade. as on 13th instant.
124th Brigade. as at present.

15th instant.

Railhead changes to CAESTRE.

No.2, 3, & 4 Companies Divisional Train draw from new Railhead.
No.4 Company will move independently of the 124th Inf. Brigade.

II BAGGAGE.

Baggage Wagons will join their Units by 5.0.p.m. on the day before the Unit moves.

III. HANDING OVER.

i. The following will be handed over to incoming units :-

Article.	Where Handed Over.
Boots, Gum, Thigh.	Those held by Units in situ. D.A.D.O.S. to D.A.D.O.S., 39th Divn.
Yukon Packs.	in situ.
Pack Saddlery.	Transport Lines.
Petrol Tins.	1. Those held by Units - in situ. 2. Divl.Reserve held by Divl.Train to 39th Divisional Train. 3. Those at NORFOLK BRIDGE in situ

Article	Where handed over
Hot Food Containers	Under Brigade arrangements.
Trench Stores	in situ

ii. Certificates will be taken from incoming units that camps, wagon lines, etc, are taken over in a clean and staisfactory condition. A guard must be left on all camps till arrival of relieving unit, if no unit takes over camp Area Commandant concerned must be given 12 hours notice.

iii. Copies of all handing over receipts will be forwarded Divisional Headquarters.

iv. Brigades will ensure that all information with regard to ammunition and supply dumps - their positions and contents - is handed over to the incoming Brigade. In this connection most particular attention must be given to S.O.S. cartridges illuminating.

IV. **BILLETING.**

A billeting schedule showing allotment of accomodation in the new area is attached.

V. **POLICE.**

A.P.M. will detail a proportion of M.M.P. to accompany Brigade Transport in all moves, to assist in maintaining march discipline.

VI. **MOBILE VETERINARY SECTION.**

No. 52 Mobile Veterinary Section will move to billets in new area on 14th instant after relief.

August 11th 1917.

Lieut Colonel,
A.A. & Q.M.G.
41st Division.

Copies to :-
- 122nd Brigade.
- 123rd Brigade.
- 124th Brigade.
- 19th Middlesex.
- C.R.A.
- C.R.E.
- Divisional Train.
- S.S.O.
- A.D.M.S.
- " G ".
- 39th Divn. Q.
- Area Com. BOESCHEPE.
- O.C.Baths.
- War Diary.
- D.A.D.V.S.
- D.A.D.O.S.
- Signals.
- Camp Commandant.
- D.M.G.O.
- A.P.M.
- 238th M.Gun Co.
- 238th Employ.Co.
- Salvage Officer.
- Xth Corps Q.
- Area Commdt Westoutre.
- Area Commdt LA CLYTTE.
- Gas Officer.
- Spare (5).

BILLETING SCHEDULE.

Areas are allotted to Groups as follows :-
in accordance with attached Maps (Sheet 27.S.E. 1/20,000.)

---

* 122nd Brigade Group.	A. Area.
228th Field Co.	R.32.c.2.3.
	R.32.d.0.9.
No.2 Co. Train.	R.19.d.5.2.
139th Field Ambulance.	X.2.b.3.2.
	X.2.b.0.6.
	R.32.d.9.5.
* 123rd. Brigade Group.	B. Area.
233rd Field Co.	X.10.b.5.7.
	X.4.c.4.3.
3 Co. Div Train.	X.4.a.8.6.
* 124th Brigade Group.	C Area.
237th Field Co.	Q.34.b.4.4.
	Q.35.c.4.3.
No.4.Co.Train.	Q.29.d.8.7.
140th Field Amb.	W.5.c.3.9.
Divl Headquarters.	BERTHEN.
* H.Q. R.E.	R.21.a.2.9.
* A.D.M.S.	BERTHEN.
* H.Q.Train.	METEREN.
* D.A.D.V.S.	METEREN.
* 19th Middlesex.	D. Area.
* Divl Machine G.Co.)	
* D A D O S.)	E. Area.

Maps only issued to those marked * .

41st Division No.Q.64/186/3.

AMENDMENT to 41st Divisional Administrative Order of today forwarded under this Office Q.64/186/1.

Para. 2 - SUPPLIES.

    Delete last para. and substitute "124th Brigade Group will continue to draw from BAILLEUL and Divisional Artillery from BRULOOZE as at present.

Para. 3 - TRANSPORT.

    All Lorries will be returned to S.M.T.O., Xth Corps on the evening of 21st instant, without fail.

[signature]
Major for
Lieut. Colonel,
A.A.& Q.M.G.,
41st Division.

19th August 1917.

Issued to all recipients of Q.64/186/1.

Appendix B
War Diary

41st Division No. Q/64/186/1.

SECRET.

ADMINISTRATIVE INSTRUCTIONS FOR MOVE TO
SECOND ARMY TRAINING AREA. Ref. 41st Divn. Order 156.

1. ACCOMODATION.

   (a). Staging Area.

122nd Infantry Brigade.	Area Commdt STAPLE
Brigade Headquarters.	T.10.b.8.9. LENIEPPE.
1 Battalion.	" "
1 Battalion.	LES TROIS ROIS.
1 Battalion.	ZUYTPEENE. S.W.
1 Battalion.	N.E. of EBBLINGHEM.
No.2 Co. Divl Train.	
M.G.Co.	
T.M.Btty.	Near LES TROIS ROIS.
Field Co. 228th	
140th Fld Amb.	

123rd Infantry Brigade.	Area Commandant STAPLE.
Brigade Headquarters.	STAPLE.
1 Battalion.	STAPLE N.
1 Battalion.	STAPLE and QUEDE d'OXELAERE.
1 Battalion.	STAPLE S.
1 Battalion.	U.5., 10, and 11.(LONGUE CROIX)
No.3 Co. Divl Train.	
M.G.Co.	
T.M.Btty.	STAPLE.
233rd Fld Co.	
139th Fld Amb.	

   | Pioneers. | RYCK HOUT CASTEEL |
   | | LES CINQRUES U.18, 19, 13. |

H.Q.Train.	
238th M.Gun Co.	LE HEYL U.8.d.
Divisional Headquarters.	
Mobile Vet Section.	

(2).

(b) **Final Area.**

Accommodation in WIZERNES and BOISDINGHEM areas.

WIZERNES.   Sub Area Commandant ESQUERDES (on
                                      SETQUES Road.)

Divisional Headquarters.)
H.Q.Train   )
Divisional M.Gun Co.   )   WIZERNES.
1 Battalion 123rd Bde.   )

Brigade Group 123rd Brigade.

Brigade Headquarters.)
1 Battalion   )
Machine Gun Co.   )   ESQUERDES.
T.M.Battery.   )
1 Co.Train.   )

1 Battalion.   )
228th Field Co.   )   SETQUES.
(alternative Bde H.Q.)   )

139th Fld Amb. and 233rd F.Co.   HALLINES.

1 Battalion.   QUELMES.

Pioneer Battalion.   (AUDEMTHUN
                                 (ETREHEN.

BOISDINGHEM.   (Sub-Area Commandant BOISDENGHEM).

Brigade Group 122nd.Inf.Bde.

Brigade Headquarters.)   BOISDINGHEM.
1 Battalion   )
1 Battalion   WESTBECOURT.
1 Battalion and T.M.B.   (ZUDAUSQUES.
                           (NOIR CARME
                           (ADSOIT
                           (LIHEUSE

1 Battalion and 1 Co.Train. (ACQUIN
                             (LE NOOURE
                             (LE POOVRE
                             (NORDAL

Spare.   BARBINGHEM.

M.Gun Co.   ZUTOVE

140th Fld.Amb.   LE WATTINE.

Advance Parties.   Billoting parties should report
to Area Commandants as above on day before their
units move to Area.

2. SUPPLIES.

123 and 123 Brigade Groups.

Rations for consumption on 20th instant will be carried on the man and First Line Transport.
Rations for consumption on 21st instant will be drawn by Supply Column lorries on 20th instant. Supply Sections will march empty and refill on the evening of the 20th instant at a point to be selected by O.C.Train, and notified to D.H.Q., S.M.T.O., and O.C.Supply Column direct. Rendezvous X roads WALLON CAPEL 3.p.m.

Railhead for 2 Brigade Groups changes from BAILLEUL to ST OMER on 21st instant.
The procedure for rations for consumption 22nd will be as for consumption 21st - Supply Column drawing from ST OMER and issuing on evening of 21st at a refilling point to be selected by O.C.Train in the Final Area. Rendezvous Road Junction E end WIZERNES 3.p.m.

124th Bde Group and Divisional Artillery will continue to draw from BAILLEUL as at present.

3. TRANSPORT.

(a). 14 lorries will be placed at the disposal of each Brigade for the period of the move and will report to :-

122nd Brigade at X.3.c.05.45. at 6.a.m. 20th inst.
123rd Brigade at X.15.d.55.75. " 6.a.m. 20th inst.

Brigades will arrange for guides to meet them.

The number 14 is arrived at as follows :-

```
Per Battalion    2 for packs    =  8.
 "      "        1 "  baggage   =  4
 "   Bde H.Q.  )
T.M.B. and M.G.C)               =  2.
                                  ----
                                   14.
                                  ====
```

The Trench Mortar Battery personnel will march.

(b). Baggage wagons, if not now with units, will join their units by 4.p.m. on the day previous to the move.

4. BUSSES.

About 80 busses will be at the disposal of the 122nd Infantry Brigade to help move Battalions on 21st to BOISDENGHEM ACQUIN and WESTBECOURT area.

These busses will arrive head of column cross roads LENIEPPE facing W. in 3 equal parties at 8., 8.30., and 9.a.m.

No kit, and not more than 25 men to be in any bus.

5. MEDICAL.

A.D.M.S. will arrange with Brigadiers 122nd and 123rd Brigades for necessary ambulances to follow Brigade Groups.

6. POLICE.

A.P.M. will detail a proportion M.M.P. to 122 and 123 Brigade Groups for the march and will leave a proportion with 124th Brigade.

Traffic Control personnel will march with Divisional Headquarters Transport.

7. ADMINISTRATIVE UNITS.

No. 52 Mobile Vet Section and Divisional H.Q. Transport will be attached to 123rd Infantry Brigade Group for accomodation in the Staging Area.

8. AREA STORES.

All tents, shelters, and other Area Stores will be left in the Area.

Certificates from Commanding Officers that areas have been left in a clean condition will be forwarded to Area Commandant BOESCHEPE.

Lieut Colonel,
A.A. & Q.M.G.
41st Division.

August 19th 1917.
(2.p.m.).

Copies to all recipients of 41st Divl Order No. 156
and 2 copies to 41st Supply Column.

41st Division No.Q.64/186/2.

AMENDMENT to 41st Divisional Administrative Order of today forwarded under this Office Q.64/186/1.

===

(1) ACCOMMODATION.

Units moving to LE HEYL, U.8.d. move to P. of W. Camp, V.8.d. (½-mile S. of HONDEGHEM).

19th Aug. 1917.

Captain,
D.A.A.G.,
41st Division.

Issued to all recipients of Q.64/196/1.

The following table shows numbers killed, wounded, missing, and evacuated sick during the month of August 1917 (to noon 31st).

UNIT.	OFFICERS.			OTHER RANKS.			EVACUATED
	Killed	Wounded	Missing.	Killed	Wounded	Missing.	Sick.
D.H.Qrs.	-	-	-	-	-	-	1
12th.E.Surrey.	2	3	2	26	101	147	104
13th.Hants.	1	5	1	19	57	8	101
11th.R.W.Kents.	-	-	-	20	189	54	118
18th.K.R.R.C.	-	2	-	25	119	37	53
122nd.M.G.Coy.	-	-	-	7	10	-	25
11th.Queen's.	1	1	1	34	97	109	76
10th.R.W.Kents.	-	1	2	27	141	56	45
23rd.Middlesex.	-	1	-	14	127	11	45
20th.Durham L.I.	1	1	2	21	345	55	57
123rd.M.G.Coy.	-	-	-	3	31	18	18
124th.Bde.H.Qrs.	-	-	-	1	-	-	1
10th.Queen's.	1	5	-	70	196	24	66
26th.R.Fusiliers.	4	5	-	14	122	29	115
32nd.R.Fusiliers.	2	5	-	50	79	5	56
21st.K.R.R.C.	1	5	-	18	210	26	105
124th.M.G.Coy.	-	2	-	9	5	-	20
19th.Middlesex.	-	1	-	2	41	-	19
228th.Field Coy.	-	-	-	1	6	-	8
233rd.Field Coy.	-	1	-	1	16	-	8
237th.Field Coy.	-	-	-	2	6	-	4
187th.Bde.R.A.	-	1	-	2	7	-	21
190th.Bde.R.A.	-	3	-	2	10	-	27
41st.D.A.C.	-	-	-	-	-	-	6
T.M.Batteries.	-	-	-	-	2	-	1
Divl.Train.	-	1	-	1	-	-	2
138th.Fld.Amb.	-	1	-	-	4	-	12
139th.Fld.Amb.	-	-	-	1	5	-	9
140th.Fld.Amb.	-	-	-	1	5	1	5
238th.M.G.Coy.	-	-	-	-	2	-	1
Gas School.	-	-	-	1	1	-	-
238th.Emp.Coy.	1	1	-	1	1	-	-
41st.Signals.	-	-	-	-	-	-	5
Supply Column.	-	-	-	-	-	-	2
TOTAL.	15	40	9	366	1934	587	1136

Appendix War Diary

41st. DIVISION.

STATEMENT SHOWING COURTS MARTIAL HELD DURING AUGUST 1917.

Unit.	No. of Cases.	Charge.	Sentence.
12th. E. Surrey.	3.	1 Drunkenness.	14 days F.P.No.1.
		1 Absence without leave.	Reduced to ranks.
		1 Leaving Post.	56 days F.P.1.
15th. Hants.	2.	1 Discharging firearms & wounding comrade.	56 days F.P.1.
		1 Neglecting to obey G.R.O.1661.	Reduced to rank of Sgt.
18th. K.R.R.C.	3.	1 Absence without leave.	42 days F.P.1.
		1 Absent from Front Line.	12mths I.H.L.
		1 Absent from Support Line.	42 days F.P.1.
11th. R.W.Kents.	1.	Discharging firearm.	Reduced to ranks and 14 days F.P.1.
20th. D.L.I.	5.	3. Desertion.	1. 1yr.I.H.L. 2. 2yrs I.H.L.
		2. Absence without leave.	Each 30 days F.P.1.
23rd. Middlesex.	1.	Cowardice before enemy.	3 mths F.P.1.
32nd. R.Fusiliers.	1.	Disobeying lawful command.	3 mths F.P.1.
187th. Bde. R.F.A.	1.	Neglect to prejudice of good order & Military discipline.	Reduced to ranks.
189th. Bde. R.F.A.	1.	Cowardice.	5 yrs. I.H.L.
233rd. Field Coy.	1.	Malingering.	Not Guilty.
A.S.C. attached 138th. Field Amb.	1.	Manslaughter.	Not Guilty.
41st. Divl. Train.	1.	Drunkenness.	Not Guilty.
28th. Army Bde R.F.A.	1.	Insubordinate language to Superior Officer.	56 days F.P.1.

Army Form C. 2118.

WAR DIARY
or
INTELLIGENCE SUMMARY.

(Erase heading not required.)

41st. DIVISION "A" & "Q".

September 1917.

Place	Date	Hour	Summary of Events and Information	Remarks and references to Appendices
WIZERNES.	Sept. 12th.		Administrative Instructions in connection with move from ST OMER Area to Forward Area, on September 14th.1917.	APPENDIX "A".
ZEVECOTEN.	Sept. 17th.		Administrative Instructions in connection with the attack on Sept 20th 1917.	APPENDIX "B".
ZEVECOTEN.	Sept. 22nd.		Administrative Instructions in connection with the move from Forward Area to CAESTRE Area on September 22nd. 1917.	APPENDIX "C".
CAESTRE.	Sept. 24th.		Administrative Instructions in connection with move from Caestre Area to Fourth Army Area. LA PANNE.	APPENDIX "D".
LA PANNE.	Oct. 4th.		Administrative Instructions in connection with move to Forward Area.	APPENDIX "E".
			A statement showing Courts Martial.	APPENDIX "F".
			A statement showing Casualties and Sick Wastage.	APPENDIX "G".

for Lieut.Colonel,
A.A.& Q.M.G.,
41st.Division.

Army Form C. 2118.

WAR DIARY
or
INTELLIGENCE SUMMARY.

41st. DIVISION "A" & "Q".

(Erase heading not required.)

September 1917.

Instructions regarding War Diaries and Intelligence Summaries are contained in F.S. Regs., Part II. and the Staff Manual respectively. Title pages will be prepared in manuscript.

Place	Date	Hour	Summary of Events and Information	Remarks and references to Appendices
WIZERNES.	Sept. 12th.		Administrative Instructions in connection with move from ST OMER Area to Forward Area, on September 14th. 1917.	APPENDIX "A".
ZEVECOTEN.	Sept. 17th.		Administrative Instructions in connection with the attack on Sept 20th 1917.	APPENDIX "B".
ZEVECOTEN.	Sept. 22nd.		Administrative Instructions in connection with the move from Forward Area to CAESTRE Area on September 22nd. 1917.	APPENDIX "C".
CAESTRE.	Sept. 24th.		Administrative Instructions in connection with move from Caestre Area to Fourth Army Area LA PANNE.	APPENDIX "D"
LA PANNE.	Oct. 4th.		Administrative Instructions in connection with move to Forward Area.	Appendix "E"
			A statement showing Courts Martial.	APPENDIX "F"
			A statement showing Casualties and Sick Wastage.	APPENDIX "G".

Lieut.Colonel,
A.A.&.Q.M.G.,
41st.Division.

SECRET.   41st Divn. Q./419/18.

ADMINISTRATIVE INSTRUCTIONS IN CONNECTION WITH 41st DIVISION INSTRUCTION No. 4 of 11/9/17.

1. **SUPPLIES.**

    (i). Railhead changes from ST.OMER to OUDERDOM on 16th instant.

    (ii). Supply Sections will march independently of Brigade Groups.

    (iii). On the 14th instant rations for consumption on that day will be carried on the man, horse and cooker.
    Rations for consumption on 15th and 16th instant will be issued on the afternoon of 14th and 15th respectively at Refilling Points to be selected and notified to all concerned by O.C. Divisional Train.

    (iv). Rendezvous will be dispensed with by arrangement between O.C. Train and O.C. Supply Column.

    (v). After refilling on 14th instant in WALLON CAPPEL area Divisional Supply Column will move to forward area, drawing at OUDERDOM Railhead on 15th instant and refilling in BERTHEN Area on 16th instant.

    (vi) From 17th instant inclusive rations will be drawn from Railhead by the Divisional Train two days in advance of the day of consumption.

2. **BAGGAGE.**

    Baggage wagons will join Units by 5.p.m. 13th instant.
    Lorries will report to Brigade Headquarters as follows:- Brigades will arrange for necessary guides to meet them.

    122nd.Inf.Bde.   14 Lorries.   6.a.m.   14th.inst.
    123rd.Inf.Bde.   11 Lorries.   6.a.m.   14th.inst.
    124th.Inf.Bde.   14 Lorries.   6.a.m.   14th.inst.

    All lorries will be returned to S.M.T.O. Xth Corps on the evening of the 16th instant. These lorries are to meet the requirements of Brigade Groups.

3. BILLETING.

Sept.13th. All billeting parties for billets in WALLON
CAPPEL Area to report to Area Commandant
STAPLE by noon.

Sept.14th. 124th.Bde.Group. Bde.H.Qrs.)
           2 Battns.) St.MARIE
           M.G.Coy &) CAPPEL.
           T.M.Bty.)
           1 Batt.   ZUYTPEENE.
           1 "   QUEUN d'OXELAERE.

           138th.Field Ambulance and No.4
           Company Train as arranged by
           Area Commandant.

     122nd.Bde.Group. Bde.H.Qrs.)
           1.Battn.) Le NIEPPE.
           M.G.Coy &)
           T.M.Bty.)
           1 Batt.   N.35.b.
           1 "   C.26.c.
           1 "   STAPLE.

           140th.Field Ambulance and No.2
           Company Train as arranged by
           Area Commandant.

     123rd.Bde.Group. Bde.H.Qrs.)
           1 Battn.)
           M.G.Coy. &) STAPLE.
           T.M.Bty.)
           1 Battn.   EBELINGHEM.
           1 "   STAPLE. S.

           1 Section 139th.Field Ambulance
           H.Qrs. and No.3 Company Train
           as arranged by Area Commandant.

(Route via LYNDE is optional)

     Transport of Signal Coy.   (St.MARIE CAPPEL
     to WALLON CAPPEL Area (East) (or TREDEGHEM.

Billeting parties for BERTHEN Area to report to
Area Commandant BERTHEN by noon.

Sept.15th. 124th.Bde.Group. Bde.H.Qrs. THIEUSHOUCK.
           Units as before.
     122nd. " " Bde.H.Qrs. S. of Le ROUKLOSHILLE.
           Units as before.
     123rd. " " Bde.H.Qrs. METEREN or
                    FONTAINE HOUCK.
           Units as before.

Billeting parties for RIDGEWOOD and MURRUMBIDGEE
to report to Area Commandant LA CLYTTE, and for
WESTOUTRE to Area Commandant WESTOUTRE by noon.

4. ACKNOWLEDGE.

                    Lieut.Colonel,
                    A.A.& Q.M.G.,
12th.September 1917.   41st.Division.

Issued to all recipients of 41st.Divisional Instruction No.4
dated 11th.September 1917.

41st Division No. Q/419/28.

ADDENDUM TO 41st DIVISIONAL ADMINISTRATIVE
INSTRUCTIONS IN CONNECTION WITH 41st DIVISION
INSTRUCTION No. 4. dated September 11th 1917.

3. BILLETING.

Units will be accomodated on the 16th instant as follows :

½ 122nd Inf.Bde (with M.G.C.& T.M.B.) ⎫
H.Q.and ½ 124th Inf.Bde.   ⎬ RIDGEWOOD.

H.Q. & ½ 122nd Inf.Bde.   ⎫
½ 124th Inf.Bde (with M.G.C. & T.M.B.) ⎬ MURRUMBIDGEE

With both Transports in ZEVECOTEN Area (Area Commandant
LA CLYTTE will arrange accomodation).

123rd Inf.Bde Headquarters.	(Ontario extension) ENINGHELST
1 Battalion.	ONTARIO CAMP.
1 Battalion	ALBERTA CAMP
1 Battalion.	WOOD CAMP.
Bde Tsport,M.G.C.,& T.M.B.-	ONTARIO CAMP.

Train Companies.

No. 1.	HURON CAMP.
No. 3.	Just South of HURON CA[MP]
No. 2.)	ZEVECOTEN AREA
No. 4.)	(Area Commandant LA CLYTTE will arrange accomodation).

D.A.D.O.S.	RENINGHELST.
Salvage Section.	RENINGHELST.
Bath Personnel.	CHIPPEWA.
Mob.Vet Section.	LION. Camp -

(signature)
Captain,
D. A. A. G.
41st Division.

September 14th 1917.

Issued to all recipients of 41st Divl Instruction No.4. dated
September 1917 and Area Commandant LA CLYTTE.

War Diary

SECRET.   41st.Divn.No.Q/419/21/S.

ADDENDUM AND CORREGENDA
TO ADMINISTRATIVE INSTRUCTIONS IN CONNECTION
WITH 41st.DIVISION INSTRUCTION No.4 of 11/9/17.
----

1. SUPPLIES.

   Sub para (v) is cancelled and the following substituted.

   (v.) The Supply Column will move to Forward Area on 15th instant and will draw from OUDERDOM Railhead on 16th instant refilling in BERTHEN Area on the 16th instant.

2. BAGGAGE.

   Lorries are now allotted as follows;-

   122nd.Inf.Brigade.   6 Lorries.
   123rd.   "   "   4   "
   124th.   "   "   6   "

3. BILLETING.

   Div.HQ Transport will move and be billeted in Staging Area with H.Qrs.Divisional Train.
   O.C.Divisional Train will notify CampCommandant time and place of rendezvous for march.

4. MARCH DISCIPLINE.

   In view of the large number of troops moving through the Army and Corps Area on the 14th,15th, and 16th instant, special precautions must be taken to ensure that no blocks occur, and that units adhere rigidly to the distances laid down.

5. ACKNOWLEDGE.

12th.September 1917.

                                           Lieut.Colonel.,
                                           A.A.&.Q.M.G.,
                                           41st.Division.

Issued to all recipients of 41st.Divisional Instruction No.4 dated 11th.September 1917.

SECRET.   41st Divn.Q./419/18.

ADMINISTRATIVE INSTRUCTIONS IN CONNECTION
WITH 41st DIVISION INSTRUCTION No. 4 of
11/9/17.

1. SUPPLIES.

   (i).   Railhead changes from ST.OMER to OUDERDOM on
           16th instant.

   (ii).   Supply Sections will march independently of
           Brigade Groups.

   (iii). On the 14th instant rations for consumption
           on that day will be carried on the man, horse
           and cooker.
           Rations for consumption on 15th and 16th
           instant will be issued on the afternoon of
           14th and 15th respectively at Refilling Points
           to be selected and notified to all concerned
           by O.C. Divisional Train.

   (iv).   Rendezvous will be dispensed with by
           arrangement between O.C. Train and O.C. Supply
           Column.

   (v).   After refilling on 14th instant in WALLON CAPPEL area.
           Divisional Supply Column will move to forward area,
           drawing at OUDERDOM Railhead on 15th instant
           and refilling in BERTHEN Area on 16th instant.

   (vi)   From 17th instant inclusive rations will be
           drawn from Railhead by the Divisional Train
           two days in advance of the day of consumption.

2. BAGGAGE,

           Baggage wagons will join Units by 5.p.m. 13th
           instant.
           Lorries will report to Brigade Headquarters as
           follows:- Brigades will arrange for necessary
           guides to meet them.

           122nd.Inf.Bde.   14 Lorries.   6.a.m.   14th.inst.

           123rd.Inf.Bde.   11 Lorries.   6.a.m.   14th.inst.

           124th.Inf.Bde.   14 Lorries.   6.a.m.   14th.inst.

           All lorries will be returned to S.M.T.O. Xth
           Corps on the evening of the 16th instant.
           These lorries are to meet the requirements of
           Brigade Groups.

3. **BILLETING.**

Sept.13th. All billeting parties for billets in WALLON CAPPEL Area to report to Area Commandant STAPLE by noon.

Sept.14th. 124th.Bde.Group. Bde.H.Qrs.)
　　　　　　　　　　　　　　　2 Battns.　) St.MARIE
　　　　　　　　　　　　　　　M.G.Coy &　) CAPPEL.
　　　　　　　　　　　　　　　T.M.Bty.　)
　　　　　　　　　　　　　　　1 Batt.　　　ZUTKERKE.
　　　　　　　　　　　　　　　1　"　　　　QUEUE d'OXELAERE.

　　　　　　　　　　　　　　　158th.Field Ambulance and No.4
　　　　　　　　　　　　　　　Company Train as arranged by
　　　　　　　　　　　　　　　Area Commandant.

　　　　　　122nd.Bde.Group. Bdo.H.Qrs.)
　　　　　　　　　　　　　　　1.Battn.　)
　　　　　　　　　　　　　　　M.G.Coy &) Le NIEPPE.
　　　　　　　　　　　　　　　T.M.Bty.　)
　　　　　　　　　　　　　　　1 Batt.　　　N.35.b.
　　　　　　　　　　　　　　　1　"　　　　O.26.c.
　　　　　　　　　　　　　　　1　"　　　　STAPLE.

　　　　　　　　　　　　　　　140th.Field Ambulance and No.2
　　　　　　　　　　　　　　　Company Train as arranged by
　　　　　　　　　　　　　　　Area Commandant.

　　　　　　123rd.Bde.Group. Bdo.H.Qrs.)
　　　　　　　　　　　　　　　1 Battn.　)
　　　　　　　　　　　　　　　M.G.Coy &) STAPLE.
　　　　　　　　　　　　　　　T.M.Bty.　)
　　　　　　　　　　　　　　　1 Battn.　　EBBLINGHEM.
　　　　　　　　　　　　　　　1　"　　　　STAPLE. S.

　　　　　　　　　　　　　　　1 Section 139th.Field Ambulance
　　　　　　　　　　　　　　　H.Qrs. and No.3 Company Train
　　　　　　　　　　　　　　　as arranged by Area Commandant.

(Route via LYNDE is optional)

　　　Transport of Signal Coy.　　　(St.MARIE CAPPEL
　　　to WALLON CAPPEL Area (East)　(or TREDEGHEM.

　　　Billeting parties for BERTHEN Area to report to
　　　Area Commandant BERTHEN by noon.

Sept.15th. 124th.Bde.Group. Bde.H.Qrs.　THIEUSHOUCK.
　　　　　　　　　　　　　　Units as before.
　　　　　　122nd.　"　　"　Bde.H.Qrs.　S. of Le ROUKLOSHILLE.
　　　　　　　　　　　　　　Units as before.
　　　　　　123rd.　"　　"　Bde.H.Qrs.　METEREN or
　　　　　　　　　　　　　　　　　　　　FONTAINE HOUCK.
　　　　　　　　　　　　　　Units as before.

　　　Billeting parties for RIDGEWOOD and MURRUMBIDGEE
　　　to report to Area Commandant LA CLYTTE, and for
　　　WESTOUTRE to Area Commandant WESTOUTRE by noon.

4. ACKNOWLEDGE.

　　　　　　　　　　　　　　　　　　　　　　[signature]
　　　　　　　　　　　　　　　　　　　　Lieut.Colonel,
　　　　　　　　　　　　　　　　　　　　A.A.&.Q.M.G.,
　　　　　　　　　　　　　　　　　　　　41st.Division.

12th.September 1917.

Issued to all recipients of 41st.Divisional Instructions
dated 11th.September 1917.

War Diary

41st Division No.Q/419/28.

ADDENDUM TO 41st DIVISIONAL ADMINISTRATIVE
INSTRUCTIONS IN CONNECTION WITH 41st DIVISION
INSTRUCTION No. 4. dated September 11th 1917.

3. BILLETING.

Units will be accomodated on the 16th instant as follows

½ 122nd Inf.Bde (with M.G.C.& T.M.B.)) RIDGEWOOD.
H.Q. and ½ 124th Inf.Bdo.)

H.Q. & ½ 122nd Inf.Bde.) MURRUMBIDGEE
½ 124th Inf.Bdo (with M.G.C. &. T.M.B.))

With both Transports in ZEVECOTEN Area (Area Commandant
LA CLYTTE will arrange accomodation).

123rd Inf.Bde Headquarters.	(Ontario extension)	RENINGHELST
1 Battalion.		ONTARIO CAMP.
1 Battalion		ALBERTA CAMP
1 Battalion.		WOOD CAMP.
Bde Tsport,M.G.C.,& T.M.B.-		ONTARIO CAMP

Train Companies.

No. 1.   HURON CAMP.
No. 3.   just South of HURON C.
No. 2.)   ZEVECOTEN AREA
No. 4.)   (Area Commandant LA CLYTTE
             will arrange accomodation).

D.A.D.O.S.   RENINGHELST.
Salvage Section. RENINGHELST.
Bath Personnel.   CHIPPEWA. ?
Mob.Vet Section. LION. Camps

Captain,
D. A. A. G.
41st Division.

September 14th 1917.

Issued to all recipients of 41st Divl Instruction No.4. dated
September 1917 and Area Commandant LA CLYTTE.

SECRET.   41st.Divn.No.Q/419/21/S.

ADDENDUM AND CORREGENDA
TO ADMINISTRATIVE INSTRUCTIONS IN CONNECTION
WITH 41st.DIVISION INSTRUCTION No.4 of 11/9/17.

---

1. **SUPPLIES.**

    Sub para (v) is cancelled and the following substituted.

    (v) The Supply Column will move to Forward Area on 15th instant and will draw from OUDERDOM Railhead on 16th instant refilling in BERTHEN Area on the 16th instant.

2. **BAGGAGE.**

    Lorries are now allotted as follows:-

122nd.Inf.Brigade.	6	Lorries.
123rd. " "	4	"
124th. " "	6	"

3. **BILLETING.**

    Div.HQ Transport will move and be billeted in Staging Area with H.Qrs.Divisional Train.
    O.C.Divisional Train will notify CampCommandant time and place of rendezvous for march.

4. **MARCH DISCIPLINE.**

    In view of the large number of troops moving through the Army and Corps Area on the 14th,15th, and 16th instant, special precautions must be taken to ensure that no blocks occur, and that units adhere rigidly to the distances laid down.

5. **ACKNOWLEDGE.**

                                               Lieut.Colonel.,
                                               A.A.&.Q.M.G.,
    12th.September 1917.   41st.Division.

    Issued to all recipients of 41st.Divisional Instruction No.4 dated 11th.September 1917.

S E C R E T.

41st Divn. No.Q/419/42.S.

INDEX TO

ADMINISTRATIVE INSTRUCTIONS ISSUED IN CONNECTION WITH
41st DIVISION ORDER No.166 dated 10th SEPT.1917.

1. AMMUNITION.
2. SUPPLY.
3. R. E. MATERIAL.
4. MEDICAL.
5. VETERINARY.
6. WATER SUPPLY.
7. ROADS & TRACKS.
8. TRAMWAYS.
9. PROVOST INSTRUCTIONS.
10. CLEARING THE BATTLEFIELD.
11. SURPLUS KITS.
12. DETAILS.
13. ACCOMMODATION.
14. ORDNANCE.

APPENDIX "A". (Ammunition).
APPENDIX "B". (Roads, Tracks & Tramways).
Appendix "C". (Traffic Circuits).
APPENDIX "D". (Burial Instructions).
APPENDIX "E". (Return of Details).

Lieut.Colonel,
A.A. & Q.M.G.,
41st Division.

17th September 1917.

Issued to -

122nd Infantry Bde.
123rd Infantry Brigade.
124th Infantry Brigade.
41st Divl.Artillery.
C. R. E.
41st Divl.Signal Coy.
"G".
A. D. M. S.
A. P. M.

Xth Corps "Q".
D.A.D.O.S.
D.A.D.V.S.
D.M.G.O.
21st Division.
23rd Division.
24th Division.
33rd Division.
39th Division.

19th Middlesex.
238th Machine Gun Coy.
41st Div. Train.
Divl.Burial Officer.
Divl.Tramway Officer.
Divl.Supply Column.
File.
War Diary.
Spares.

(1). S.A.A., GRENADES, and L.T.M. AMMUNITION.

(a). Divisional Dump will be at N.4.c.5.2. BARDENBRUG.

(b). Brigade Dumps will be established

    Right Brigade at CANADA STREET.

    Left Brigade at HEDGE STREET.

(c). Battalion Dumps will be formed

    Right Brigade Sector:-

    Left Brigade Sector :-   J.19.c.4.2.
                                       J.25.a.5.9.
                                       J.19.d.4.8.

Appendix "A" shows amounts allotted for operations at Divisional Dump, Brigade and Battalion Dumps.

It is hoped to be able to get up the whole of the Brigade and Battalion allotments before the Division takes over the Line.

(2). SUPPLIES.

Rations.

(a). Each man will start on Attack Day carrying the current days ration and his Iron Ration.

(b). It is not proposed to dump Barrage Rations for any Unit, but in order to save Transport on the road and movement in the assembly area, two days rations for consumption on Attack Day - 1 and Attack Day will be taken up by Units moving to area North of YPRES - COMINES CANAL on night of Attack Day - 2 days/Attack Day -1 day. Rations for Units, or portions of units, who have been holding the line previous to the preliminary assembly will be sent up evening Attack Day - 2, they should be sent up as early as possible, to clear roads and tracks leading to the front by the time movement of troops commences. To provide for the two days rations to be carried up on night Attack Day - 2/ Attack Day - 1, Divisional Train will ▸

    On 17th instant deliver rations for consumption 18th instant for the whole Division.

    On 18th instant deliver rations for consumption 19th and 20th instant for 122nd & 124th Infantry Brigades;
    and for consumption 19th instant for 123rd Infantry Brigade and Divisional Troops.

    On 19th instant deliver rations for consumption 20th instant for 123rd Infantry Brigade and Divisional Troops.

    On 20th instant deliver rations for consumption 21st instant for the whole Division.

(3). R. E. STORES.

Main Divisional Dump	VOORMEZEELE I.31.a.4.4.
Advanced Divisional Dump.	JACKSONs DUMP I.28.b.0.3.
Consolidation Stores.	J.25.a.95.95.
	J.25.a.7.2.

(4). MEDICAL.

R. A. Ps.

    Left Brigade Sector. No.1. J.19.c. 4.3.
                                  No.2. J.25.a. 3.8.

    Right Brigade Sector. No.3. I.30.b. 9.3.
                                   No.4. I.30.b. 9.3.

Advanced Collecting Posts.

    Right Brigade Sector.   CANADA STREET.

    Left Brigade Sector.   HEDGE STREET.

Collecting Post.   LARCH WOOD.

Advanced Dressing Stations.   LOCK 8.

                                      VOORMEZEELE.

Main Dressing Station. (Seriously Wounded).

                                      CHIPPEWA M.6.a.8.8.

MAIN Dressing Station. (lightly Wounded).

                                      LA CLYTTE N.7.c.4.5.

(5). V E T E R I N A R Y.
==========================

VETERINARY.

An Advanced Veterinary Aid Post will be formed at near KRUISTRAAT KOEK, H.30.c. 3.7. Mobile Veterinary Section will be at LA CLYTTE, N.7.a.8.5.

(6). W A T E R.

(A) Forward Water Cart Refilling Point VOORMEZEELE.

(B) There is no pipe line in Divisional Area.

(C) Controller of mines is driving headings and installing 10 shallow bore holes to feed two 400 gallon tanks at each of the following places:-

    MT.SORREL.   I. 30.a. 70.15.

    HEDGE STREET. I. 30.b. 4.8.

    LARCH WOOD.   I. 29.c. 1.9.
by pipe from well at I.29.c.5.3. (If pipe is broken, water can be drawn at well).

Estimated daily supply from each of these points is 1000-1500 gallons.

(D) Tanks are being installed at about I.29.a.Central, on the KNOLL ROAD, and will be kept full by the Xth Corps by Water Lorry.

(E) Petrol Tins will be available as follows, and can be drawn from S.S.O. 41st Divisional Train any time after noon 16th instant:-

For formation of Forward Dumps 500 per Brigade.	1000.
20 per Battery.	400.
D.M.G.O.	80.
To be issued to Transport to enable water to be delivered by Pack 500 for each Brigade.	1500.
Divisional Water Dump at I.29.c.1.9.	800

(F) Brigades will be responsible for getting up their own reserve supplies of water by Attack Day.

(7). R O A D S   &   T R A C K S.
===

Map "Appendix "B" ", shows all roads

and tracks in the Divisional Area.

SECRET.   41st Division No.Q/419/47.

ADDENDUM TO ADMINISTRATIVE INSTRUCTIONS ISSUED IN CONNECTION WITH 41st DIVISION ORDER No. 166 dated 10th September 1917.

(8). TRAMWAYS.

On the **afternoon of Attack** Day the Headquarters of the Trench **Tramway Officer**, and the **Tramway Base** will move to the vicinity of LARCH WOOD.

[signature]
Major for

Lieut.Colonel,
A.A. & Q.M.G.,
41st Division.

18th September 1917.

Issued to all recipients of 41st Division
No.Q/419/10.S, dated 11/9/17.

(8). TRAMWAYS.

(i). Map, Appendix "B" shows Tramway System in Divisional Area.

(ii). 2/Lt. B. M. CARPENTER, 19th Middlesex, is appointed Divisional Tramway Officer, Headquarters, VOORMEZEELE I.31.a.1.6.

All indents for trucks will be made to him.

(iii). All rolling stock will be based on VOORMEZEELE, and when not in use will be accommodated in the various sidings. All trucks will be drawn from this point, and units are responsible for returning them to VOORMEZEELE on completion of the service.

(iv). In the event of mule traction being desirable the unit concerned will provide the mules except as in para.(v).

(v). Six mules from the Field Ambulances will be provided by the A.D.M.S. for drawing stretcher trucks, and will be accommodated about I.28.b.9.0. in the Railway Cutting.
Each Infantry Brigade will detail two Transport Drivers to tend those mules. The Drivers should report at A.D.M.S. Office as soon after the receipt of these orders as is practicable.

(vi). Rolling Stock exists as follows :-

    Ordinary Trucks   71.
    Stretcher Trucks.   48. plus 10 on indent.
    Trucks fitted with
    100 gallon water
    tanks.   4.

SECRET.

41st Division No. Q/419/45S.

ADDENDUM TO ADMINISTRATIVE INSTRUCTIONS
ISSUED IN CONNECTION WITH 41st DIVISION
ORDER No. 166 DATED 10th SEPTEMBER 1917.

1. Sub-Para. "C" Traffic: add the following :-

"Ambulance Cars and all horsed transport may for the present use any road in either direction.

Lorries and Tractors must follow the Battle Traffic Circuits.

In case of bad weather it may be necessary to make Horse Transport adhere to the circuits."

Please acknowledge.

Lieut.-Colonel,
18th September, 1917. A.A. & Q.M.G., 41st Division.

(9). PROVOST INSTRUCTIONS.

A. BATTLE STRAGGLER POSTS.

(1). A Battle Straggler Post will be established at Lock 8. I.32.a.8.5. in touch with posts of Division on Right at I.32.d.8.5. -Division on Left at I.20.c.4.3.

(2). Collecting Station for Stragglers will be at VOORMEZEELE I.31.c.4.9. from where they will be sent to the Depot Battalion of their Brigade.

(3). The A.P.M. will detail 2 Policemen of whom one must be an M.M.P. to be on duty at each of the following:-
  LARCH WOOD TUNNELS.
  HEDGE STREET "
  CANADA STREET "

These Police will be responsible for constantly searching those Tunnels, and seeing that no stragglers shelter in them. They will report to the Senior Officer in the Tunnels, and be instructed by him as to who are authorised to be in the Tunnels.

B. PRISONERS OF WAR.

Divisional Prisoners of War Collecting Station will be established at KRUISSTRAAT HOEK H.36.b.1.9. whore all prisoners will be sent.

C. TRAFFIC.

(1). The traffic circuits shown on attached map "Appendix" C" will be adhered to by all wheeled traffic in the forward area, subject to following regulations:-

The SHRAPNEL CORNER -VERBRANDEN -ZILLEBEKE road is not to be used by transport on the day or night preceding and the day or night of Attack Day.

No Transport except what is absolutely necessary is to move EAST of the KRUISSTRAATHOEK -VIERSTRAAT road on those two days and nights.

Any transport that has to proceed NORTH of the CANAL during the above period is to return by the MIDDLESEX ROAD.

(2). Advanced Transport Aid Posts are established at N.6.c.90.95. (100 yards W. of DEAD DOG FARM)
H.30.d.35.23.(KRUISSTRAAT HOEK)

When any vehicle M.T. or Horse drawn breaks down, or is ditched, notice is to be sent at once to the nearer of the Advanced Aid Posts, in order that the vehicle may be removed, and the road cleared without delay.

If any vehicle has to be towed back, the A.T.A.P. will bring it back to their post, and notify the Unit concerned, who must arrange to fetch it.

(10). CLEARING THE BATTLEFIELD.

A. BURIAL OF THE DEAD.

(1). The following Cemeteries exist in the Area :-

    VOORMEZEELE.
    SPOIL BANK BRIDGE.
    LARCH WOOD.

The amount of Burial which can be done under Divisional arrangements depends largely on the outcome of operations, but a large proportion must of necessity be carried out by the fighting troops under Brigade and Battalion arrangements.

(2). 2/Lieut. E.S.L.GREAR, 23rd.Middlesex Regiment is appointed Divisional Burial Officer.
He will
- (a) issue discs, rods, forms for burial return, bags for effects to Brigades vide attached instructions.
- (b) Units will send in their Burial Returns to him as soon as possible.
- (c) Supervise burials at all recognised cemeteries.

(3). Units will carry out the attached instructions, Appendix "D" as far as practicable, special care being taken to mark the graves at the time of burying or as soon after as possible.

(4). A supply of Notice Boards will be issued to Brigades for marking sites selected for burying. Graves should be grouped together.

B. SALVAGE.

Main Divisional Dump.	LA CLYTTE.
Divisional Dumps.	RIDGEWOOD.
	VOORMEZEELE.
	LOCK 8.
	JACKSON's DUMP. I. 28.b.03.
	CANADA STREET.
	HEDGE STREET.

Units will collect to these Dumps, and clear them by returning ration vehicles, tramway, or carrying parties.

Should an advance take place, Brigades will establish advanced dumps in the captured area, and clear these by returning carrying or working parties to previously existing Divisional Dumps.

If the returning ration transport etc. is insufficient to clear Divisional Dumps, Salvage Officer will indent on Divisional Headquarters for such additional transport as is required.

(11). SURPLUS KITS.
=====================

Packs and Surplus Kits will be stored under Battalion arrangements at Battalion Transport Lines.

SECRET.   41st. Division No.Q/419/23.S.

      122nd.Infantry Brigade.   21st. Division.
      123rd.Infantry Brigade.   23rd. Division.
      124th.Infantry Brigade.   24th. Division.
      41st. Divisional Artillery.   33rd. Division.
      C.R.E.   39th. Division.
      41st.Divisional Signal Co.   19th. Middlesex.
      "G"   238th.Machine Gun Co.
      A.D.M.S.   Xth. Corps "Q".
      A. P. M.   41st. Divisional Train.
      D.M.G.O.   D.A.D.O.S.
      Divl.Burial Officer.   D.A.D.V.S.
      Divl.Tramway Officer.   File.
                                 War Diary.

                    ****

        Administrative Instructions reference 41st.Division Order No. 166 of the 10th.instant forwarded under this Office No.Q/419/20. heading No. 12. "DETAILS" para 4. for Appendix "D" read

        Appendix "E".

Appendix "E" is forwarded herewith.

Please acknowledge.

                                          Lieut. Colonel,
                                          A.A. & Q. M. G.
September 13th. 1917.   41st. Division.

(12). DETAILS.

The personnel left out under S.S.135., with any reinforcements arriving during operations will be organized by each Brigade into a Depot Battalion of 4 Companies, one Company being found from the details of each Battalion. A Senior Officer of the Brigade being placed in Command. He will be responsible for the training and administration of the details, whilst the Brigade is in the line.

Before going into the line Brigades will report to Divisional Headquarters the name of Officer Commanding Depot Battalion and the numbers of Officers and Other Ranks by Battalions who it is proposed to leave out. Officers and Other Ranks now on Courses of Instruction should be counted in the proportion of Specialists to be left out.

The Depot Battalions will be accomodated at or near the Brigade Transport Lines.

Senior Officer Commanding will render Return, Appendix "D" to Divisional Headquarters by 4.p.m. daily, and no men are to be sent to join their Units without sanction from Divisional Headquarters.

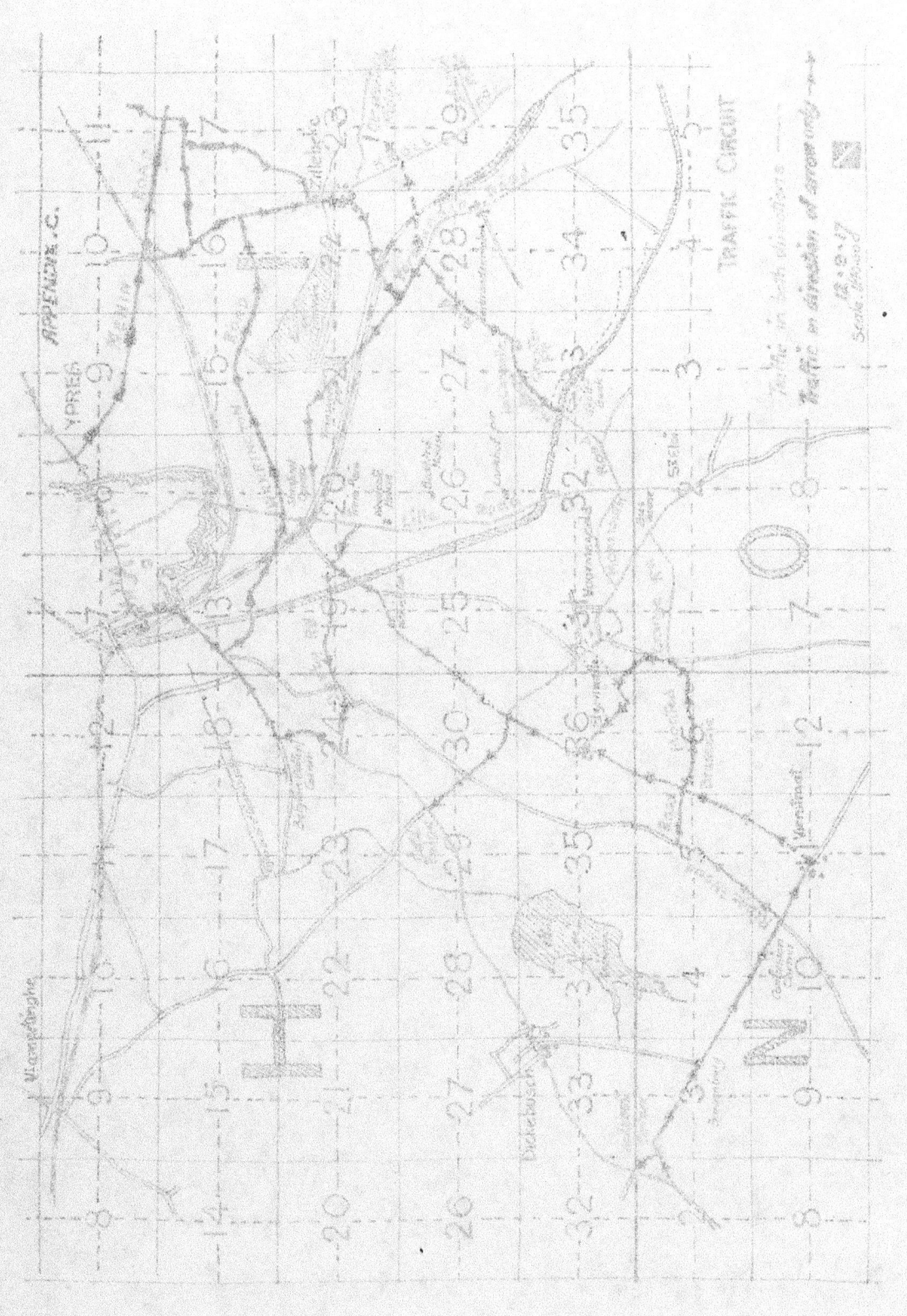

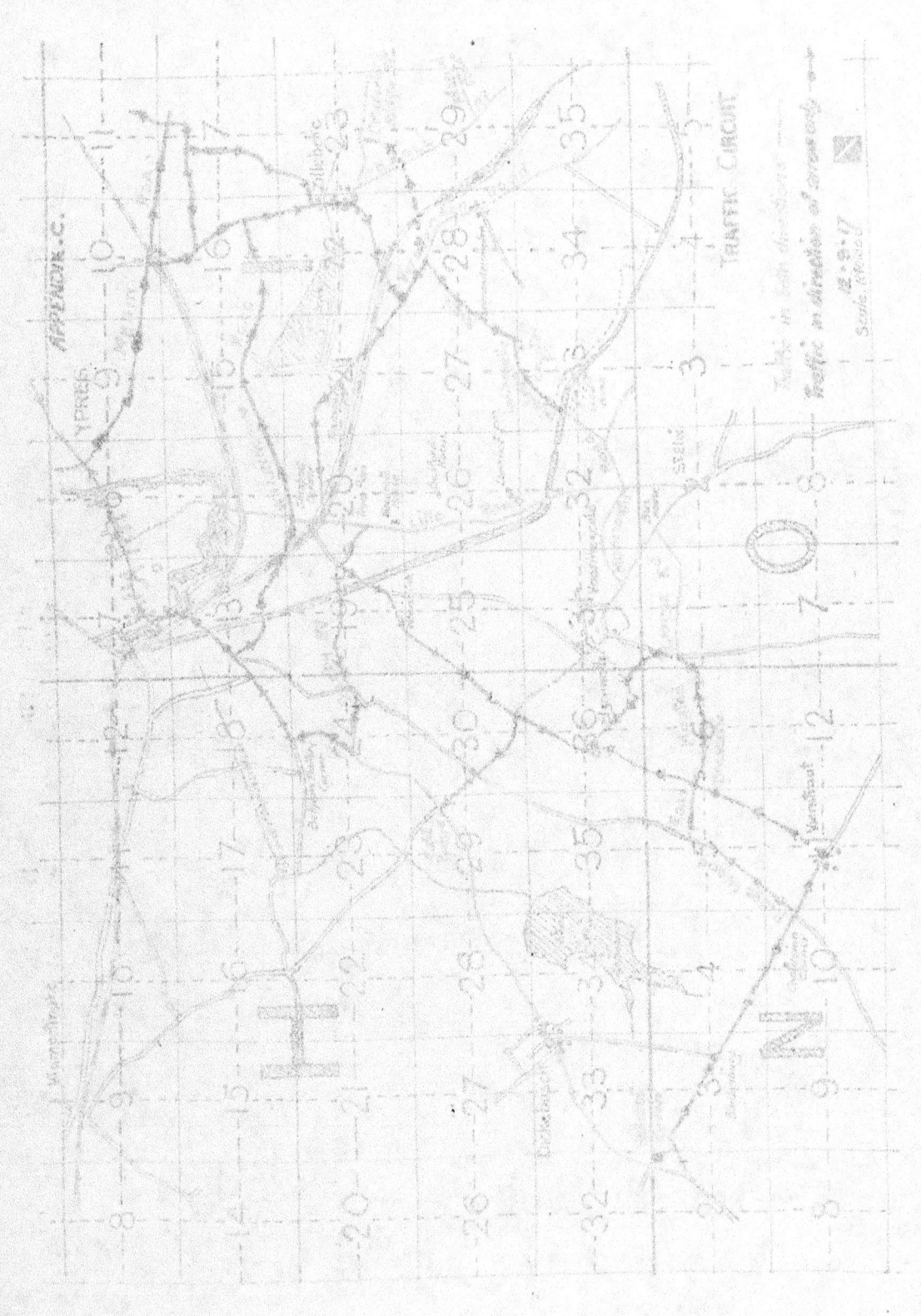

APPROXIMATE CONTENTS OF AMMUNITION DUMPS SHOWN ON REVERSE.

	S.A.A.	Mills Hand Grenades.	Mills Rifle Grenades.	Stokes. 3".	Cartridges Illuminating. 1"	Cartridges Illuminating. 1½"	S.O.S. Signals.	"P" Grenades.	Flares. Red.	Webley Pistol.
R.	150,000	3,000	1,800	1,000	1,000	500	20	50	200	500.
S.	100,000	2,500	2,500	500	1,000	1,000	20	50	200	200.
T.	50,000	1,000	600	Nil	500	Nil.	15	150	500	Nil.
V.	30,000	300	500	Nil.	250	Nil.	15	130	300	Nil.
W.	30,000	500	300	Nil.	250	Nil.	10	100	200	Nil.
X.	50,000	1,000	200.	120	400	350	20	200	400	150.
Y.	50,000	1,000	200	130	400	250	20	200	400	150.
Z.	50,000	500	100	60	150	100	Nil	Nil	Nil	Nil.

– COMMUNICATIONS – 41st DIVISION — – SECRET. – MAP. "B."

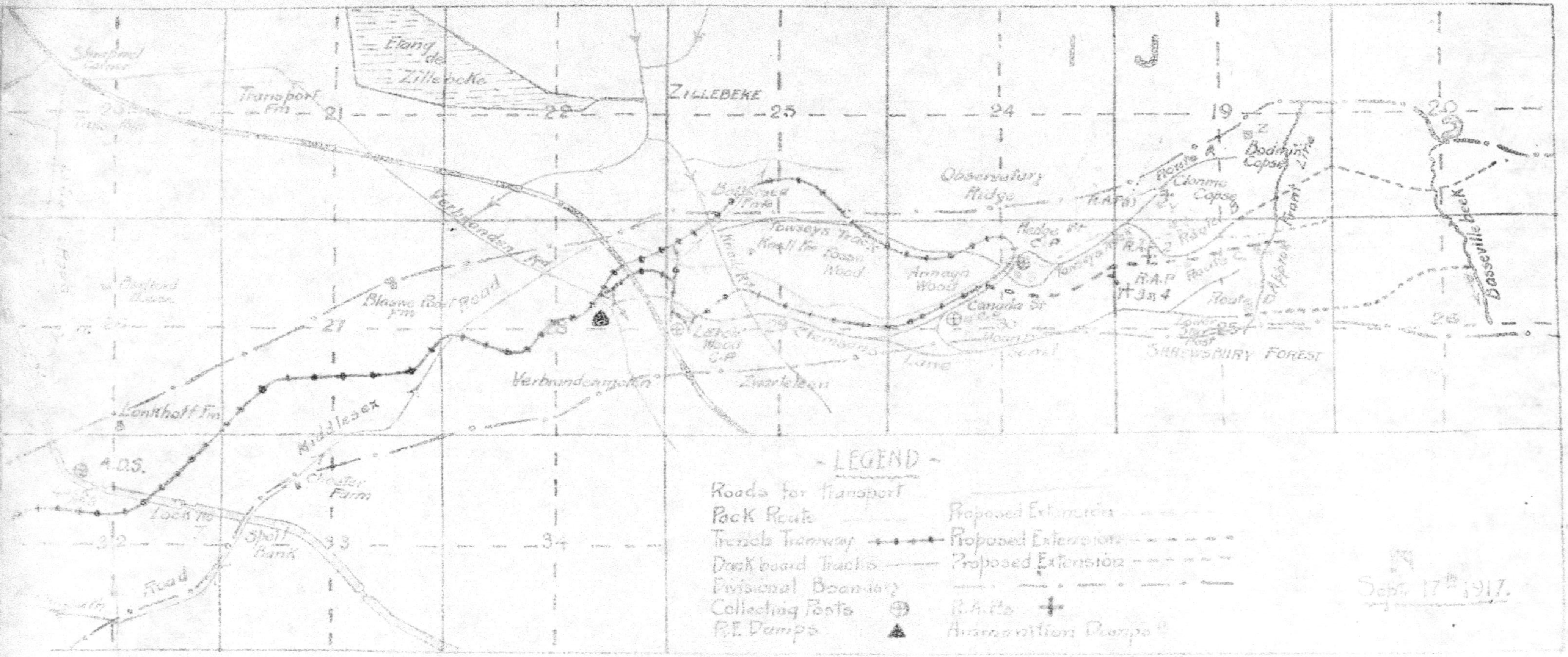

APPENDIX "D"

BURIAL INSTRUCTIONS.

(1). MARKING OF GRAVES AND EFFECTS.

1. Graves will be marked with a disc hung on a wire rod which will be stuck in the ground at the head of the grave :-

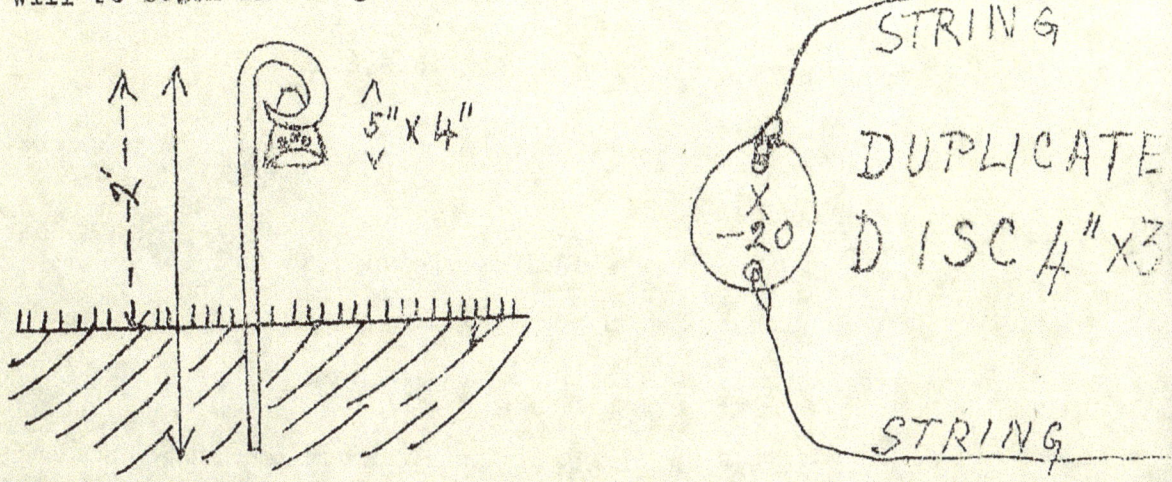

2. A number of these rods and discs will be issued to units, who will be held responsible that every disc not returned is accounted for on a roll (vide pro-forma below).
    Discs and rods will be supplied by the Divisional Burial Officer.

(2). SYSTEM OF BURIAL.

1. Burial Officers will be held responsible that burials are carried out in accordance with these instructions.

2. Burial parties must observe the following routine:-
    (a) Remove nothing from the dead until ready to place into the grave.
    (b) Bury British, French, and German separately.
    (c) Bury Officers with men except General Officers.
    (d) Collect all personal effects and the RED Identity disc and place them in a ration bag or packet and tie it up. The GREEN identity disc will be left on the man's body and buried with it.
    (e) Mark each grave (whether containing one or more bodies) with wire rod and disc.
    (f) Return sandbags containing effects of British and send them to the Divisional Burial Officer.
    (g) Mark sandbags containing effects of Germans "Xth Corps" and send them at once to the Divisional Burial Officer.

(14). ORDNANCE.

Ordnance Refilling Point G.35.a.8.5.

The following special equipment is available and can be drawn by Brigades.

    Pack Saddlery.   85 additional sets per Brigade.

    Yukon Packs.   50 per Brigade.

    Water Crates   for Pack animals 60 pairs per Brigade.

The following articles of equipment will not be taken into the line by Battalions.

    50% of Binoculars on charge.

    Any Rangefinders or telescopic rifles.

    Those Lewis Gun Parts enumerated in 41st Division No. Q.21/90/4 of 17/9/17.

(ii).

5.   The Officer in charge of a Burial Party on completion of his work will make a nominal roll in the following form :-

Xth Corps Graves No. & Map Reference.	Regtl. No.	Rank.	Name.	Regt.	Religion.
X /20	100	Pte.	T. JONES,	1st. D.L.I.	C. of E.
E.36.d.4.2.					

==

       He will sign and date the roll and <u>print</u> his own name and Regiment.

       He will send the sandbags and roll to his Divisional Burial Officer who will forward them to the Corps Burial Officer.

       The Corps Burial Officer will send

(a).   The sandbags to the Corps Salvage Officer who will be responsible for despatching such effects to the Base and obtaining receipts from the R.T.O. which will be forwarded to   Division "A".

(b).   The rolls to   Division "A".

APPENDIX "E".

RETURN OF PERSONNEL......................INFANTRY BRIGADE.

Battalion.	Details left behind by Brigades		Reinforcements who have not been out before.		Reinforcements who have been out before.		Sent up to join Units.		Remarks.
	Offrs.	O.Ranks.	Offrs.	O.Ranks.	Offrs.	O.Ranks.	Offrs.	O.Ranks.	

Date............................

O. i/c Personnel..................Inf. Brigade.

B

S[E]CRET.

41st Divn. No. Q/419/42.S.

INDEX TO

ADMINISTRATIVE INSTRUCTIONS ISSUED IN CONNECTION WITH
41st DIVISION ORDER No.166 dated 10th SEPT, 1917.

1. AMMUNITION.
2. SUPPLY.
3. R. E. MATERIAL.
4. MEDICAL.
5. VETERINARY.
6. WATER SUPPLY.
7. ROADS & TRACKS.
8. TRAMWAYS.
9. PROVOST INSTRUCTIONS.
10. CLEARING THE BATTLEFIELD.
11. SURPLUS KITS.
12. DETAILS.
13. ACCOMMODATION.
14. ORDNANCE.

APPENDIX "A". (Ammunition).
APPENDIX "B". (Roads, Tracks & Tramways).
Appendix "C". (Traffic Circuits).
APPENDIX "D". (Burial Instructions).
APPENDIX "E". (Return of Details).

Lieut.Colonel,
A.A. & Q.M.G.,
41st Division.

17th September 1917.

Issued to -

122nd Infantry Bde.	Xth Corps "Q".	19th Middlesex.
123rd Infantry Brigade.	D.A.D.O.S.	238th Machine Gun Coy.
124th Infantry Brigade.	D.A.D.V.S.	41st Div. Train.
41st Divl. Artillery.	D.M.G.O.	Divl. Burial Officer.
C. R. E.	21st Division.	Divl. Tramway Officer
41st Divl. Signal Coy.	23rd Division.	Divl. Supply Column.
"G".	24th Division.	File.
A. D. M. S.	33rd Division.	War Diary.
A. P. M.	39th Division.	Spares.

(1). S.A.A., GRENADES, and L.T.M.AMMUNITION.

(a). Divisional Dump will be at N.4.c.5.2. BARDENBRUG.

(b). Brigade Dumps will be established
        Right Brigade at CANADA STREET.
        Left Brigade at HEDGE STREET.

(c). Battalion Dumps will be formed
        Right Brigade Sector:-

        Left Brigade Sector :-   J.19.c.4.2.
                                            J.25.a.5.9.
                                            J.19.d.4.8.

Appendix "A" shows amounts allotted for operations at Divisional Dump, Brigade and Battalion Dumps.
It is hoped to be able to get up the whole of the Brigade and Battalion allotments before the Division takes over the Line.

(2). SUPPLIES.

Rations.

(a). Each man will start on Attack Day carrying the current days ration and his Iron Ration.

(b). It is not proposed to dump Barrage Rations for any Unit, but in order to save Transport on the road and movement in the assembly area, two days rations for consumption on Attack Day - 1 and Attack Day will be taken up by Units moving to area North of YPRES - COMINES CANAL on night of Attack Day - 2 days/Attack Day -1 day. Rations for Units, or portions of units, who have been holding the line previous to the preliminary assembly will be sent up evening Attack Day - 2, they should be sent up as early as possible, to clear roads and tracks leading to the front by the time movement of troops commences. To provide for the two days rations to be carried up on night Attack Day - 2/ Attack Day - 1, Divisional Train will.

    On 17th instant deliver rations for consumption 18th instant for the whole Division.

    On 18th instant deliver rations for consumption 19th and 20th instant for 122nd & 124th Infantry Brigades:
    and for consumption 19th instant for 123rd Infantry Brigade and Divisional Troops.

    On 19th instant deliver rations for consumption 20th instant for 123rd Infantry Brigade and Divisional Troops.

    On 20th instant deliver rations for consumption 21st instant for the whole Division.

(3). R. E. STORES.

Main Divisional Dump	VOORMEZEELE I.31.a.4.4.
Advanced Divisional Dump.	JACKSONs DUMP I.28.b.0.3.
Consolidation Stores.	J.25.a.95.95.
	J.25.a.7.2.

(4). MEDICAL.

R. A. Ps.

    Left Brigade Sector. No.1. J.19.c. 4.3.
                           No.2. J.25.a. 3.8.

    Right Brigade Sector. No.3. I.30.b. 9.3.
                            No.4. I.30.b. 9.3.

Advanced Collecting Posts.

    Right Brigade Sector.   CANADA STREET.

    Left Brigade Sector.   HEDGE STREET.

Collecting Post.   LARCH WOOD.

Advanced Dressing Stations.   LOCK 8.

                                      VOORMEZEELE.

Main Dressing Station. (Seriously Wounded).

                                      CHIPPEWA M.6.a.8.8.

MAIN Dressing Station. (lightly Wounded).

                                      LA CLYTTE N.7.c.4.5.

(5). V E T E R I N A R Y.

VETERINARY.

An Advanced Veterinary Aid Post will be formed at near KRUISTRAAT KOEK, H.30.c.3.7. Mobile Veterinary Section will be at LA CLYTTE, N.7.a.8.5.

(6). W A T E R.

(A) Forward Water Cart Refilling Point VOORMEZEELE.

(B) There is no pipe line in Divisional Area.

(C) Controller of mines is driving headings and installing 10 shallow bore holes to feed two 400 gallon tanks at each of the following places:-

    MT. SORREL.   I. 30.a. 70.15.

    HEDGE STREET. I. 30.b. 4.8.

    LARCH WOOD. I. 29.c. ▓. 1.9.

by pipe from well at I.29.c.5.3. (If pipe is broken, water can be drawn at well).

Estimated daily supply from each of these points is 1000-1500 gallons.

(D) Tanks are being installed at about I.29.a.Central, on the KNOLL ROAD, and will be kept full by the Xth Corps by Water Lorry.

(E) Petrol Tins will be available as follows, and can be drawn from S.S.O. 41st Divisional Train any time after noon 16th instant:-

    For formation of Forward Dumps
        500 per Brigade.   1000.

    20 per Battery.   400.

    D.M.G.O.   80.

    To be issued to Transport to enable water
    to be delivered by Pack 500 for each Brigade. 1500.

    Divisional Water Dump at I.29.c.1.9.   800

(F) Brigades will be responsible for getting up their own reserve supplies of water by Attack Day.

(7). R O A D S & T R A C K S.

Map "Appendix "B" ", shows all roads

and tracks in the Divisional Area.

SECRET. 41st Division No. Q/419/47.

ADDENDUM TO ADMINISTRATIVE INSTRUCTIONS ISSUED IN
CONNECTION WITH 41st DIVISION ORDER No. 166
dated 10th September 1917.

(8). TRAMWAYS.

On the afternoon of Attack Day the Headquarters of the Trench Tramway Officer, and the Tramway Base will move to the vicinity of LARCH WOOD.

18th September 1917.

Ericoh...
Major for

Lieut.Colonel,
A.A. & Q.M.G.,
41st Division.

Issued to all recipients of 41st Division
No. Q/419/10.S, dated 11/9/17.

(8). T R A M W A Y S.

(i).   Map, Appendix "B" shows Tramway System in Divisional Area.

(ii).   2/Lt. B. H. CARPENTER, 19th Middlesex, is appointed Divisional Tramway Officer, Headquarters, VOORMEZEELE I.31.a.1.6.

All indents for trucks will be made to him.

(iii). All rolling stock will be based on VOORMEZEELE, and when not in use will be accommodated in the various sidings. All trucks will be drawn from this point, and units are responsible for returning them to VOORMEZEELE on completion of the service.

(iv).   In the event of mule traction being desirable the unit concerned will provide the mules except as in para.(v).

(v).   Six mules from the Field Ambulances will be provided by the A.D.M.S. for drawing stretcher trucks, and will be accommodated about I.28.b.9.0. in the Railway Cutting.
Each Infantry Brigade will detail two Transport Drivers to tend these mules. The Drivers should report at A.D.M.S. Office as soon after the receipt of these orders as is practicable.

(vi).   Rolling Stock exists as follows :-

Ordinary Trucks	71.	
Stretcher Trucks.	48.	plus 10 on indent.
Trucks fitted with 100 gallon water tanks.	4.	

SECRET.

41st Division No. Q/419/45S.

ADDENDUM TO ADMINISTRATIVE INSTRUCTIONS
ISSUED IN CONNECTION WITH 41st DIVISION
ORDER No. 166 DATED 10th SEPTEMBER 1917.

1. Sub-Para. "C" Traffic: add the following :-

"Ambulance Cars and all horsed transport may for the present use any road in either direction.

Lorries and Tractors must follow the Battle Traffic Circuits.

In case of bad weather it may be necessary to make Horse Transport adhere to the circuits."

Please acknowledge.

Lieut.-Colonel,
18th September, 1917.   A.A. & Q.M.G., 41st Division.

(9). PROVOST INSTRUCTIONS.

A. **BATTLE STRAGGLER POSTS.**

(1). A Battle Straggler Post will be established at Lock 8. I.32.a.8.5. in touch with posts of Division on Right at I.32.d.8.5. -Division on Left at I. 20.c.4.3.

(2). Collecting Station for Stragglers will be at VOORMEZEELE I.31.c.4.9. from where they will be sent to the Depot Battalion of their Brigade.

(3). The A.P.M. will detail 2 Policemen of whom one must be an H.M.P. to be on duty at each of the following:-
LARCH WOOD TUNNELS.
HEDGE STREET "
CANADA STREET "

These Police will be responsible for constantly searching those Tunnels, and seeing that no stragglers shelter in them. They will report to the Senior Officer in the Tunnels, and be instructed by him as to who are authorised to be in the Tunnels.

B. **PRISONERS OF WAR.**

Divisional Prisoners of War Collecting Station will be established at KRUISSTRAAT HOEK H.36.b.1.9. whene all prisoners will be sent.

C. **TRAFFIC.**

(1). The traffic circuits shown on attached map "Appendix "C" will be adhered to by all wheeled traffic in the forward area, subject to following regulations:-

The SHRAPNEL CORNER -VERBRANDEN -ZILLEBEKE road is not to be used by transport on the day or night preceding and the day or night of Attack Day.

No Transport except what is absolutely necessary is to move EAST of the KRUISSTRAATHOEK -VIERSTRAAT road on those two days and nights.

Any transport that has to proceed NORTH of the CANAL during the above period is to return by the MIDDLESEX ROAD.

(2). Advanced Transport Aid Posts are established at N.6.c.20.95. (100 yards W. of DEAD DOG FARM)
H.30.d.35.23.(KRUISSTRAAT HOEK)

When any vehicle M.T. or Horse drawn breaks down, or is ditched, notice is to be sent at once to the nearer of the Advanced Aid Posts, in order that the vehicle may be removed, and the road cleared without delay.

If any vehicle has to be towed back, the A.T.A.P. will bring it back to their post, and notify the Unit concerned, who must arrange to fetch it.

(10). CLEARING THE BATTLEFIELD.

A. **BURIAL OF THE DEAD.**

(1). The following Cemeteries exist in the Area :-

   VOORMEZEELE.
   SPOIL BANK BRIDGE.
   LARCH WOOD.
   The amount of Burial which can be done under Divisional arrangements depends largely on the outcome of operations, but a large proportion must of necessity be carried out by the fighting troops under Brigade and Battalion arrangements.

(2). 2/Lieut. E.S.L.GREAR, 23rd.Middlesex Regiment is appointed Divisional Burial Officer.
   He will
   (a) issue discs, rods, forms for burial return, bags for effects to Brigades vide attached instructions.
   (b) Units will send in their Burial Returns to him as soon as possible.
   (c) Supervise burials at all recognised cemeteries.

(3). Units will carry out the attached instructions, Appendix "D" as far as practicable, special care being taken to mark the graves at the time of burying or as soon after as possible.

(4). A supply of Notice Boards will be issued to Brigades for marking sites selected for burying. Graves should be grouped together.

B. **SALVAGE.**

Main Divisional Dump.	LA CLYTTE.
Divisional Dumps.	RIDGEWOOD.
	VOORMEZEELE.
	LOCK 8.
	JACKSON's DUMP. I. 28.b.03.
	CANADA STREET.
	HEDGE STREET.

Units will collect to these Dumps, and clear them by returning ration vehicles, tramway, or carrying parties.

Should an advance take place, Brigades will establish advanced dumps in the captured area, and clear these by returning carrying or working parties to previously existing Divisional Dumps.

If the returning ration transport etc. is insufficient to clear Divisional Dumps, Salvage Officer will indent on Divisional Headquarters for such additional transport as is required.

(11). SURPLUS KITS.

Packs and Surplus Kits will be stored under Battalion arrangements at Battalion Transport Lines.

War Diary

SECRET.   41st. Division No.Q/419/23.S.

    122nd. Infantry Brigade.   21st. Division.
    123rd. Infantry Brigade.   23rd. Division.
    124th. Infantry Brigade.   24th. Division.
    41st. Divisional Artillery.   33rd. Division.
    C.R.E.   39th. Division.
    41st. Divisional Signal Co.   19th. Middlesex.
    "G"   238th. Machine Gun Co.
    A.D.M.S.   Xth. Corps "Q".
    A.P.M.   41st. Divisional Train.
    D.H.G.O.   D.A.D.O.S.
    Divl. Burial Officer.   D.A.D.V.S.
    Divl. Tramway Officer.   File.
                                  War Diary.

****

        Administrative Instructions reference 41st. Division Order No. 166 of the 10th. instant forwarded under this Office No.Q/419/20. heading No. 12. "DETAILS" para 4. for Appendix "D" read

        Appendix "E".

Appendix "E" is forwarded herewith.

Please acknowledge.

                                        Lieut. Colonel,
                                        A.A. & Q.M.G.
September 13th. 1917.   41st. Division.

(12). DETAILS.

The personnel left out under S.S.135., with any reinforcements arriving during operations will be organized by each Brigade into a Depot Battalion of 4 Companies, one Company being found from the details of each Battalion. A Senior Officer of the Brigade being placed in Command. He will be responsible for the training and administration of the details, whilst the Brigade is in the line.

Before going into the line Brigades will report to Divisional Headquarters the name of Officer Commanding Depot Battalion and the numbers of Officers and Other Ranks by Battalions who it is proposed to leave out. Officers and Other Ranks now on Courses of Instruction should be counted in the proportion of Specialists to be left out.

The Depot Battalions will be accomodated at or near the Brigade Transport Lines.

Senior Officer Commanding will render Return, Appendix "D" to Divisional Headquarters by 4.p.m. daily, and no men are to be sent to join their Units without sanction from Divisional Headquarters.

(14).   O R D N A N C E.
=====================================

Ordnance Refilling Point G.35.a.8.5.

The following special equipment is available and can be drawn by Brigades.

Pack Saddlery.   85 additional sets per Brigade.

Yukon Packs.   30 per Brigade.

Water Crates   for Pack animals   60 pairs per Brigade.

The following articles of equipment will not be taken into the line by Battalions.

50% of Binoculars on charge.

Any Rangefinders or telescopic rifles.

Those Lewis Gun Parts enumerated in 41st Division No. Q.21/90/4 of 17/9/17.

APPROXIMATE CONTENTS OF AMMUNITION DUMPS SHOWN ON REVERSE.

	S.A.A.	Mills Hand Grenades.	Mills Rifle Grenades.	Stokes. 3".	Cartridges Illuminating. 1".	Cartridges Illuminating. 1½".	S.O.S. Signals.	"P". Grenades.	Flares. Red.	Webley Pistol.
R.	150,000	3,000	1,800	1,000	1,000	300	20	50	200	500
S.	100,000	2,500	2,500	500	1,000	1,000	20	50	200	200
T.	60,000	1,000	600	Nil	500	Nil.	15	150	500	Nil.
V.	30,000	300	500	Nil.	250	Nil.	15	150	500	Nil.
W.	30,000	500	300	Nil.	250	Nil.	10	100	300	Nil.
X.	50,000	1,000	200	120	400	250	20	200	400	150
Y.	50,000	1,000	200	120	400	250	20	200	400	150
Z.	50,000	500	100	60	150	100	Nil	Nil	Nil	Nil

— COMMUNICATIONS — 41st DIVISION — — SECRET — MAP "B"

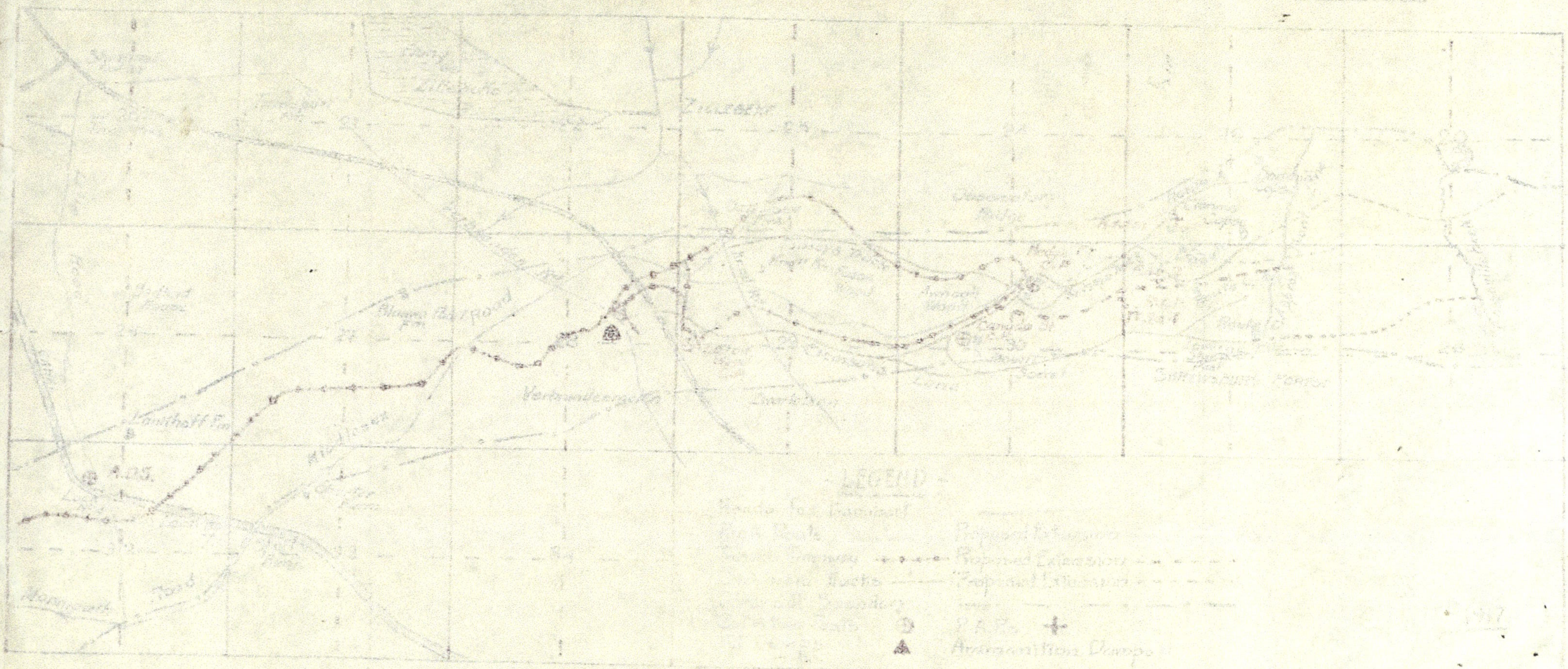

41st DIVISION.
STATEMENT SHOWING COURTS MARTIAL HELD DURING SEPTEMBER 1917.

Unit.	No. of Cases.	Charge.	Sentence.
18th K.R.R.C.	2.	2. Desertion.	Death.
11th R.W.Kent.	3.	1. Discharging firearm wounding himself.	28 Days F.P.1.
		1. Absent without Leave.	1 Year I.H.L.
		1. Desertion.	5 Years P.S.
20th Durham L.I.	1.	Absent without leave.	90 Days F.P.1.
11th Queens.	1.	Desertion.	Death commuted 10 Years I.H.L.
10th R.W.Kents.	1.	Drunkenness.	28 Days F.P.1.
26th R.Fusiliers.	1.	Absence without leave.	1 Year I.H.L.
32nd R.Fusiliers.	2.	1. Desertion.	Death commuted 10 Years I.H.L.
		1. Drunkenness & striking a soldier.	Reduced to ranks.
187th Bde.RFA.	2.	1. Civil Offence Theft.	Not Guilty.
		1. Desertion.	Death commuted 10 Years I.H.L. (suspended).
122nd M.G.Coy.	1.	Conduct to prejudice of good order and Military discipline.	21 Days F.P.2.
189th Bde.RFA.	1.	Insubordinate language to Superior Officer.	56 Days F.P.1.
1st Divl.Train.	1.	Drunkenness.	Not Guilty.

41st DIVISION.
STATEMENT SHOWING COURTS MARTIAL HELD DURING SEPTEMBER 1917.

Unit.	No. of Cases.	Charge.	Sentence.
18th K.R.R.C.	2.	2. Desertion.	Death.
11th R.W.Kent.	3.	1. Discharging firearm wounding himself.	28 Days F.P.1.
		1. Absent without Leave.	1 Year I.H.L.
		1. Desertion.	3 Years P.S.
20th Durham L.I.	1.	Absent without leave.	90 Days F.P.1.
11th Queens.	1.	Desertion.	Death commuted 10 Years I.H.L.
10th R.W.Kents.	1.	Drunkenness.	28 Days F.P.1.
26th R.Fusiliers.	1.	Absence without leave.	1 Year I.H.L.
32nd R.Fusiliers.	2.	1. Desertion.	Death commuted 10 Years I.H.L.
		1. Drunkenness & striking a soldier.	Reduced to ranks.
187th Bde.RFA.	2.	1. Civil Offence Theft.	Not Guilty.
		1. Desertion.	Death commuted 10 Years I.H.L. (suspended).
122nd M.G.Coy.	1.	Conduct to prejudice of good order and Military discipline.	21 Days F.P.2.
189th Bde.RFA.	1.	Insubordinate language to Superior Officer.	56 Days F.P.1.
41st Divl.Train.	1.	Drunkenness.	Not Guilty.

The following table shows numbers killed, wounded, missing, and evacuated sick during the month of September 1917 (to noon 30th)

Unit.	OFFICERS.			OTHER RANKS.			Evacuated Sick.
	Killed.	Wounded.	Missing.	Killed.	Wounded.	Missing.	
12th East Surreys.	7	5	1	55	190	37	40.
15th Hants.	4	6	-	41	263	49	54.
11th R.W.Kent.	2	11	-	31	193	53	49.
18th K.R.R.C.	2	5	-	55	200	30	39.
122nd M.Gun Coy.	-	3	-	6	52	5	7.
11th Queens R.W.S.	5	2	-	11	35	7	38.
10th R.W.Kent.	2	9	-	52	109	24	30.
23rd Middlesex.	2	10	-	21	200	25	41.
20th Durham L.I.	1	13	-	44	205	49	40.
123rd M.Gun Coy.	2	5	-	9	33	1	5.
10th Queens R.W.S.	2	22	3	26	199	39	42.
26th Royal Fusrs.	7	9	3	34	212	27	52.
32nd Royal Fusrs.	2	14	-	30	213	43	43.
21st K.R.R.C.	3	3	-	56	181	87	33.
124th M.Gun Coy.	2	2	-	8	29	-	12.
238th M.Gun Coy.	-	4	-	10	31	-	4.
19th Middlesex.	1	2	-	4	61	3	2.
228th Field Coy.	-	1	-	-	17	-	5.
233rd Field Coy.	-	-	-	4	8	-	2.
237th Field Coy.	-	-	-	4	4	-	3.
Signal Coy.	-	1	-	-	17	-	4.
138th Field Amb.	-	-	-	1	1	1	10.
139th Field Amb.	-	-	-	-	12	-	6.
140th Field Amb.	-	3	-	5	45	-	5.
182th Bde.R.F.A.	-	5	-	14	36	-	20.
199th Bde.R.F.A.	-	1	-	-	4	-	17.
Div.Amm.Colm.	-	-	-	-	-	-	1.
Trinity.	-	-	-	-	-	-	2.
258th Emply.Co.	-	-	-	1	1	-	2.
Divisional Train.	-	-	-	-	-	-	6.
Div.Headquarters.	-	-	-	1	1	-	1.
Artillery H.Qrs.	-	1	-	-	-	-	1.
Totals	42.	136.	7.	474.	2468.	582.	611.

The following table shows numbers killed, wounded, missing, and evacuated sick during the month of September 1917 (to noon 30th)

Unit.	OFFICERS.			OTHER RANKS.			Evacuated Sick.
	Killed.	Wounded.	Missing.	Killed.	Wounded.	Missing.	
...h East Surreys.	7	5	1	55	190	57	40.
...h Hants.	4	6	—	41	253	42	54.
...h R...Kent.	2	11	—	31	195	53	49.
...h R.F.K.C.	2	5	—	55	200	30	39.
...nd M.Gun Coy.	1	3	—	6	32	3	7.
...h Queens R...S.	—	8	—	11	35	7	38.
...h R...Kent.	5	9	—	32	109	24	30.
...d Middlesex.	2	10	—	21	200	25	41.
...h Durham L.I.	2	13	—	44	205	49	40.
...rd M.Gun Coy.	1	—	—	9	33	1	5.
...h Queens R...S.	2	5	—	26	179	39	42.
...th Royal Fusrs.	7	22	3	34	212	97	52.
...rd Royal Fusrs.	2	9	3	30	213	43	43.
...t R.K.C.	3	14	—	36	161	87	33.
...th M.Gun Coy.	2	3	—	8	29	—	12.
...th M.Gun Coy.	1	2	—	10	31	—	4.
...h Middlesex.	—	4	—	4	61	3	2.
...th Field Coy.	1	2	—	1	17	—	5.
...th Field Coy.	—	—	—	4	8	—	2.
...rd Field Coy.	—	—	—	—	4	—	3.
...nal Coy.	—	1	—	1	17	1	4.
...th Field Amb.	—	—	—	1	1	—	10.
...th Field Amb.	—	—	—	—	12	—	6.
...th Field Amb.	—	3	—	5	45	—	3.
...th Rde.A.F.A.	—	5	—	14	26	—	20.
...th Ide.R.F.A.	—	1	—	—	4	—	17.
...l.Amm.Col'n.	—	—	—	—	—	—	1.
...Rty.	—	—	—	—	—	—	2.
...th Emploi.Co.	—	1	—	1	—	—	2.
...isional Train.	—	—	—	1	3	—	6.
...l.Headquarters	—	—	—	1	—	—	1.
...illery H.Qrs.	—	1	—	1	3	—	1.
Totals	42.	138.	7.	464.	2468.	558.	611.

APPENDIX "D"

BURIAL INSTRUCTIONS.

(1). **MARKING OF GRAVES AND EFFECTS.**

1. Graves will be marked with a disc hung on a wire rod which will be stuck in the ground at the head of the grave :-

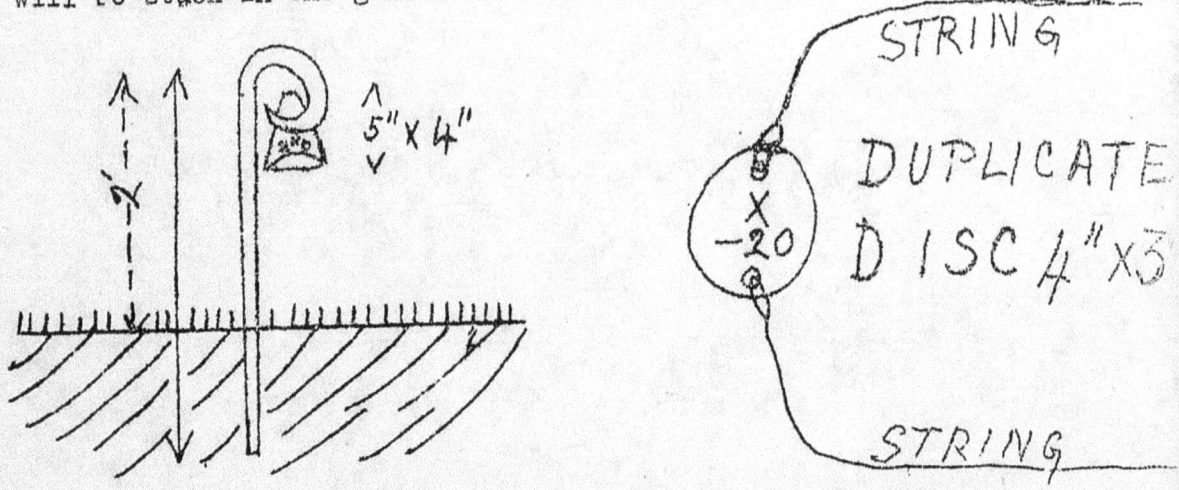

2. A number of these rods and discs will be issued to units, who will be held responsible that every disc not returned is accounted for on a roll (vide pro-forma below).

Discs and rods will be supplied by the Divisional Burial Officer.

(2). **SYSTEM OF BURIAL.**

1. Burial Officers will be held responsible that burials are carried out in accordance with these instructions.

2. Burial parties must observe the following routine:-
 (a) Remove nothing from the dead until ready to place into the grave.
 (b) Bury British, French, and German separately.
 (c) Bury Officers with men except General Officers.
 (d) Collect all personal effects and the RED Identity disc and place them in a ration bag or packet and tie it up. The GREEN identity disc will be left on the man's body and buried with it.
 (e) Mark each grave (whether containing one or more bodies) with wire rod and disc.
 (f) Return sandbags containing effects of British and send them to the Divisional Burial Officer.
 (g) Mark sandbags containing effects of Germans "Xth Corps" and send them at once to the Divisional Burial Officer.

(11).

3. The Officer in charge of a Burial Party on completion of his work will make a nominal roll in the following form :-

Xth Corps Graves No. & Map Reference.	Regtl. No.	Rank.	Name.	Regt.	Religion.
X./20 E.36.d.4.2.	100	Pte.	T. JONES,	1st. D.L.I.	C. of E.

He will sign and date the roll and <u>print</u> his own name and Regiment.

He will send the sandbags and roll to his Divisional Burial Officer who will forward them to the Corps Burial Officer.

The Corps Burial Officer will send

(a). The sandbags to the Corps Salvage Officer who will be responsible for despatching such effects to the Base and obtaining receipts from the R.T.O. which will be forwarded to Division "A".

(b). The rolls to Division "A".

APPENDIX "E".

RETURN OF PERSONNEL.................INFANTRY BRIGADE.

Battalion.	Details left behind by Brigades		Reinforcements who have not been out before.		Reinforcements who have been out before.		Sent up to join Units.		Remarks.
	Offrs.	O.Ranks.	Offrs.	O.Ranks.	Offrs.	O.Ranks.	Offrs.	O.Ranks.	

O. i/c Personnel................Inf.Brigade.

Date................

SECRET.      41st Divn. No.Q.64/187/1.

ADMINISTRATIVE INSTRUCTIONS IN CONNECTION WITH 41st DIVISION ORDER No. 175.

I. **MOVE.**

The Division less R.A., R.E., Pioneer Battalion, 2 M.G.Coy No.1 Company Divisional Train, and 2 Field Ambulances will move to the CAESTRE area on 23rd instant.

Units will entrain as follows :-

Entraining Station.	Time.	Unit.		No. allowed.
OUDERDOM.	9.0.a.m.	D.H.Q. & Divl. Observers.		110
		A.P.M.		100
		Salvage Coy.		40
		Details 122.Bde.		360
		" 123.Bde.		660
		" 124.Bde.		730
OUDERDOM.	4.0.p.m.	123rd. Brigade. (less M.G.C.)		1400
		124.Bde.(H.Q.		28.
		(Signal Coy.		103.
		(M.G.Coy.		83
		(10.Queens.		181
		(26th R.F.		181
				1976.
OUDERDOM.	6.30.p.m.	124.Bde.(T.M.B.		41
		(32nd.R.F.		185
		(21st K.R.R.		183
		122.Bde.		1400
		132 Field Ambulance.		180

In all cases Units will report to R.T.O. OUDERDOM one hour before scheduled time of departure of the Train (shown above).

Personnel equipment and packs will be carried on the man except as detailed in para.II - Baggage. No other Baggage whatsoever may be taken in these trains.

Entrainment will be directed by the D.A.Q.M.G.

Detrainment will be directed by the D.A.A.G.

2. BAGGAGE.

Baggage Wagons will report to Units by 6.p.m. 23rd inst.

6 Lorries will report at each Brigade Transport Lines at 8.a.m. 23rd inst.- these must also be used to carry Packs of Casualties which have not yet been disposed of.

3. SUPPLIES.

RAILHEAD will change to CAESTRE on 24th inst.

The Supply Column will draw from OUDERDOM on 23rd inst. and will issue to the Divisional Train in the new area on the evening of 23rd inst. at Refilling Points to be selected and notified to all concerned by the O.C. Divisional Train.

Supplies will be drawn from CAESTRE on 24th inst. by Horse Transport.

4. TRANSPORT.

Divisional Train less No. 1 Company and first Line Transport of Units will proceed to CAESTRE Area by road, in accordance with attached March Table.

Transport will be met at GODEWAERSVELDE by a representative of Divisional Headquarters "Q" who will direct to respective billeting areas.

A distance of 200 yards will in all cases be maintained between the Transport of each Unit.

The A. P. M. will send a proportion of Mounted Policemen with the transport of each Brigade Group, to assist in maintaining march discipline.

5. HANDING OVER.

Brigades will hand over to relieving Brigades all possible information re. Ammunition and Ration Dumps, Water and Tramway Services etc.

The following articles will also be handed over :-

Petrol Tins.

    With Brigades & Units – to Relieving Unit. Total Available.

    At Divisional Dump LARCHWOOD, under
    Lieutenant CARPENTER.   "   "

    Held by S.S.O.   "   "

Hot Food Containers held by Units.   "   "

                  held by D.A.D.O.S. – to
                  D.A.D.O.S. 39th Division.   53

Yukon Packs. will be retained by Units.

Packsaddlery.   ) Will be handed in to D.A.D.O.S.
) 41st Division before leaving area.
Water Tin Crates.)

    WATER CARTS.   Will be handed over to O.C. Xth
                              Corps Reinforcement Camp ABEELE
                              Station R.2.a.9.8. on 24th inst.
                              under arrangements to be made by
                              C.R.A.

6. BILLETING.

Billeting parties will travel by the 9.0.a.m. train and must be supplied from Brigade Details. Particulars as to Billeting Areas will be forwarded later.

7. DETAILS.

Details will proceed as laid down in para.1. Any surplus to the numbers therein shown will march with the first line transport.

[signature]
Major

Lieut.Colonel,
A.A. & Q.M.G.
41st Division.

22nd September 1917.

MARCH TABLE.

DIVISIONAL TRANSPORT.

To accompany No.Q.64/187/1. 22nd Sept,1917.

UNIT.	FROM.	TO.	STARTING POINT.	TIMES.	ROUTE.
123rd I.Bde Group. Divisional H.Q.Transport 41st Divl.Signal Coy.R.E.	ZEVECOTEN.	CAESTRE AREA.	ZEVECOTEN Road Junc.	9.a.m.	RENINGHELST
1st Line Transport 123rd I.B.	LION CAMP.	"	G.34.d.8.3.	9.15 a.m.	Cross roads 300 yards S. of ABEELE STATION
124th Inf.Bde Group. 1st Line Transport 124th.I.B.	N.1.a.7.3.	"	"	9.45 a.m.	Junction of BOESCHEPE ABEELE & BOESCHEPE GODEWAERSVELDE roads -GODEWAERSVELDE.
122nd Inf.Bde Group. 1st Line Transport 122nd.I.B.	N.1.d.5.6.	"	"	10.25 a.m.	
Divisional Train Group. Divisional Train.	N,1.a. and M.11.a.	"	"	10.55.a.m.	"
139th Field Ambulance.	LA CLYTTE.	"	"	11.15.a.m.	
No.52 M.V.S.	LA CLYTTE.	"	"	11.25.a.m.	

NOTE :- 200 yards interval to be maintained between Transport of Units, and Train Coys. There will be a halt of ten minutes at ten minutes to each clock hour.

41st Divn.No.Q.64/187/1.
==========================

Copy No. 1. 122nd Infantry Brigade.
2. 123rd Infantry Brigade.
3. 124th Infantry Brigade.
4. Transport Officer.122nd.Inf.Bde.
5. Transport Officer.123rd.Inf.Bde.
6. Transport Officer.124th.Inf.Bde.
7. 238th Machine Gun Coy.
8. 19th Middlesex.
9. C. R. A.
10. C. R. E.
11. A. D. M. S.
12. D. A. D. V. S.
13. Divisional Train.
14. D. A. D. O. S.
15. A. P. M.
16. Camp Commandant.
17. Salvage Officer.
18. D. M. G. O.
19. 39th Division "Q".
20. N.C.O. i/c Divl.Post Office.
21. S. S. O.
22. 41st Divl.Signal Coy.
23. "G".
24. Xth Corps "Q".
25. O.C. Divl. Baths.
26. Gas Officer.
27. Employment Company (Divl).

28. Forward Area Commandant. LA CLYTTE.
29. File.
30.)
31.)Spares.
32.)

SECRET.   41st Divn. No.Q.64/187/1.
==========   ================================

ADMINISTRATIVE INSTRUCTIONS IN CONNECTION
WITH 41st DIVISION ORDER No. 175.

I. MOVE.

    The Division less R.A., R.E., Pioneer Battalion, 2 M.G.Coys
No.1 Company Divisional Train, and 2 Field Ambulances
will move to the CAESTRE area on 23rd instant.

    Units will entrain as follows :-

Entraining Station.	Time.	Unit.	No.allowed.
OUDERDOM.	9.0.a.m.	D.H.Q. & Divl. Observers.	110
		A.P.M.	100
		Salvage Coy.	40
		Details 122.Bde.	360
		" 123.Bde.	660
		" 124.Bde.	730
OUDERDOM.	4.0.p.m.	123rd. Brigade. (less M.G.C.)	1400
		124.Bde.(H.Q.	28.
		(Signal Coy.	103.
		(M.G.Coy.	83
		(10.Queens.	181
		(26th R.F.	181
			1976.
OUDERDOM.	6.30.p.m.	124.Bde.(T.M.B.	41
		(32nd.R.F.	185
		(21st K.R.R.	183
		122.Bde.	1400
		132 Field Ambulance.	180

In all cases Units will report to R.T.O. OUDERDOM one
hour before scheduled time of departure of the Train
(shown above).

Personnel equipment and packs will be carried on the man
except as detailed in para.II - Baggage. No other
Baggage whatsoever may be taken in these trains.

Entrainment will be directed by the D.A.Q.M.G.

Detrainment will be directed by the D.A.A.G.

2. BAGGAGE.

Baggage Wagons will report to Units by 6.p.m. 23rd inst.

6 Lorries will report at each Brigade Transport Lines at 8.a.m. 23rd inst.-these must also be used to carry Packs of Casualties which have not yet been disposed of.

3. SUPPLIES.

RAILHEAD will change to CAESTRE on 24th inst.

The Supply Column will draw from OUDERDOM on 23rd inst. and will issue to the Divisional Train in the new area on the evening of 23rd inst. at Refilling Points to be selected and notified to all concerned by the O.C. Divisional Train.

Supplies will be drawn from CAESTRE on 24th inst. by Horse Transport.

4. TRANSPORT.

Divisional Train less No. 1 Company and first Line Transport of Units will proceed to CAESTRE Area by road, in accordance with attached March Table.

Transport will be met at GODEWAERSVELDE by a representative of Divisional Headquarters "Q" who will direct to respective billeting areas.

A distance of 200 yards will in all cases be maintained between the Transport of each Unit.

The A. P. M. will send a proportion of Mounted Policemen with the transport of each Brigade Group, to assist in maintaining March discipline.

5. HANDING OVER.

Brigades will hand over to relieving Brigades all possible information re. Ammunition and Ration Dumps, Water and Tramway Services etc.

The following articles will also be handed over :-

Petrol Tins.

   With Brigades & Units - to Relieving Unit. Total Available.

   At Divisional Dump LARCHWOOD, under
   Lieutenant CARPENTER.   "   "

   Held by S.S.O.   "   "

Hot Food Containers held by Units.   "   "

                      held by D.A.D.O.S. - to
                      D.A.D.O.S. 39th Division.   53

Yukon Packs. will be retained by Units.

Packsaddlery.   } Will be handed in to D.A.D.O.S.
                       } 41st Division before leaving area.
Water Tin Crates. }

   WATER CARTS.   Will be handed over to O.C. Xth
                        Corps Reinforcement Camp ABEELE
                        Station R.2.a.9.8. on 24th inst.
                        under arrangements to be made by
                        C.R.A.

6. BILLETING.

Billeting parties will travel by the 9.0.a.m. train and must be supplied from Brigade Details. Particulars as to Billeting Areas will be forwarded later.

7. DETAILS.

Details will proceed as laid down in para.1. Any surplus to the numbers therein shown will march with the first line transport.

                                                       Lieut.Colonel,
                                                       A.A. & Q.M.G.
22nd September 1917.   41st Division.

MARCH TABLE.

DIVISIONAL TRANSPORT.

To accompany No.Q.64/187/1. 22nd Sept.1917.

UNIT.	FROM.	TO.	STARTING POINT.	TIMES.	ROUTE.
123rd I.Bde Group. Divisional H.Q.Transport) 41st Divl.Signal Coy.R.E.)	ZEVECOTEN.	CAESTRE AREA.	ZEVECOTEN Road Junc.	9.a.m.	RENINGHELST -
1st Line Transport 123rd I.B.	LION CAMP.	"	G.34.d.8.3.	9.15 a.m.	Cross roads 300 yards S. of ABEELE STATION -
124th Inf.Bde Group. 1st Line Transport 124th.I.B.	N.1.a.7.3.	"	"	9.45 a.m.	Junction of BOESCHEPE ABEELE & BOESCHEPE
122nd Inf.Bde Group. 1st Line Transport 122nd.I.B.	N.1.d.3.6.	"	"	10.25 a.m.	GODEWAERSVELDE roads - -GODEWAERSVELDE.
Divisional Train Group. Divisional Train.	N.1.a. and M.11.a.	"	"	10.55.a.m.	"
139th Field Ambulance.	LA CLYTTE.	"	"	11.15.a.m.	
No.52 M.V.S.	LA CLYTTE.	"	"	11.25.a.m.	

NOTE :- 200 yards interval to be maintained between Transport of Units, and Train Coys. There will be a halt of ten minutes at ten minutes to each clock hour.

41st Divn.No.Q.64/187/1.
===========================

Copy No. 1. 122nd Infantry Brigade.
      2. 123rd Infantry Brigade.
      3. 124th Infantry Brigade.
      4. Transport Officer.122nd.Inf.Bde.
      5. Transport Officer.123rd.Inf.Bde.
      6. Transport Officer.124th.Inf.Bde.
      7. 238th Machine Gun Coy.
      8. 19th Middlesex.
      9. C. R. A.
     10. C. R. E.
     11. A. D. M. S.
     12. D. A. D. V. S.
     13. Divisional Train.
     14. D. A. D. O. S.
     15. A. P. M.
     16. Camp Commandant.
     17. Salvage Officer.
     18. D. M. G. O.
     19. 39th Division "Q".
     20. N.C.O. i/c Divl.Post Office.
     21. S. S. O.
     22. 41st Divl.Signal Coy.
     23. "G".
     24. Xth Corps "Q".
     25. O.C. Divl. Baths.
     26. Gas Officer.
     27. Employment Company (Divl).

     28. Forward Area Commandant. LA CLYTTE.
     29. File.
     30.)
     31.)Spares.
     32.)

SECRET.   41st Division No.Q/420/1.

ADMINISTRATIVE INSTRUCTIONS REFERENCE 41st DIVISION WARNING ORDER No.16 DATED 24th SEPTEMBER 1917.

(1). SUPPLIES.

(a). Serial No.1.
Rations for consumption 26th will be delivered to units on 25th before transport leaves.
No. 3.Company Divisional Train will refill before marching with rations for consumption 27th instant.
Section of Divisional Supply Column to feed troops in Serial 1 will draw CAESTRE last time on 26th instant rations for consumption 28th instant, dump in New Area and draw first time ADINKERKE-OOSTHOEK on 27th for consumption 29th instant.

(b). Serial No.2.
Rations for consumption 27th will be delivered to units on 26th instant before Transport leaves.
No.2. Company Divisional Train will refill before marching 26th instant with rations for consumption 28th instant
Section of Divisional Supply Column to feed troops in Serial No.2. will draw CAESTRE last time 27th inst with rations for consumption 29th inst. dump in New Area and draw ADINKERKE-OOSTHOEK for first time on 28th instant for consumption 30th instant.

(c). Serial No.3.
Rations for consumption 28th instant will be delivered to units on 27th instant before transport leaves.
No.4.Company Divisional Train will refill before marching 27th instant with rations for consumption 29th instant.
Section of Divisional Supply Column to feed troops in Serial No.3. will draw CAESTRE for last time 28th instant with rations for consumption 30th instant and will dump on arrival in New Area drawing first time ADINKERKE-OOSTHOEK on 29th instant for consumption 1st October.

(d). A preserved ration will be issued to troops for consumption on day of embussment.

(2). BAGGAGE.

Baggage wagons will remain with units until completion of move.
6 lorries will report to each Brigade as follows :-
    122 Brigade   7.a.m. 27th inst. Bde H.Q. CAESTRE.
    123 Brigade. 7.a.m. 26th inst. Bde.H.Q. HONDEGHEM.
    124 Brigade. 7.a.m. 28th inst. Bde H.Q. BORRE.

These lorries must return to S.M.T.O. on the same day that they are detached.

/3.

(2).

(3). TRANSPORT.

Transport will move under orders of Brigadiers concerned and Officer Commanding Train as laid down in 41st Division Warning Order No.16. of 24th instant.

The hour of start should not be till after the dinner hour.

An interval of 200 yards is to be maintained between the Transport of units or Train Companies.

No.52nd Mobile Veterinary Section and Headquarters Divisional Train will march with Transport of Serial No.2. as separate units.

Motor Ambulances will move to new area in one stage under orders of A.D.M.S.

(4). ACCOMMODATION.

Details as to accommodation in new area will be issued later.

Billeting parties (on bicycles) should report to Area Commandant TETEGHAM or GHYVELDE on evening day before their units are due to arrive.

(5). POLICE.

The A.P.M. will detach a proportion of police to assist in maintaining march discipline in transport of each serial No.

(6). EMPUSSMENT.

Orders regarding embussment will be issued later.

September 24th 1917.

Lieut Colonel,
A.A.&.Q.M.G.
41st Division.

Issued to all recipients of 41st Division Warning Order No.16 and Divisional Supply Column, N.C.O. i/c Posts.

SECRET.   41st Division No.G/420/2.

INSTRUCTIONS FOR EMBUSSING in continuation
of 41st Division Administrative Instructions
reference 41st Division Warning Order No. 18.
dated 24th September 1917.

(i).   Units will embuss in accordance with the table given
         below.

(ii).   All vehicles will be numbered in CHALK - numbers painted
         on vehicles should be ignored.

(iii).   In each case vehicles numbers 1 to 84 inclusive will be
         loaded at the rate of 25 men per vehicle - from 85
         inclusive onwards at the rate of 20 men per vehicle.

(iv).   Vehicles will draw up on the road at 6 vehicles per 80 yards.

(v).   Brigades will arrange for units to be drawn up on the left
         of the road facing the direction in which the busses will
         proceed vide table, at least 15 minutes before schedule
         time for embussing, at approximately correct intervals
         to bring them opposite the busses allotted to them.

(vi).   No one will embuss until orders have been given by the
         Divisional Staff Officer directing embussing.

(vii).   Brigades will issue the necessary orders to all units
         in their convoys for the concentration on the embussing
         point - with the exception of Divisional Headquarters.

(viii). An extra vehicle will be placed between buss No.52 and
         buss No.53 on the 26th instant to convey the party to
         BRAY DUNES as detailed in 41st Division Order No.176
         para.3.

(ix).   On arrival at destination :-
         (1) Personnel will not debuss except under orders of the
             Divisional Staff Officer directing debussing.
         (2). After debussing units will form up at once if possible
             clear of the road, and will not move off until the
             busses are clear.

(x).   Embussing will be directed by the D.A.Q.M.G.
         Debussing will be directed by the D.A.A.G.

                                              Eric White
                                              Major

                                              Lieut Colonel,
                                              A.A. & Q.M.G.
September 25th 1917.   41st Division

Copies to all recipients of above order and O.C. No. 18
Aux.Bus Company.

Date.	Time of embussing.	Embussing Point.	Position of leading Bus.	Unit.	Strength.	Bus numbers allotted. all inclusive.
26th.	7.a.m.	Squa&o CAESTRE.	-	D.H.Q. H.Qrs., Sig. Coy.	400	1 - 16
26th.	7.a.m.	St Sylvester Cappell - Hazebrouck Road.	V.5.a.9.4 facing North.	19th Msex.	890.	17 - 52
				123 Bde H.Q. Sig.Section 123 T.M.B.	240.	53 - 62
				A.Battln.	784	63 - 96
				B.Battln.	645	97 - 129
				C.Battln.	582	130 - 158
				D.Battln.	517	159 - 184
				233 Fld.Co 139 Fld Amb.	450	185 - 206
27th	7.a.m.	CASSELL - CAESTRE Road.	Q.25.c.0.1 facing West.	122 Bde H.Q. Sig.Secn. 122 T.M.B. 122 M.G.C.	236.	1 - 10
				A.Battln	437	11 - 28
				B.Battln.	806	29 - 60
				C.Battln.	551	61 - 82
				D.Battln.	490	83 - 106
				228 Fld Co. 138 Fld Amb	390	107 - 126
28th	7.a.m.	HAZEBROUCK - BORRE Road.	V.24.a.4.0 facing West.	124 Bde H.Q. Sig Secn. 124 M.G.C 124 T.M.B.	233	1 - 10
				A.Battln.	813	11 - 43
				B Battln.	442	44 - 61
				C Battaln.	612	62 - 86
				D.Battln.	510	87 - 112
				237 Fld.Co. 140 Fld Amb.	410	113 - 135

SECRET.   41st Division No.Q/420/1.

ADMINISTRATIVE INSTRUCTIONS REFERENCE 41st DIVISION WARNING ORDER No.16 DATED 24th SEPTEMBER 1917.

(1). **SUPPLIES.**

  (a). *Serial No.1.*
   Rations for consumption 26th will be delivered to units on 25th before transport leaves.
   No. 3.Company Divisional Train will refill before marching with rations for consumption 27th instant.
   Section of Divisional Supply Column to feed troops in Serial 1 will draw CAESTRE last time on 26th instant rations for consumption 28th instant, dump in New Area and draw first time ADINKERKE-OOSTHOEK on 27th for consumption 29th instant.

  (b). *Serial No.2.*
   Rations for consumption 27th will be delivered to units on 26th instant before Transport leaves.
   No.2. Company Divisional Train will refill before marching 26th instant with rations for consumption 28th instant
   Section of Divisional Supply Column to feed troops in Serial No.2. will draw CAESTRE last time 27th inst with rations for consumption 29th inst. dump in New Area and draw ADINKERKE-OOSTHOEK for first time on 28th instant for consumption 30th instant.

  (c). *Serial No.3.*
   Rations for consumption 28th instant will be delivered to units on 27th instant before transport leaves.
   No.4.Company Divisional Train will refill before marching 27th instant with rations for consumption 29th instant.
   Section of Divisional Supply Column to feed troops in Serial No.3. will draw CAESTRE for last time 28th instant with rations for consumption 30th instant and will dump on arrival in New Area drawing first time ADINKERKE-OOSTHOEK on 29th instant for consumption 1st October.

  (d). A preserved ration will be issued to troops for consumption on day of embussment.

(2). **BAGGAGE.**

   Baggage wagons will remain with units until completion of move.
   6 lorries will report to each Brigade as follows :-
      122 Brigade   7.a.m. 27th inst. Bde H.Q. CAESTRE.
      123 Brigade.   7.a.m. 26th inst. Bde.H.Q. HONDEGHEM.
      124 Brigade.   7.a.m. 28th inst. Bde H.Q. BORRE.

   These lorries must return to S.M.T.O. on the same day that they are detached.

(2).

(3). TRANSPORT.

Transport will move under orders of Brigadiers concerned and Officer Commanding Train as laid down in 41st Division Warning Order No.16. of 24th instant.

The hour of start should not be till after the dinner hour.

An interval of 200 yards is to be maintained between the Transport of units or Train Companies.

No.52nd Mobile Veterinary Section and Headquarters Divisional Train will march with Transport of Serial No.2. as separate units.

Motor Ambulances will move to new area in one stage under orders of A.D.M.S.

(4). ACCOMMODATION.

Details as to accommodation in new area will be issued later.

Billeting parties (on bicycles) should report to Area Commandant TETEGHAM or GHYVELDE on evening day before their units are due to arrive.

(5). POLICE.

The A.P.M. will detach a proportion of police to assist in maintaining march discipline in transport of each serial No.

(6). EMBUSSMENT.

Orders regarding embussment will be issued later.

September 24th 1917.

Lieut Colonel,
A.A.&.Q.M.G.
41st Division.

Issued to all recipients of 41st Division Warning Order No.16 and Divisional Supply Column, N.C.O. i/c Posts.

S E C R E T.

41st Division No.G/420/2.

INSTRUCTIONS FOR EMBUSSING in continuation of 41st Division Administrative Instructions reference 41st Division Warning Order No. 16. dated 24th September 1917.

(i). Units will embuss in accordance with the table given below.

(ii). All vehicles will be numbered in CHALK - numbers painted on vehicles should be ignored.

(iii). In each case vehicles numbers 1 to 84 inclusive will be loaded at the rate of 25 men per vehicle - from 85 inclusive onwards at the rate of 20 men per vehicle.

(iv). Vehicles will draw up on the road at 6 vehicles per 80 yards.

(v). Brigades will arrange for units to be drawn up on the left of the road facing the direction in which the busses will proceed vide table, at least 15 minutes before schedule time for embussing, at approximately correct intervals to bring them opposite the busses allotted to them.

(vi). No one will embuss until orders have been given by the Divisional Staff Officer directing embussing.

(vii). Brigades will issue the necessary orders to all units in their convoys for the concentration on the embussing point - with the exception of Divisional Headquarters.

(viii). An extra vehicle will be placed between buss No.52 and buss No.53 on the 26th instant to convey the party to BRAY DUNES as detailed in 41st Division Order No.176 para.3.

(ix). On arrival at destination :-
  (1) Personnel will not debuss except under orders of the Divisional Staff Officer directing debussing.
  (2). After debussing units will form up at once if possible clear of the road, and will not move off until the busses are clear.

(x). Embussing will be directed by the D.A.Q.M.G.
Debussing will be directed by the D.A.A.G.

September 25th 1917.

Lieut Colonel,
A.A. & Q.M.G.
41st Division

Copies to all recipients of above order and O.C. No. 18 Aux.Bus Company.

Date.	Time of embussing.	Embussing Point.	Position of leading Bus.	Unit.	Strength.	Bus numbers allotted. all inclusive.
26th.	7.a.m.	Square CAESTRE.	-	D.H.Q. H.Qrs.,Sig. Coy.	400	1 - 16
				19th Msex.	890.	17 - 52
				123 Bde H.Q. Sig.Section. 125 T.M.B.	240.	53 - 62
26th.	7.a.m.	St Sylvester Cappell - Hazebrouck Road.	V.5.a.9.4 facing North.	A.Battln.	784	63 - 96
				B.Battln.	645	97 - 129
				C.Battln.	582	130 - 158
				D.Battln.	517	159 - 184
				233 Fld.Co 139 Fld Amb.	430	185 - 203
27th	7.a.m.	CASSELL - CAESTRE Road.	Q.25.c.0.1 facing West.	122 Bde H.Q. Sig.Secn. 122 T.M.B. 122 M.G.C.	236.	1 - 10
				A.Battln	437	11 - 28
				B.Battln.	606	29 - 60
				C.Battln.	551	61 - 82
				D.Battln	490	83 - 106
				228 Fld Co. 138 Fld Amb	390	107 - 126
28th	7.a.m.	HAZEBROUCK - BORRE Road.	V.24.a.4.0 facing West.	124 Bde H.Q. Sig Secn. 124 M.G.C 124 T.M.B.	233	1 - 10
				A.Battln.	813	11 - 43
				B Battln.	442	44 - 61
				C Battaln.	612	32 - 86
				D.Battln.	510	87 - 112
				237 Fld.Co. 140 Fld Amb.	410	113 - 135

WAR DIARY
or
INTELLIGENCE SUMMARY

(Erase heading not required.)

Army Form C. 2118

41st Division A & Q

Sept 15

Place	Date	Hour	Summary of Events and Information	Remarks and references to Appendices
SL IPASWICH	Sep 28		Orders to move into Reserve Area issued	Appendix A
	Sep 29, 30, 31		Divisions equipping to establishment prior to moving by rail to Italian front. A statement showing barracks & their contago is attached	Appendix B

Submitted

L. Luin Col
aa & ng
41 Divn

Secret

WAR DIARY
or
INTELLIGENCE SUMMARY
(Erase heading not required.)

41st Division   Army Form C. 2118

A & Q

Place	Date	Hour	Summary of Events and Information	Remarks and references to Appendices
ST OMER AREA	Oct 29		Orders to move into Reserve Area received	Appendix A
	Oct 30, 31		41 Division equipping prior to moving by rail to Italian front.	
			A statement showing Casualties & Sick Wastage is attached	Appendix B

Submitted
J Lewis
Lt

41st Division No. 103/1/1.

41st Division Administrative Instructions in connection
with Warning Order No. 12   dated October 28th 1917.
❋❋❋❋❋❋❋❋❋❋❋❋❋❋❋❋❋❋

1. TRANSPORT.

Transport of 124th Infantry Brigade, 237th Field Company R.E.,
138th Field Ambulance and No. 4 Company A.S.C., will move by
road to TETEGHEM area via LA PANNE and ADINKERKE on the afternoon
of the 28th instant.

124th Infantry Brigade will arrange for sufficient wagons to
remain to move offices etc of units in the trenches. These
wagons will follow as soon as possible.

On arrival at TETEGHAM they will report to Area Commandant's
office (see para. 4.) where their own billeting representatives
will meet them and guide them to their lines.

2. SUPPLIES.

Change of Railhead will be notified later.
Supply Column will draw tomorrow 29th instant from present
railhead and deliver to refilling points to be selected by
O.C.Divisional Train in TETEGHAM and GHYVELDE areas for 124th
Infantry Brigade, 237th Field Company R.E., 138th Field Ambulance,
No. 4 Company A.S.C., and 1 Section per Battery R.A. respectively.
Supply Column will probably draw for whole Division on 30th
instant. Further information regarding this will be forwarded.

3. EMBUSSING.

170 busses will be on road ZEAPANNE - ST IDASBALDE - COXYDE
BAINS after 3.p.m. 28th instant to convoy 124th Infantry Brigade
Group to TETEGHAM area. In order to facilitate embussing
all parties will report to an Officer from 41st Divisional
Headquarters at COXYDE BAINS cross roads V.6.a.9.5. who will
give them full instructions as to which busses they are to use.
Busses will proceed in convenient convoys when loaded to
UXEM, halting on the W. side and clear of the village. They
will be met at this point by their own billeting
representatives who will direct the busses to their billets.

4. BILLETING.

Billeting parties should report to Area Commandants (Infantry
to TETEGHAM, Artillery to GHYVELDE) as near to 3.p.m. as possible.
The two battalions of the 124th Infantry Brigade out of the Line
will be sent to COUDERKQUE and TETEGHEM if possible.

5. LORRIES and BLANKETS.

10 lorries will be sent to 124th Infantry Brigade Rear
Headquarters at about 4.p.m. 28th instant to convey blankets
and surplus kit to the TETEGHAM area.

(2).

6. TRENCH STORES.

All Trench Stores, Gum Boots, including those held by
D.A.D.O.S. will be handed over to relieving units.
D.A.D.O.S. will demand the necessary lorries today from
D.H.T.O.XVth Corps and dump 2nd blanket per man for units
of 124th Infantry Brigade at a convenient point at TEETGHAM.
He will send a N.C.O. forward with the blankets and he
will notify 124th Infantry Brigade position of dump.
The 124th Infantry Brigade will draw them without fail on the
29th instant.

7. ENTRAINING STRENGTHS.

All units will wire this office by 6.p.m. tonight without
fail entraining strengths to include all men detached in
this Corps Area under the following headings :-

  A. Officers.
  B. Other ranks.
  C. Riding Horses.
  D. Light Draught and Mules.
  E. Pack animals.
  F. Heavy Draught.
  G. Vehicles.(Showing whether G.S.limbered etc etc.).

Any alteration in these figures to be wired by 6.p.m. daily
until further notice.

8. Administrative Instructions with regard to the move of
other units of the Division will be issued later.

9. ACKNOWLEDGE.

        [signature] Capt.

            Lieut Colonel,
            A.A. & Q.M.G.
October 28th 1917.   41st Division.

Issued at 11.a.m.

Copies to :- File.   A.D.M.S.
    War Diary.   D.A.D.O.S.
    XV Corps Q.   D.A.D.V.S.
    41st Divn.Artillery. A.P.M.
    122nd Inf.Brigade. Divl Observation Offr.
    123rd " "   D.M.G.O.
    124th " "   42nd Divn.
    19th Middlesex   9th Division Q.
    C.R.E.   Camp Commdt.
    41st Divl Signal Co. Salvage Offr.
    41st Divl Train.   Baths Officer
    "Q".   41st Divl Supply Col
    N.C.O. i/c Posts. 41st Divl Wing.

41st Division No. 103/1/1.

41st Division Administrative Instructions in connection
with Warning Order No. 18   dated October 28th 1917.

1. TRANSPORT.

Transport of 124th Infantry Brigade, 237th Field Company R.E.,
158th Field Ambulance and No. 4 Company A.S.C., will move by
road to TETEGHEM area via LA PANNE and ADINKERKE on the afternoon
of the 28th instant.

124th Infantry Brigade will arrange for sufficient wagons to
remain to move officers etc of units in the trenches. These
wagons will follow as soon as possible.

On arrival at TETEGHEM they will report to Area Commandant's
office (see para. 4.) where their own billeting representatives
will meet them and guide them to their lines.

2. SUPPLIES.

Change of Railhead will be notified later.

Supply Column will draw tomorrow 29th instant from present
railhead and deliver to refilling points to be selected by
O.C. Divisional Train in TETEGHEM and GHYVELDE areas for 124th
Infantry Brigade, 237th Field Company R.E., 158th Field Ambulance,
No. 4 Company A.S.C., and 1 Section per Battery R.A. respectively.

Supply Column will probably draw for whole Division on 30th
instant. Further information regarding this will be forwarded.

3. EMBUSSING.

170 busses will be on road ZEAPAENE - ST IDASBALDE - COXYDE
BAINS after 3.p.m. 28th instant to convey 124th Infantry Brigade
Group to TETEGHEM area. In order to facilitate embussing
all parties will report to an Officer from 41st Divisional
Headquarters at COXYDE BAINS cross roads W.6.a.9.5. who will
give them full instructions as to which busses they are to use.
Busses will proceed in convenient convoys when loaded to
UXEM, halting on the W. side and clear of the village. They
will be met at this point by their own billeting
representatives who will direct the busses to their billets.

4. BILLETING.

Billeting parties should report to Area Commandants (Infantry
to TETEGHEM, Artillery to GHYVELDE) as near to 3.p.m. as possible.
The two battalions of the 124th Infantry Brigade out of the Line
will be sent to COUDERKQUE and TETEGHEM if possible.

5. LORRIES and BLANKETS.

10 lorries will be sent to 124th Infantry Brigade Rear
Headquarters at about 4.p.m. 28th instant to convey blankets
and surplus kit to the TETEGHEM area.

(2).

6. TRENCH STORES.

All Trench Stores, Gum Boots, including those held by D.A.D.O.S. will be handed over to relieving units. D.A.D.O.S. will demand the necessary lorries today from D.H.T.O. XVth Corps and dump 2nd Blanket per man for units of 124th Infantry Brigade at a convenient point at TETEGHAM. He will send a N.C.O. forward with the Blankets and he will notify 124th Infantry Brigade position of dump. The 124th Infantry Brigade will draw them without fail on the 29th instant.

7. ENTRAINING STRENGTHS.

All units will wire this office by 6.p.m. tonight without fail entraining strengths to include all men detached in this Corps Area under the following headings:-

     A.   Officers.
     B.   Other ranks.
     C.   Riding Horses.
     D.   Light Draught and Mules.
     E.   Pack animals.
     F.   Heavy Draught.
     G.   Vehicles.(Showing whether G.S.limbered etc etc.).

Any alteration in these figures to be wired by 6.p.m. daily until further notice.

8. Administrative Instructions with regard to the move of other units of the Division will be issued later.

9. ACKNOWLEDGE.

[signature] Capt.

                           Lieut Colonel,
                           A.A. & Q.M.G.
October 28th 1917.   41st Division.

Issued at 11.a.m.

Copies to :- File.   A.D.M.S.
         War Diary.   D.A.D.O.S.
         XV Corps Q.   D.A.D.V.S.
         41st Divn.Artillery. A.P.M.
         122nd Inf.Brigade.   Divl Observation Offr.
         123rd "   "   D.M.G.O.
         124th "   "   42nd Divn.
         19th Middlesex   9th Division Q.
         C.R.E.   Camp Commdt.
         41st Divl Signal Co. Salvage Offr.
         41st Divl Train.   Baths Officer
         "G".   41st Divl Supply Col
         N.C.O. i/c Posts.   41st Divl Wing.

41st. DIVISION.

Statement showing Casualties and Sick Evacuations during the month of October.

Unit.	Killed Officers.	Killed O.Ranks.	Wounded Officers.	Wounded O.Ranks.	Missing Off.	Missing O.R.	Evacuated Sick.
12th.E.Surrey.Regt.	-	-	-	4	-	-	13
15th.Hants Regt.	-	-	1	20	-	-	8
11th.R.W.Kent Regt.	-	-	-	2	-	-	8
18th.K.R.R.Corps.	-	-	-	-	-	-	18
122nd.M.G.Coy.	-	2	-	-	-	-	5
11th.R.W.Surrey Regt.	-	-	-	20	-	-	22
10th.R.W.Kent Regt.	-	1	-	12	-	-	13
23rd.Middlesex Regt.	-	2	1	5	-	-	10
20th.Durham L.I.	-	-	-	-	-	-	16
123rd.M.G.Coy.	-	-	-	4	-	-	3
10th.R.W.Surrey Regt.	1	5	-	11	1	-	23
26th.R.Fusiliers.	-	2	1	5	-	-	10
32nd.R.Fusiliers.	-	-	-	-	-	-	15
21st.K.R.R.Corps.	-	-	-	10	-	-	10
124th.M.G.Coy.	-	-	-	4	-	-	4
9th.Middlesex Regt.	-	2	-	10	-	-	11
87th.Brigade R.F.A.	-	10	3	24	-	-	7
80th.Brigade R.F.A.	-	15	-	32	-	-	2
D.A.C.	-	2	-	11	-	-	1
228th.Field Coy.R.E.	-	1	-	3	-	-	3
237th.Field Coy.R.E.	-	-	-	3	-	-	6
138th.Field Amb.ce.	-	-	-	-	-	-	2
139th.Field Amb.ce.	-	-	-	-	-	-	2
140th.Field Amb.ce.	-	-	-	1	-	-	1
Divisional Train.	-	-	-	-	-	-	3
41st.Signals.	-	-	-	-	-	-	2
238th.Employment Coy.	-	-	-	1	-	-	-
Divisional Headquarters.	-	-	-	-	-	-	1
41st.T.M.Btys.	-	2	-	10	-	-	-
TOTAL.	1	45	8	180	1	-	221

41st. DIVISION.

Statement showing Casualties and Sick Evacuations during the month of October.

Unit.	Killed. Officers.	Killed. O.Ranks.	Wounded. Officers.	Wounded. O.Ranks.	Missing. Off.	Missing. O.R.	Evacuated. Sick.
12th.E.Surrey Regt.	-	-	-	4	-	-	13
13th.Hants Regt.	-	-	1	20	-	-	8
11th.R.W.Kent Regt.	-	-	-	2	-	-	8
18th.K.R.R.Corps.	-	-	-	-	-	-	15
22nd.M.G.Coy.	-	2	-	1	-	-	5
11th.R.W.Surrey Regt.	-	-	-	20	-	-	22
10th.R.W.Kent Regt.	-	1	-	12	-	-	13
23rd.Middlesex Regt.	-	2	1	5	-	-	10
20th.Durham L.I.	-	-	-	4	-	-	16
23rd.M.G.Coy.	-	-	-	-	-	-	3
10th.R.W.Surrey Regt.	1	5	-	11	1	-	10
26th.R.Fusiliers.	-	2	-	5	-	-	15
32nd.R.Fusiliers.	-	-	-	-	-	-	10
21st.K.R.R.Corps.	-	-	-	1	-	-	4
24th.M.G.Coy.	-	2	-	10	-	-	11
9th.Middlesex Regt.	-	10	-	24	-	-	7
87th.Brigade R.F.A.	-	15	3	32	-	-	2
90th.Brigade R.F.A.	-	2	-	11	-	-	1
D.A.C.	-	1	-	2	-	-	3
228th.Field Coy.R.E.	-	1	-	3	-	-	6
237th.Field Coy.R.E.	-	-	-	1	-	-	2
138th.Field Amb.	-	-	-	-	-	-	2
139th.Field Amb.	-	-	-	1	-	-	1
140th.Field Amb.	-	-	-	-	-	-	3
Divisional Train.	-	-	-	-	-	-	2
41st.Signals.	-	-	-	-	-	-	1
238th.Employment Coy.	-	-	-	-	-	-	1
Divisional Headquarters.	-	-	-	-	-	-	-
41st.T.M.Btys.	-	2	-	10	-	-	-
TOTAL.	1	45	8	180	1	1	221

SECRET.

41st Divn.No.Q.64/187/5.

ADMINISTRATIVE INSTRUCTIONS
Reference 41st Division Order No.177 of 4th Oct.1917.

4th October 1917.

1. ACCOMMODATION.

On completion of relief the Division will be accommodated as shown in attached Schedule.

2. S.A.A. - GRENADES.

    Divisional Dump is at R.33.b.2.0.
    Main Brigade Dump. M.14.c.2.2.
    Additional Brigade Dump. M.20.a.9.0.

123rd Infantry Brigade will detail an officer, 1 N.C.O, and 8 men to take charge of the Divisional Dump (until arrival of Divisional Artillery) on 5th instant.

3. SUPPLIES.

Supply Railhead changes to ST.IDESBALDE (Light Railway) W.17.b.5.5. on 7th instant.

Supply Refilling Point and Fuel Dumps will be at W.17.b.5.5.

4. WATER.

There is no difficulty regarding water in this area, numerous water points and horse troughs exist.

5. ROADS & TRACKS.

The two roads OOST DUNKERQUE BAINS - NIEUPORT BAINS and OOST DUNKERQUE - M.20.d. are both fit for wheeled traffic by day as far E. as OOST DUNKERQUE - OOST DUNKERQUE BAINS Road, and by night to near Battalion H.Q. at M.19.b.1.9. and M.20.b.8.4.
There are no tracks for transport.

6. TRAMWAYS.

A map will be issued later showing Light Railways and Tramways in the Divisional Area.
It is however more convenient under present circumstances to deliver both ammunition and rations by Horse Transport.

7. MEDICAL.

    A. D. S.   X.4.c.7.2.
                  M.13.d.4.2.
    Ambulance H.Q. R.27.c.5.3.

8. R.E. STORES.

    Divisional Dump.   X.8.d.3.8.
    Advanced Dumps No.1. R.23.d.4.4.
                    No.2. M.25.c.1.9.

9. COOKING.

The Battalion in the Line use Trench Cookhouses. No hot Food Containers yet available.

10.

10. ORDNANCE.

   D.A.D.O.S. Store and Ordnance R.P. is at W.10.d.8.8.

11. VETERINARY.

   No.52nd Mobile Veterinary Section will move to
   COXYDE BAINS in relief of No.19 Mobile Vety.Section,
   42nd Division on the 7th instant.

12. SALVAGE.

   Dumps are situated -

   Main Divisional Dump.   W.10.d.8.6.

   Brigade Dumps.   N.1.a.2.9.
                                 R.27.c.5.5.

   Divisional Salvage Officer will arrange with
   Salvage Officer 42nd Division as to taking over.

13. BATHS.

   Divisional Baths are at ST.IDESBALDE.
   There are also some disused baths at OOST DUNKERQUE
   BAINS.
   Divisional Baths Officer will arrange with Divisional
   Baths Officer 42nd Division to take over on 7th
   instant.

14. TRENCH STORES.

   Brigade in the Line will render to D.H.Q. "Q" by
   10th instant a return of :-

   (a).   All trench stores taken over.
   (b).   Total quantities of ammunition, fireworks
          etc. in sector.
   (c).   Locations of Dumps, giving contents.

                                        Lieut.Colonel,
                                        A.A. & Q.M.G.,
                                        41st Division.

Copy No. 1.	File.	Copy No. 19.	52nd Division "Q".
" " 2.	War Diary.	" 20.	42nd Division "Q".
" " 3.	XVth Corps "Q".	" 21.	4th Army A.A.Group.
" " 4.	41st Divl.Artillery.	" 22.	34th Squadron R.F.C.
" " 5.	122nd Inf.Bde.	" 23.	184th Tun.Coy.R.E.
" " 6.	123rd Inf.Bde.	" 24.	256th Tun.Coy. R.E.
" " 7.	124th Inf.Bde.		
" " 8.	C. R. E.	" 25.	2nd Aus.Tun.Coy.R.E.
" " 9.	41st Divl.Signal Coy.	" 26.	409th Field Coy.R.E.
" " 10.	41st Divl.Train.	" 27.	O.C., Divl.Baths.
" " 11.	"G".	" 28.	O.C., Salvage.
" " 12.	A. D. M. S.	" 29.	O.C., 236th Emp.Coy.
" " 13.	D. A. D. O. S.	" 30.	O.C., 41st Supply Col
" " 14.	D. A. D. V. S.	" 31.	Gas Officer.
" " 15.	A. P. M.	" 32.	N.C.O. i/c P.O.
" " 16.	Divl.Observ.Officer.	" 33.)	
" " 17.	Divl.M.G.Officer.	" 34.)	Spare.
" " 18.	Camp Commandant.	" 35.)	

S E C R E T.
========

LOCATION OF UNITS 41st DIVISION.

Unit.	Location.	Transport Lines.
Divisional H.Q.	ST. IDESBALDE.	With Unit.
C. R. E.	"	"
41st Signal Coy.	"	"
A. D. M. S.	"	"
D. A. D. V. S.	"	"
H.Q. Divisional Train.	"	"
D. A. D. O. S.	W.10.d.8.8.	
122nd Inf.Bde.H.Q.	W.10.d.7.3.	W.10.d.5.3.
1 Battalion.	W.10.d.3.7.	W.10.c.5.5.
1 Battalion.	W.11.c.3.6.	W.11.c.2.7.
1 Battalion.	W.5.c.1.1.	W.11.c.1.7.
1 Battalion.	W.10.b.4.7.	W.10.d.3.9.
122nd Machine Gun Coy.	W.6.a.6.4.	W.6.a.6.3.
122nd L.T.M.Battery.	W.10.a.6.3.	-----
124th Inf.Bde.H.Q.	W.6.b.8.6.	With Unit.
1 Battalion.	X.1.b.(Wiltshire Camp).	X.1.b.1.8.
1 Battalion.	R.27.d.80.20.	R.33.a.4.2.
1 Battalion.	W.6.a.75.60.	W.6.b.2.6.
1 Battalion.	LA PANNE.	W.15.a.5.1.
124th Machine Gun Coy.	R.32.c.5.6.	R.32.c.5.6.
124th T.M.Batty.	X.1.b.(Wiltshire Camp).	-------
123rd Inf.Bde.H.Q.	R.24.a.6.6. (Adv.).	R.33.d.7.9.
	R.33.d.7.9. (Rear).	
1 Battalion.	M.19.b.1.9.	R.32.b.8.3.
1 Battalion.	X.3.a.9.1.	X.3.a.9.1.
1 Battalion.	R.27.c.3.3.	R.32.b.8.3.
1 Battalion.	M.20.b.8.4.	X.1.a.2.7.
123rd M. G. Coy.	R.24.a.3.5.	W.6.a.8.6.
123rd T. M. Batty.	R.32.b.2.4.	------

R. E.

1 Field Company.	R.32.a.5.0.	R.31.d.6.5.
1 Field Company.	R.20.c.8.3.	R.27.c.8.3.
1 Field Company.	M.15.a.7.3.	R.27.c.6.2.

R. A. M. C.

1 Field Ambulance.	X.25.b.7.8.(GROOTE KWINTE FARM)	With Unit.
1 Field Ambulance.	OOST DUNKERKE BAINS.	"
1 Field Ambulance.	ST. IDESBALDE.	"

A. S. C.

1 Company A.S.C.	W.18.c.5.9.	With Unit.
1 Company A.S.C.	W.18.a.2.5.	"
1 Company A.S.C.	W.18.a.2.5.	"

238th Div.Emp.Coy.	ST. IDESBALDE.	----
52nd Mobile Vety.Section.	COXYDE BAINS.	----

SECRET.   41st Divn.No.Q.64/187/5.

ADMINISTRATIVE INSTRUCTIONS
Reference 41st Division Order No.177 of 4th Oct.1917.

4th October 1917.

1. ACCOMMODATION.

    On completion of relief the Division will be accommodated as shown in attached Schedule.

2. S.A.A. - GRENADES.

    Divisional Dump is at R.33.b.2.0.
    Main Brigade Dump.   M.14.c.2.2.
    Additional Brigade Dump. M.20.a.9.0.

    123rd Infantry Brigade will detail an officer, 1 N.C.O. and 8 men to take charge of the Divisional Dump (until arrival of Divisional Artillery) on 5th instant.

3. SUPPLIES.

    Supply Railhead changes to ST.IDESBALDE (Light Railway) W.17.b.5.5. on 7th instant.

    Supply Refilling Point and Fuel Dumps will be at W.17.b.5.5.

4. WATER.

    There is no difficulty regarding water in this area, numerous water points and horse troughs exist.

5. ROADS & TRACKS.

    The two roads OOST DUNKERQUE BAINS - NIEUPORT BAINS and OOST DUNKERQUE - M.20.d. are both fit for wheeled traffic by day as far E. as OOST DUNKERQUE - OOST DUNKERQUE BAINS Road, and by night to near Battalion H.Q. at M.19.b.1.9. and M.20.b.8.4.
    There are no tracks for transport.

6. TRAMWAYS.

    A map will be issued later showing Light Railways and Tramways in the Divisional Area.
    It is however more convenient under present circumstances to deliver both ammunition and rations by Horse Transport.

7. MEDICAL.

    A.D.S.   X.4.c.7.2.
                M.13.d.4.2.
    Ambulance H.Q. R.27.c.5.3.

8. R.E. STORES.

    Divisional Dump.   X.8.d.3.8.
    Advanced Dumps No.1. R.23.d.4.4.
                   No.2. N.25.c.1.9.

9. COOKING.

    The Battalion in the Line use Trench Cookhouses. No hot Food Containers yet available.

10.

10. ORDNANCE.

D.A.D.O.S. Store and Ordnance R.P. is at W.10.d.8.8.

11. VETERINARY.

No.52nd Mobile Veterinary Section will move to COXYDE BAINS in relief of No.19 Mobile Vety. Section, 42nd Division on the 7th instant.

12. SALVAGE.

Dumps are situated:-

    Main Divisional Dump.   W.10.d.8.6.

    Brigade Dumps.   X.1.a.8.9.
                            R.27.c.5.5.

Divisional Salvage Officer will arrange with Salvage Officer 42nd Division as to taking over.

13. BATHS.

Divisional Baths are at ST.IDESBALDE.
There are also some disused baths at OOST DUNKERQUE BAINS.
Divisional Baths Officer will arrange with Divisional Baths Officer 42nd Division to take over on 7th instant.

14. TRENCH STORES.

Brigade in the Line will render to D.H.Q. "Q" by 10th instant a return of :-

    (a). All trench stores taken over.
    (b). Total quantities of ammunition, fireworks etc. in sector.
    (c). Locations of Dumps, giving contents.

[signature]
Lieut-Colonel,
A.A. & Q.M.G.
41st Division.

Copy No. 1.	File.	Copy No. 19.	32nd Division "Q".
" " 2.	War Diary.	" " 20.	42nd Division "Q".
" " 3.	XVth Corps "Q".	" " 21.	4th Army A.A.Group.
" " 4.	41st Divl.Artillery.	" " 22.	34th Squadron R.F.A.
" " 5.	122nd Inf.Bde.	" " 23.	184th Tun.Coy.R.E.
" " 6.	123rd Inf.Bde.	" " 24.	256th Tun.Coy. R.E.
" " 7.	124th Inf.Bde.		
" " 8.	C.R.E.	" " 25.	2nd Aus.Tun.Coy.R.E.
" " 9.	41st Divl.Signal Coy.	" " 26.	409th Field Coy.R.E.
" " 10.	41st Divl.Train.	" " 27.	O.C., Divl.Baths.
" " 11.	"G".	" " 28.	O.C., Salvage.
" " 12.	A.D.M.S.	" " 29.	O.C., 238th Emp.Coy.
" " 13.	D.A.D.O.S.	" " 30.	O.C., 41st Supply Col
" " 14.	D.A.D.V.S.	" " 31.	Gas Officer.
" " 15.	A.P.M.	" " 32.	N.C.O. i/c P.O.
" " 16.	Divl.Observ.Officer.	" " 33.)	
" " 17.	Divl.M.G.Officer.	" " 34.)	Spare.
" " 18.	Camp Commandant.	" " 35.)	

SECRET.
==========

LOCATION OF UNITS 41st DIVISION.

Unit.	Location.	Transport Lines.
Divisional H.Q.	ST. IDESBALDE.	With Unit.
C. R. E.	"	"
41st Signal Coy.	"	"
A. D. M. S.	"	"
D. A. D. V. S.	"	"
H.Q. Divisional Train.	"	"
D. A. D. O. S.	W.10.d.8.8.	"
122nd Inf.Bde.H.Q.	W.10.d.7.3.	W.10.d.5.3.
1 Battalion.	W.10.d.3.7.	W.10.c.5.5.
1 Battalion.	W.11.c.3.6.	W.11.c.2.7.
1 Battalion.	W.5.c.1.1.	W.11.c.1.7.
1 Battalion.	W.10.b.4.7.	W.10.d.3.9.
122nd Machine Gun Coy.	W.6.a.6.4.	W.6.a.6.3.
122nd L.T.M.Battery.	W.10.a.6.3.	-----
124th Inf.Bde.H.Q.	W.6.b.8.6.	With Unit.
1 Battalion.	X.1.b.(Wiltshire Camp).	X.1.b.1.8.
1 Battalion.	R.27.d.80.20.	R.33.a.4.2.
1 Battalion.	W.6.a.75.60.	W.6.b.2.6.
1 Battalion.	LA PANNE.	W.15.a.5.1.
124th Machine Gun Coy.	R.32.c.5.6.	R.32.c.5.6.
124th T.M.Batty.	X.1.b.(Wiltshire Camp).	------
123rd Inf.Bde.H.Q.	R.24.a.6.6. (Adv.)	R.33.d.7.9.
	R.33.d.7.9. (Rear).	
1 Battalion.	M.19.b.1.9.	R.32.b.8.3.
1 Battalion.	X.3.a.9.1.	X.3.a.9.1.
1 Battalion.	R.27.c.3.3.	R.32.b.8.3.
1 Battalion.	M.20.b.8.4.	X.1.a.2.7.
123rd M. G. Coy.	R.24.a.3.5.	W.6.a.8.6.
123rd T. M. Batty.	R.32.b.2.4.	------

R. E.

1 Field Company.	R.32.a.5.0.	R.31.d.6.5.
1 Field Company.	R.27.c.8.3.	R.27.c.8.3.
1 Field Company.	M.15.a.7.3.	R.27.c.6.2.

R. A. M. C.

1 Field Ambulance.	X.25.b.7.8.(GROOTE KWINTE FARM)	With Unit.
1 Field Ambulance.	OOST DUNKERKE BAINS.	"
1 Field Ambulance.	ST. IDESBALDE.	"

A. S. C.

1 Company A.S.C.	W.18.c.5.9.	With Unit.
1 Company A.S.C.	W.18.a.2.5.	"
1 Company A.S.C.	W.18.a.2.5.	"

238th Div.Emp.Coy.	ST. IDESBALDE.	----
52nd Mobile Vety.Section.	COXYDE BAINS.	----

==*=*=*=*=*=*=*=*=*=*=*=*